ENEMY OF THE EMPIRE

Life as an International Undercover IRA Activist

EAMON McGUIRE

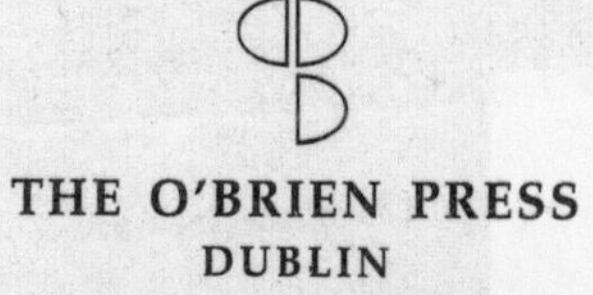

THE O'BRIEN PRESS
DUBLIN

First published 2006 by The O'Brien Press Ltd,
12 Terenure Road East, Rathgar, Dublin 6, Ireland.
Tel: +353 1 4923333; Fax: +353 1 4922777
E-mail: books@obrien.ie
Website: www.obrien.ie

ISBN-10: 0-86278-909-5

ISBN-13: 978-0-86278-909-1

Many thanks to Colman Doyle and Brendan Murphy
for permission to use copyright photographs.

British Library Cataloguing-in-Publication Data
McGuire, Eamon
Enemy of the empire : life as an international undercover IRA activist
1. McGuire, Eamon 2. Terrorists - Ireland - Biography
I. Title
364.1'092

1 2 3 4 5 6 7 8 9 10
06 07 08 09 10 11 12

Layout and design: The O'Brien Press Ltd.
Printing: Nørhaven Paperback A/S

ACKNOWLEDGEMENTS

Thanks to Richard Johnson for the cover photo (front, top); Kathleen O'Brien for holding the manuscript; Kelly for typing; Suzanne Bunting for scanning; Sharon Pollock for copying; and Íde ní Laoghaire, my editor, without whose help this book would never have been published.

Dedication

To all my fallen comrades

Contents

Introduction

In prison you do all your travelling in your mind. When I was locked up in South Africa, Ireland and the United States I had to condition myself so as to use my mind to travel out of my cell and wander through all the places in the world where I had worked or visited.

In 1992 my life had taken an unusual but possibly predictable turn. One morning I was working as an aircraft engineer in Mozambique, that night I was in solitary confinement in Pretoria prison in South Africa. Here the isolation was broken only by the action of food being pushed through a hatch in the door twice a day. The removal of all stimulation from a very active mind can cause a high level of frustration. To remain healthy, it became essential to find a means of occupying the mind. I found too that to depend on mental activity alone was not helpful and I had to do physical exercises as best I could in the cell. If I walked in a figure eight, I could take ten steps. I counted the steps and worked out the mileage; I recorded the miles and after each one I did a set of forty military-style push-ups. Then for the mental bit: after five miles I lay down on my cot and went travelling in my mind. When I was able to get writing paper I started to record the things I remembered to slow down the brain-storming process going on in my head. Later, in prison in the United States, I was in a cell with a man who had a doctorate in English from Cambridge in England; he looked at what I was doing and suggested that I put it into a book some day.

This book is a product of those sheets of paper that were written from memory in prison. It takes the reader on a journey through various countries and events that took place during the last sixty years of the twentieth century, from my childhood days in Ulster, military service, working on contract in British colonies and emerging nations, and involvement in the conflict in Northern Ireland. I lived in countries along the equator, from the Caribbean in the west to Borneo in the east, and I listened with interest to stories about historical events and figures. I was in a position to observe the local people and their customs and the effects of colonialism and its decline, as the British Empire retreated, often painfully, to its last bastion in the six counties of Northern Ireland. My deep involvement in dismantling its last foothold there was a secret life I carried with me for over twenty years around the world.

PART I
PRISON LIFE – SOUTH AFRICA, IRELAND, THE USA

Chapter 1

Arrest

I started work at 6.30am on the morning of 13 December 1992 at Maputo airport in Mozambique. It was mid-summer and the height of the rainy season, and I had put my travel plans on hold until late afternoon. When I finally decided to travel I came under so much pressure at Departures for 'dash' (an illegal payment, or bribe) that I turned and walked away until I was finally called back by the official and waved through. I have thought about that incident since and wondered what way my life would have progressed if I had kept going.

The small twin-engine aircraft droned incessantly as we flew slowly over bush country on our way to the South African border. Such a flight can be boring, even hypnotic, but the man in the cockpit seat beside me was familiar with the run and was able to point out places of interest, including areas controlled by anti-government Renamo forces. Increasing altitude, we flew over the Lebombo mountain ridge along which runs the electrified and heavily guarded South African border; from the air it is possible to see the double-wire fencing as it runs north along the Kruger National Park and south to Swaziland. Crossing the line presents such a contrast that it shocks the senses: one moment you are over a jungle floodplain, the next you feel that you have been transported to Europe or California where healthy crops form a beautiful multi-coloured pattern across the country.

Familiar things tend to relax you and I felt myself dropping down a couple of gears as we covered the sixty miles from the border to Nelspruit. This small town is on the main road and rail line that runs to Johannesburg and Pretoria from Maputo in Mozambique. The remnants of the Boer army and government retreated along the route after Pretoria fell to the British in 1900. It is said that Paul Kruger, on his way to exile, stopped the train here and unloaded wooden crates that contained the contents of the state mint at Pretoria to prevent it falling into the hands of the advancing British. All this gold is supposed to be buried somewhere between Nelspruit and Barberton. It was also the town where earlier in 1992 Tiso Leballo, Winnie Mandela's driver, and five other alleged robbers were killed in an ambush by Eugene De Kock and other members of Vlakplaas. De Kock was a former police colonel who commanded an assassination squad that killed opponents to apartheid. They then blew up Leballo's body with explosives. Not the most pleasant of policemen to bump into on arrival in South Africa.

The grass airstrip at Nelspruit is on rocky bush land, raised slightly above the surrounding countryside, which allows a clear, smooth approach and relatively easy landing. We taxied across the bumpy surface and parked beside a couple of light aircraft located some distance from the take-off strip. As I stepped out of the plane I instinctively scanned the area: one small building, but quite a few people – some walking, others standing. Why so many? Normally these places are deserted. Another survey of the people seemed to indicate a containment ring. I felt that I was in the centre. When you are exposed to danger for a long time it sharpens your mental faculties – some people call it 'being jumpy' – and you develop an instinct for imminent danger in a way that people living under normal, civilised conditions can hardly imagine. A kind of sixth sense warns you of impending danger while at the same time it allows you to weigh up the chances of escape.

I bent down on one knee and went through the motions of tying my shoelace while I suppressed my feelings and evaluated my options. This period of slow breathing allowed me to clear my mind and prevent myself from reaching the level of tension when things go so quiet you can hear your own heartbeat. The distance between each individual was less than the radius of the circle; it would have to be twice that, at least, to give me a fifty-fifty chance of a surprise break out. I did not see a rifle, but a short-arm would take me down in such circumstances on open ground. After twenty years of active involvement in guerrilla warfare, I did not fear death, only the method of its coming. And it brought no sorrow. But how bitter it would be to die on this glorious sunny day in a land I had dreamt of in my childhood.

My instincts could be wrong, of course. It would be better to wait for more favourable odds and some cover. I picked up my hold-all, placed it on my shoulder and walked slowly to the building to check in. As I walked I observed the people for positional changes and tried to put myself inside the mind of the man in charge. Where would I try to take a person like myself? Not in the open, too dangerous; not in the building, that could end in a stand-off with a hostage. There would have to be protection, concealment and cover. If my instincts were correct, it had to be close to the building before I entered it or when I came out the other side. Remain calm! If a fifty-fifty opportunity of escape presents itself should I take it? The vegetation on this dry, rocky outcrop was low thorn-bush and shrub. To move at speed through such vegetation would inflict severe surface injury. It was a relatively small area with open farmland beyond. And if I made the initial break could I survive the long pursuit that would follow? I was well acquainted with the African involvement in the hunt for me; and lack of drinking water, insects and wild life would be a problem too. If I could reach a large urban area I could survive on the fifteen hundred dollars in my pocket. In the final analysis, the decision to go or stay would be an instinctive, split-second reaction.

I entered the small building. The ring, if it existed, must have extended out on to the entrance road behind. The lone official who performed the duty of control, immigration and customs officer went through my papers and bag too carefully – a bad sign, but he did not know if I had a firearm on my person. I stood at the exit door and looked around. The area was deserted. The only other structure was a car-hire portacabin situated across the narrow entrance road. The bush started directly behind it and I could see no fencing. There was a chimpanzee family in the tall bushes behind, which seemed to indicate that there was nobody positioned there. Then, again, they are very inquisitive and might have been attracted by a human's presence.

I moved across the road to the car-hire shack and as I reached the three-quarter point I heard a step behind. Keep going! As my hand reached for the door handle the voice called out, 'Mr McGuire!' Brilliant timing and strategy on their part: I was up against a structure with no possibility of getting into the bush. I turned to see at least four men, two in protected positions and two in line about ten yards from me. As the back-up man moved I saw his gun strapped to his ankle and I suppressed the urge to bolt. The lead man spoke again: 'My name is Colonel Myburgh. I have a United States warrant for your arrest.' I remained silent. 'We can do this the easy way or the hard way. Put your bag down and step away.' I obeyed the order.

The back-up man moved around and picked up my bag as a total of seven men appeared from various points around me. I was searched and taken to the small veranda of the shack. Here I leaned against a support and pondered what lay ahead while the group engaged in a discussion. They were obviously watching me very closely because they must have reported to the United States that I looked tired: this appeared in the *Boston Globe* newspaper about a week later on 21 December 1992:

> When he was taken into custody at the airport in Johannesburg last week Peter Eamon Maguire [sic], allegedly the Irish Republican Army's chief technical expert, looked tired. Federal agents who had tracked Maguire to his clandestine meetings in New England years ago had thought the same thing as they listened in on bugged conversations. Maguire was tired. But then, maybe he was. At fifty-six, he had for two decades lived what authorities say was an extraordinary double life: mild-mannered engineer in public, dedicated revolutionary in private. And for the past three years he has lived the life of a wanted IRA man on the run in Africa.

* * *

I was led back on to Nelspruit airfield and put on board a security-force aircraft. During the flight, members of the group took turns trying to involve me in conversation. One particular man may have been military intelligence. His approach was friendly. Playing the Irish card, he asked, 'What can you do for us?' Others wanted to know the purpose of my visit to South Africa. 'Why do you need fifteen hundred dollars?' I ignored them and observed the navigation system through the cockpit door. The two military pilots were flying west. My escort became aware of where my interest lay and tried to involve me in conversation about such systems. But I was in a bad situation; speaking could only make it worse.

After two hours of flying we landed at a military airfield and taxied to an area that seemed to be reserved for this type of operation. The time and direction in which we were flying led me to believe that we were going to Johannesburg, but when I was moved by car I found myself in Pretoria, the capital. I was taken to the police headquarters in the centre of the city. It was a Sunday evening and the place was practically deserted. I memorised the names on the doors as we moved along the corridors. One was General Nells; when I met him he was not happy with me and made his feelings known. When we reached Col. Myburgh's office I received permission to make a phone call home and to ring Maputo where I was expected back at work three days later. Col. Myburgh made long phone calls, presumably to the United States and to his superiors, informing them that the operation was successful. When he had finished he laughingly said, 'Let us bring Mr McGuire to his hotel.' On our way to Pretoria prison I asked for food, as I had not eaten since six-thirty that morning. They stopped at a take-away and purchased a burger and coffee for me. The next day was my fifty-sixth birthday.

It was almost midnight on a Sunday night when we reached the prison. It is a rather foreboding structure and grey walls restrict vision from inside and out. The place was locked and it required many phonecalls before the police gained entry. When the formalities of checking the body and paperwork were finished I was led along a corridor which had overhead grating where an armed guard patrolled. The doors were controlled from a central security point and access had to be requested at each door. When we reached the wing where I was to be housed I was taken up through three gates to the second floor which had six cells. Except for the occasional shower, or a walk up and down from the security gate past the six cells to the end wall, I would spend twenty-four hours a day in my cell here. I was told that I was dangerous by one of the prison officers and he always had his gas canister at the ready when dealing with me. Since he was over six feet tall and fourteen stone I said a person like myself, five feet nine and ten-and-a-half stone, did not pose much of a threat to him. He replied that the special forces taught you not to underestimate or misjudge people. It was about midnight when I was put into the cell. I did not pay too much attention to it and just lay down on the cot and went to sleep.

I was woken up by the intercom in my cell after what seemed like five minutes and handed a plate of Indian corn or maize meal porridge and told to prepare for a court appearance. I was the only person in the paddy wagon that brought me to the city-centre courthouse. A large metal gate opened and I entered a large auditorium that was crowded with young Africans who drifted up and down in small bunches. The only other European there was an old man who obviously lived rough. Dirt in his long grey hair, he shuffled about in his tattered clothes and worn-out shoes, carrying a small suitcase. The young Africans, always full of devilment and fun, were as curious as I was about what was in the case. (They had already removed my golf cap from my hip pocket; feeling it being removed gently I turned and it was tossed back to me when my reaction was seen to be friendly.) Eventually the clasp of the suitcase was slipped open after many failed passes and out fell another pair of worn-out shoes. This generated shrieks of laughter that lifted the gloom of the place.

When my turn came I was led up to a courtroom where the judge quickly checked my detention documents and asked if I was represented. I said no. I was remanded and told to apply for legal aid. This I did before being returned to prison. Now I had all the time in the world to view that prison block that would be my world for the next few months.

This was a political wing of Pretoria prison – the prison as a whole housed twelve thousand regular prisoners. The floor beneath me had, up until recently, held a South African naval admiral who had spied for the Russians; below that on the ground floor there were white extremist prisoners.

As cells go it was clean and I did not have to share it with anybody else. The bed was a standard metal military cot that I was familiar with from my army training days. A hand basin, toilet bowl, a small shelf on the wall and a chair completed the furnishing. The window was about one foot wide and three feet high; if you stood on the chair you could look out through the three bars. The door had an inner metal barred gate and an outer metal door with one-way-view glass. Communications were conducted through a two-way speaker system from the control centre. I suspect that this system could be used as a listening device if you were inclined to talk to yourself.

The toilet had a nasty habit of not shutting off after you flushed it. There must have been a common cistern for the six cells in the row. The flush was so vicious that it continued and overflowed the bowl, flooding the cell. The second time this happened I threw a folded army-type blanket over the bowl, put down the cover and sat on top of it until the pressure closed the valve.

This was high summer in South Africa and it was extremely hot. The block in which I was housed was built of brick and in the evening the sun shone on the window and wall of my cell. The brick held the heat well into the night, making things very uncomfortable, and you generally lay on your cot in a pool of your own sweat. The only ventilation was through the small window and a tiny gap under the metal door. To make things worse, you had no control over the light as the switch was outside the cell door. At night when the light was on, you had to close the window because the light attracted mosquitoes that entered the cell to eat you alive.

An incident occurred which finally deprived me of the little air that came in under the door. The prison diet generally consisted of maize or Indian cornmeal porridge with some milk for breakfast; at twelve-thirty potatoes or more maize cooked more solidly, plus a vegetable (beetroot was the most recognisable) and a form of meat which tasted like the rind of bacon on most occasions. With this I got two thick slices of brown bread cut from a small-sized loaf. That was it for the day. Perhaps there was more food available that I could have foraged for if I had not been locked up all the time. In any case, I saved the two slices of bread and ate one at seven in the evening and the other in the morning with water from the tap. I woke up one night to what I thought was the sound of a small pig grunting and felt something pulling at my hair. I instinctively brushed my hand over my hair, thinking to myself: You are dreaming or beginning to lose it, then went back to sleep. Next morning, when I went for my slice of bread there was nothing but a few crumbs on the chair and floor. It was not my imagination after all; I had had a visitor during the night. Whatever kind of beast it was, I did not want it chewing on my hair as I slept so I decided to sit up on the chair close to the door and see what arrived the following night. After waiting for ages I got tired and decided to lie down on the bed, but I managed to stay awake. Eventually a head appeared under the metal door and a large rat pushed his flattened body in. Since I was at the furthest point from the door I allowed him to come right in before I hopped up with my shoe as a weapon. The rodent's quick reaction allowed him to escape before I could reach him and I was not able to inflict serious injury. To prevent the rodent or one of his friends returning, I stuffed another grey blanket between the gate and the bottom of the door. The closing off of all sources of air to the cell made the nights very hot and difficult.

The twenty-four-hour confinement generated a feeling of day stacked upon day, and in the sameness of the prison routine days and weeks seemed to merge into an infinite river of time, where it was difficult to remember what day it was or what day some incident had occurred. This was new to me and I decided I needed some strategies to deal with it. The routine of rising in the morning, having porridge, washing my underpants and T-shirt, waiting for the midday meal and going to bed was now to be broken by physical activity. I would do press-ups in groups of forty at regular intervals and I found that I could take ten steps in the cell if I walked in a figure of eight. I counted the steps for hours and worked out the number of miles I covered. I then tried to recall all the information I had about South Africa and repeat it to myself in my head. The only distraction I had was when darkness fell. Although the windows were very narrow the young Africans in the main prison next door climbed up, opened the windows and put their legs out through the bars and hung on there. Their cries rose up like a continuous wail as they shouted into the night or communicated with friends in various parts of the prison. It reminded me of the wildlife sounds of the bush, but was more concentrated, and it went on for a couple of hours.

After a couple of weeks Col. Myburgh called to tell me that foreigners were not allowed legal aid. I was allowed to phone Dublin to see if the legal association there could recommend somebody in Pretoria to represent me. Within a few days I had a visit from a bright young lawyer called Chris Niehouse who worked in Webster Wentzel law firm in Johannesburg. They requested fifty thousand rand up-front before they would handle my case. He visited me a couple of times to prepare my case and it helped to break up my life of solitary confinement. When I returned to court in Pretoria, J.A. Louw and C. Jordan represented me as advocates. They made a dynamic defence team who did not believe for one minute they could lose. Their first move was to insist that the hearing take place in the district in which I was arrested. When this was allowed, I would have to wait for a date to be arranged for the hearing in Nelspruit. While I was waiting for the outcome of these discussions I was told that the South African security services had uncovered a plot to poison me and they showed me a photograph of a blond-haired girl who was supposed to be involved in the plot. The image was similar in style to one taken of me by federal agents in New England three years previously – taken with a long surveillance lens and saturated with grain, the subject's face was too blurred to be identified. I wondered what this was about, but that was the last I heard about the plot. Shortly after that the media somehow managed to gain access to the room where I was held and when the authorities realised what was happening I was quickly removed from the courthouse and returned to prison.

I continued my routine in my cell. My thoughts focused on my childhood dream of visiting Africa and how this and my political ideas had clashed, resulting in me ending up in a Boer prison. For two decades of war I had prepared myself for the possibility of prison or death, and now I had to adjust to my new circumstances. That would take time. I felt no anger or desire for recrimination, and as time passed I became more efficient at using mental discipline to escape the endless, aching boredom that occurs in the early months of first imprisonment. I learned to travel outside the walls using memory and imagination. I learned to make this a vivid experience.

It felt strange being in a Boer prison and I had many conflicting feelings about it. After all, I was a Republican, and Republicans had fought on the Boer side during the Boer War; even John McBride, who was executed after the 1916 Rising, fought with the Irish Brigade here in South Africa. Perhaps Republicans saw British imperial expansion taking over the Boer Transvaal state because it had suddenly become rich on gold and diamonds; the repugnant apartheid laws were still a generation in the future.

I would often recall the old British soldier of my childhood who sold the African dream to me. He had fought against the Boers. So did about thirty thousand other Irish men drawn from the Connaught Rangers, Inniskilling Fusiliers, Dublin Fusiliers and other outfits. I recalled that there was a 'traitor's gate' at the Dawson Street entrance to St Stephen's Green in the heart of Dublin – it commemorates members of the Dublin Fusiliers who fought and died for the British at Spion Kop, Ladysmith, Tugela, Mafeking, Talana and other battlefields. Lord Kitchener of Kartoom, the British commander-in-chief, was also an Irishman – it was he who promoted the concentration camp idea where one in five died. The logic of some people, including public figures in Ireland, defies my understanding: they decry northerners for using force to get civil and human rights and equality, yet they see no problem about their grandfathers, fathers and sons being paid by the British to kill people who never did anything to them. My feeling is that they feel it is fine 'out there', but they don't want their comfortable life in Ireland disturbed no matter what people have to suffer, even their own people.

* * *

On the morning of 25 January 1993 Col. Myburgh and his team arrived to take me to court in Nelspruit. For security reasons I was always transported by air, but this time there was a sting in the tail: we had to use the local airforce base to depart from Pretoria and, as an additional restraint, I would be blindfolded. I had had blindfolds on before, but not in a hostile environment, where people who could not be regarded as friendly control your every movement; this definitely increases your sense of insecurity and vulnerability. In some office, however, I assume the flight commander's, I was treated with great respect. I expect they were aware of my past military experience and every effort was made to make me feel among friends. I was provided with coffee and scones, but the blindfold and chains remained in place.

The background to all of this was my involvement with the 'Boston Three'. Although there were five of us involved in that IRA cell, it was always referred to as the 'Boston Three' because by the time a support system had been set up I was on the run and the fifth person had already left prison. This cell was a technical one, and was in the process of producing a guided missile system. Three charges were brought against me after the American security services uncovered our cell.

They were:

1 conspiracy to violate Arms Export Control Act

2 conspiracy to injure or destroy property

3 conspiracy to destroy helicopters located in Northern Ireland and belonging to the United Kingdom, a country with which the United States is at peace.

Due to lapses in security over the years, the FBI were able to pinpoint the main participants in the cell and bug their phones and accommodation. But in the end, in a strange twist, one of our own engineers, Richard Johnson, almost had the FBI agents arrested! Johnson was walking along a corridor in his workplace when he saw two men interfering with his car in the carpark. He called Security and had the men arrested because he thought they were trying to steal his car. When arrested, the men showed their FBI credentials and one of them called the field office on the car-phone and asked for instructions. According to Ronald Kessler in his book, *The FBI*, the assistant US Attorney, Richard G Stearns, who was handling the case, replied: 'You can either arrest the two agents for car theft or you can arrest Johnson. I recommend the latter.' That was the beginning of the end. Four members of the cell were arrested in 1989, but I was in Ireland at the time.

When I arrived in the courthouse in Nelspruit my defence team informed me that the state was not pursuing two of the United States' charges and it all hinged on the remaining one – conspiracy to injure or destroy property of a foreign government. I did not think being extradited to the United States on *that* charge – which carried a maximum term of imprisonment of three years – was so bad. That was before I understood how the United States' justice system works. All day, the respective counsels put forward arguments about the presence of a corresponding charge in South Africa, or its absence. Finally the judge ended the hearing and said he would deliver his judgement the following day.

I was lodged in Nelspruit police jail for the night. The cell where I was held seemed to have once been a deluxe unit. It was a twelve-foot-square exercise area with a barred metal gate. The walls were very high and it was open to the sky. A few moments after I was placed there I heard a woman's voice in the adjoining unit, asking: 'Where are you from? Do you have any cigarettes?' She could put her hand around the wall to my entrance gate, but when there was nothing to be gained she went silent, which suited me. The cell opened into the yard and I found that the latch had long since broken and hadn't been replaced. It would not remain in the closed position. The bed had nothing but a mattress on it that seemed to have been there since the building was constructed. It was just a lot of lumps contained in a dirty cover. There was a small hand-basin, where the water dribbled continuously. The toilet was encrusted with so much excrement that it was difficult to determine what the original colour was.

The good part was the deep-fried fish *goujons* and the couple of slices of bread that were passed through the gate to me, and the walk around the little compound in the balmy night air with the postage-stamp sky above. Eventually I decided to chance the bed. For a few decades during my active involvement I had been used to sleeping in rough situations with my clothes on; now I simply removed my T-shirt, placed it under my head, settled in between the lumps and went to sleep.

During the night I thought I heard a baby crying. Such non-threatening sounds do not fully wake me up and usually I sink back into sleep, often assuming that I am dreaming. However, next morning when I was having a fried-egg sandwich and coffee in the holding area, an African woman with a baby in her arms walked up from the cells. I saw her watching me hungrily as I ate. I did not speak but pointed to the plate, and she nodded her head. I passed the plate to her as the escort arrived to take me to court. There were looks of disapproval, but nothing was said.

The judge arrived in court at ten o'clock. He immediately went through the submissions from the state and the defence of the previous day, and gave his reasons why he agreed or disagreed with their points of view. In the end, his judgement was in favour of the defence's argument and I was discharged.

I felt it was a pyrrhic victory. This was the United States' third attempt to apprehend me and on each occasion they were getting closer to their objective. Having me in custody and knowing exactly where I was for the first time allowed them to stay on top of me from this moment on. Denying me the facilities to travel could also control my movements – flights could always be full, and countries could be encouraged to refuse me entry. If I could reach home, then I might be able to remain free.

When my passport was handed back to me it was useless as the visa for South Africa had expired long ago. My possessions were in Pretoria prison and I had no alternative but to return to Pretoria in the security force's aircraft. I would have preferred to have crossed the border into Mozambique, war or no war, but my passport had to be validated and on a Friday evening it would require somebody with authority to demand that. After collecting my hold-all and cash from prison, I had to return to police headquarters for validation. There my passport was validated for a further three-day stay in the country. Before I left for Johannesburg, General Nells made it clear that I would not be welcome in his country in the future.

I was able to get an Air France flight to Paris on Sunday evening, 27 January. As I checked in, the attendant picked up the phone and said, 'Mr McGuire has arrived.' No effort was made to conceal what she was saying. I would not be travelling alone, it seemed. But would they have time to prepare a warrant in Paris on Sunday evening? The French! Perhaps not.

Chapter 2

In Prison in Ireland

Mountjoy

There was no problem with the authorities at Paris airport and I was able to make it back to Ireland. I suspected that the Americans rated their chances of extraditing me from Ireland higher than from France. I decided to lie low for a while, then on a dark, wet Friday evening in February 1993 I visited the home where I normally lived with my wife. My daughter was returning from overseas that weekend and I had not seen her for a number of years. We were having a meal in the kitchen when a face appeared at the rear window; the Special Branch had the house surrounded. They obviously had tracked me at the request of the United States agents who shadowed me on my return journey from South Africa.

My daughter opened the door to them and they presented a warrant for my arrest. I continued to eat while being observed by individuals who, in their anxiety, had beads of sweat breaking out on their top lips. It was not long before I was being led down that infamous tunnel from the Bridewell police station to the local District Court in Dublin. The judge checked my arrest papers and the US extradition request, and remanded me in custody for a week. Around midnight the procedure was over and, much to my surprise, I was taken to that relic of Victorian times, Mountjoy prison. I was expecting to be lodged in Portlaoise where political prisoners were held at that time, but since I was not charged with an offence in the state it seems that a ministerial order would be required to send me there and I would have to remain in Mountjoy until it was available. During my stay in Portlaoise, each time a court remanded me I was returned to the confines of Mountjoy while a dispatch rider returned from the minister's office with the signed order.

I was led in through Mountjoy's well-known main entrance door into a reception area where my clothes were taken from me and replaced by bits and pieces of old prison clothes. From there I was taken into the prison proper. The sheer volume of the building surprised me. Four cavernous wings with three tiers radiated out in a half-circle from a central hub. Metal stairs in the middle of each unit that led up to the landings was the only break in the vast emptiness. I became conscious of the fact that I was following in the footsteps of so many political prisoners before me and wondered what they had felt when their eyes looked on this for the first time.

I didn't feel much one way or the other – this had been coming down the line for a long time. I was prepared for it. One of the most frequent questions asked by people who never experienced prison is, 'How did you feel when the metal door slams behind you?' Some of my male visitors could not return because the sound of the main gate closing as they entered unnerved them. This sound stirred no emotions whatsoever in me. In fact, most times I was glad to hear the cell door close behind me. I accepted it as inevitable, one of the lesser risks you take for being 'involved'. And if you had a cell to yourself, you had privacy; if you had a vivid imagination with this privacy – then you could let your mind roam through your images of the outside world without distraction.

As I stood staring, a senior prison officer's voice jerked me back to the present. 'Would you prefer to share a cell with a convicted prisoner rather than going up to the druggies in the remand wing?' he asked. Since I was given the choice I said I would, and added, 'Don't worry, I will be okay.' He surprised me when he replied, 'The last man who said that to me left here with a bunch of his friends in a helicopter!' He was referring to the famous republican prisoner escape that took place in the 1970s when a helicopter landed in the exercise yard of Mountjoy, in the heart of Dublin city, and whisked away three republican prisoners. He wandered off and left me standing there and the surroundings caused the ghosts of the past to flood in on me.

In 1850 when the prison was built it was expected to house the normal run-of-the-mill prisoners such as robbers, thieves, drunks and prostitutes, but within ten years it was also used to suppress political dissent. Many Fenians were held here, including O'Donovan Rossa and John O'Leary. Over the next hundred and fifty years it was seen by those in power as an important weapon in a series of political upheavals. This placed the prison at the focal point of the struggle for independence. Hunger strikes, executions and escapes imprinted it on the national conciousness. Well- known figures like Sean Lemass, Ernie O'Malley, Sean McBride, Dan Breen, Oscar Traynor and Robert Duggan, to name but a few, spent time here during the Civil War in the 1920s. Many activists were executed here by the British and later the Irish Free State.

'Come with me,' the prison officer's voice interrupted my thoughts again. He led me down D wing that still had the execution room at the end. I was put into an INLA (Irish National Liberation Army) man's cell; though we had very different views about how to conduct the struggle in the north, he could, to a small degree, be seen as a fellow traveller. He had no objections to me sleeping on a mattress on the floor of his nine-by-seven-foot cell. Together with the mattress and blanket, I was handed an aluminium chamber pot to use as a toilet during the twelve-hour lock-up. I was told that each cell had had a toilet bowl when the prison was built one hundred and fifty years previously, but it seems that they were removed shortly afterwards because the sewage system was so bad the 'flow back' frequently soiled the cells. Now the pots had to be carried along the landings to a disposal area and this created an unbelievable daily mess. The prison was dark and looked dirty, but this was due more to design than neglect. Very little light entered the cell and during the day it remained twilight.

Morning arrives sooner than most people wish even in prison, and we had to line up to receive our breakfast from containers positioned in the centre of the wing. We then returned to our cells to eat and the cell doors were again locked. Later in the morning and again in the afternoon the doors were unlocked to allow people to attend various activities. Those who had been assigned work were free to come and go as the job dictated.

During my short periods at Mountjoy I met only one unpleasant officer. When my clothes were exchanged for prison garb I was not given an overcoat to replace the one they taken from me. When I had left South Africa it was summer and the temperature was in the mid-thirties day and night. The temperature in Dublin was about four degrees centigrade. When it came to exercise time in the yard I explained my position to the guard who said, 'Well, you should have stayed in South Africa, out you go.' That was exactly what I had to do and I was engulfed in a blanket of cold, damp air that chilled me to the bone.

On Monday morning all services were operational again. I was taken to the doctor for the standard check-up. This was more of an interview than a medical examination. I informed him that I had an appointment with a skin specialist for that day and asked if he could arrange for me to attend – the years spent in the tropics and in deserts had damaged my skin, and as time passed some cells were showing signs of becoming cancerous. He said he would do his best, but said I was due to be moved to Portlaoise later in the day. With much inconvenience to the specialist, who had to contend with venue and time changes for security reasons, I was attended to before I was moved to Portlaoise in a high-speed military, police and prison cavalcade. In a very short time I would return to Dublin in the same manner to have further treatment. On that occasion I would be attended to by my own doctor – and unfortunately this created a difficult situation for her. The army sealed off the area and the special police entered to check the surgery before I arrived. But she was not there. Patients in the waiting room assumed that she was being arrested! Her husband was in the kitchen and when asked who he was and where he was from, he replied that he was the husband and was from Belfast, which raised the temperature. You can imagine what went through their minds: is he one of them too? Then, the roadblock was holding the doctor up on her return until she managed to explain that she was the reason for the traffic chaos and she was escorted through. In the surgery I could see that the presence of people with guns was unnerving her and I was glad to be soon on the road at high speed again.

Portlaoise

Portlaoise prison is constructed of grey stone that looks depressing even on a bright sunny day. A cold February night makes it worse and the military installations added over the previous twenty years give it a sinister look from outside. The wagon in which I was transported was reversed into the prison as soldiers took up defensive positions. I was led in through a large barred gate covered in sheet metal into a huge archway. A prison officer who had opened the first entrance released the lock on a small door in a massive solid metal door in the centre of the arch. He then signalled to a second officer on the other side to release a similar lock before the door was opened. Passing through this we entered the inner half of the archway. Here my papers were checked and the delivery party's responsibility for me ended.

As this process was taking place I had an opportunity to have a good look at the huge central steel door with its three large sliding bars and securing locks. I had heard stories from IRA prisoners who spent many years here during the bad times in the 1970s and 1980s. These stories are always circulated among activists; in fact, escape is seen as a political act, part of the struggle one is engaged in. The concept of escape is extremely important in keeping morale high in prison.

During an escape attempt years previously, prisoners had stood before this very door and had to accept the awful reality that they had failed in their attempt. They had managed to get through a combination of eight doors and gates and across open ground guarded by soldiers, to this door. The three explosive charges removed the locks but in the process it distorted the bars and it was impossible to slide them open even with the assistance of an iron bar.

The price for failure can be high. All the prisoners, regardless of involvement or not, were herded into the yard and remained there all day while the authorities took each cell apart, including every door which was partly wooden. Later, prisoners were taken in, one at a time, and strip-searched, and great force was used on those who put up any resistance.

But in October 1974 nineteen prisoners did escape from Portlaoise by using explosives to blow out the wall. Some years later, during another failed attempt, one prisoner was shot dead by soldiers.

When my papers were checked I was led through the third door of the archway into an open area where there was a collection of portacabins. One of these was used as a reception facility where I went through a partial strip-search. All my property was then returned to me except my footwear, which was X-rayed and returned later. From here I was taken to the Provisional wing of the top security block where a cell had been organised for me.

The Provisionals were housed together on the top two floors of the building and a command structure, similar to that outside, was maintained within the prison. Previously, in the seventies and eighties, their numbers were so large that they filled the whole block. But now the numbers were small and only one floor was used by them. The floor below us housed political prisoners from other groups, including Dominic McGlinchey. The ground floor accommodated high-risk criminals who were transferred here for security reasons. Others such as the 'Border Fox' (Dessie O'Hare) were in the bunker, the equivalent of the 'hole' in American prisons. The other block housed low-security prisoners who received time off their sentence for agreeing to come here to carry out routine prison work.

I was told that the culture of the prison I entered bore little resemblance to that which existed in the seventies and eighties. One man who was there at that time described it as 'a prison notorious for its ill-treatment of republican prisoners'. Then prison discipline was based on a system that slowly degraded the prisoner. Scheduled and random strip-searching and harassment produced an atmosphere of oppression and resentment. The smooth running of any prison is based on a high level of tacit cooperation between officers and prisoners. When highly disciplined political prisoners rescind on this, the prison administration has an impossible task. If it resorts to imposing harsh and cruel rules to make people conform, the prison becomes a battleground. Prisoners will expend their energy probing the system and the facility for weak points to disrupt the running of the place – or to escape.

This was the case in the mid-seventies when a new system of visiting was introduced. The prisoner stood with two prison officers behind him in one half of a visiting box measuring six feet by ten. Between him and his visitors were two wire meshes about three feet apart. The grid in the wire was about one inch by a half-inch wide and a sheet of perspex came up half way on the inside of the wire. This arrangement formed a cage, inside which sat a prison officer who could observe both parties at all times.

If a prisoner made any reference to any matter concerning the prison or anything else that the officers did not like, he was immediately grabbed and dragged out, and the visit was terminated. This harsh regime had sad consequences for some prisoners. One man's wife had a child shortly after he arrived in. He was never able to physically touch the baby when it was brought in on a visit. Later, on the way to the prison, the baby was involved in an accident and thrown out on to the road and killed.

During that terrible period in the 1970s and 1980s a cell search was carried out before a prisoner was out of bed in the morning when he had little or no clothes on him. On other random occasions, when prisoners were locked up during the day, a general search would be carried out. When this happened, a call went around the cells and a full-scale protest swung into action. The prisoners usually dismantled the metal frames of their beds and used the tubular end to beat the cell doors. Depending on how strong the man was it was possible to break through the metal inside skin and smash the wood on the outside of the door. The doors soon became useless and the authorities decided to replace them with strong metal ones that had six bars that were operated by a key and slid into holes in a metal jamb, similar to a safe.

One prisoner, examining the door for weak points, found that when the door was locked a plastic knife jammed in between the door and the metal frame into which the six metal bolts slipped could prevent the guard opening it – the load put on the bolts was too great for the key to overcome. This knowledge was kept secret from the prison authorities until a large-scale search was imminent and the prisoners jammed the doors with their plastic knives. The doors remained secured until the governor agreed to negotiate with the prisoners' commanding officer.

Around 1985 the Provisional officer commanding the prisoners negotiated a new visiting arrangement. It was agreed that a prisoner could have one open visit every month, and further visits using the old system if he wanted. The old system of visits was rejected and everybody agreed to the one open visit per month in the hope that they could expand on that. It was felt that if they continued with the old-style visits they would never be able to increase the number of open visits. Visits were very important, especially for married men with young children. It was how they retained some connection with their children as the years passed, often up to twenty or more. The cost of travel made it impossible for families from the far north and south to visit more than once a month and it could be a traumatic experience for young children. After prisoners were released many marriages were just not viable because the partner had lived a separate life for so long. For me, visits were not as essential – I was used to being away from Ireland on my own for extended periods of time and my children were nearly thirty years of age. Still, my wife, some of my brothers and sisters and visitors from across the world and their children came to see me. This worked out as a visit a week, which broke the monotony of prison, and I was glad to have it.

John Lonergan was posted to Portlaoise prison in around 1988 as governor. He was a man who believed in a more humane regime. The IRA found that they could negotiate with him more easily, not that they were looking for much. The prisoners always conducted educational classes and he introduced better facilities. He facilitated studies in the Open University to degree level and allowed teachers to come in from outside to help the prisoners to better themselves. The old form of caged visiting was dispensed with and the atmosphere in the prison changed for the better. One prisoner who had been there for fifteen years when I arrived said that the legacy of John Lonergan was the educational facilities that he had introduced.

* * *

This was the type of prison that I arrived in and I expected to remain here for two years during which I would fight my extradition. The extradition attempt had failed under South African law, but the law in Ireland was different – this may be due to the laws in South Africa being more lax in order to circumvent trade sanctions that were in full swing at the time.

My cell was on the top level and on the west side of the block. The small window was very high up and if you stood on the metal bed you could look out across the country, but not nearby. Over the years some of the three-inch-square glass panes had broken and the wind blew in through the holes and out under the metal door. The walls and curved ceiling were painted regularly but the long metal heating pipe that ran through cell after cell did not produce enough heat to dry the moisture that seeped through the stone construction. The paint soon flaked and fell like fine snow on to your bed. Sleeping at night was not always easy as the soldiers who manned the general-purpose machine guns on the flat roof got cold at night and, intentionally or not, stomped their boots above your head. (One soldier, at least, who once patrolled up there made the transition to guerrilla fighter and was now in a cell with us! There was also one former Garda in prison with us during my short time there.)

While I was waiting for my extradition hearing in the District Court, an application for bail on my behalf went to the High Court on 19 February 1993. Unfortunately, the court accepted the State's argument that I would flee the jurisdiction if I were allowed bail. That was quite untrue – I had already been free and did not have to return to Ireland.

When my extradition hearing took place the question before the court was: Could I claim political offence exception in respect of activities in the United States, a third state, which I had no political dispute with and which was not involved in the conflict? All such previous cases across the world had returned a No verdict and I did not expect a favourable result. The judge handed down his decision on 19 April 1993:

> In the instant case I therefore hold that the United States are seeking the extradition of the fugitive in order to try him on ordinary criminal charges. I am satisfied that his extradition is not prohibited by part II of the extradition act 1965 or by the relevant extradition provisions.

> Accordingly I propose to make an order under section 29 subsection I committing Peter Eamon McGuire to prison there to await the order of the Minister for Justice for his extradition.

As expected, I was to be extradited. I could delay its implementation by appealing the verdict all the way to the Supreme Court. That option could mean that I would spend more time in prison. In order to have more time to consider my options, I appealed the verdict to the High Court and I expected to spend many months in Portlaoise prison before the case would be heard.

When you are waiting for court cases time is inclined to drag. It is difficult to settle down and do something useful with your time. The removal of the brutal culture that had existed meant that most people were now fully occupied with staff duties, education, recreation and administration of the landings. This left people in my position in a kind of limbo. The area in which I lived my life was very small. Inside, we were confined to two landings. At one end of the top one there were toilets and showers, and a disposal unit for the contents of chamber pots. The other end had small classrooms, showers, library and gym. The other landings were similar, but did not have the library or gym.

A twenty-foot wall and razor wire surrounded the block and exercise yards. The exercise yards had to be time-shared with other groups. This cut down the time you could spend outside because they were closed at dusk. Most mornings I ran around the yard for exercise. The tarmac surface was very hard on the joints and most longterm prisoners have to give it up eventually and rely on the gym. It took about fifty circuits to complete four miles. To reduce the effect on the legs of running in a tight circle we would run half the distance in the each direction. When the weather permitted it was possible to play basketball, handball and football, using a limited number of men.

There was time to observe the different types of people confined in this small area. We were all equal here, all volunteers. Prison stripped people of every disguise they have developed – now they were judged only on their behaviour, outlook and discipline in prison. Looking at them it was hard to guess their background, profession or education. These were all men who had learned to be very secretive because the struggle had lasted so long, and little was known about their past involvements except the charge that got them here.

A person's accent, of course, gave an indication of what part of the country they came from. Counties that fought well during the War of Independence in the south were still well represented – Cork, Kerry, Tipperary, Limerick, Waterford, Kilkenny, Laois, Offaly, Meath, Dublin, Louth and, of course, all the counties of Ulster. Farmers and country people spoke softly, mostly listening and observing. Men from towns carried an air of confidence not always warranted. The city men, particularly Belfast and Dublin, were more adaptable and outgoing. They were used to the proximity of many people and had quick wits; they played games and pranks that helped to keep spirits high.

Time passed, and I was still waiting for the High Court decision on my extradition. I did not believe that I could prevent extradition, so contact was made with Mr Bachman, a lawyer from the United States who had represented one of the 'Boston Three' in their trial in Boston some years previously. I was the last person indicted in what had become known as the 'Boston Three Case'. The other four lost their case and went to prison in 1990. Bachman was coming to Ireland on a visit and agreed to see me. When he arrived in the first week of December he surprised us when he said that the US prosecuting attorney on the case had travelled with him and would I agree to see them both? This idea was discussed with the senior Provisional staff in Portlaoise and the commanding officer agreed that the meeting could take place with a staff member present. Two meetings took place. The United States were anxious to close the long-standing case; as they saw it, I was the last loose end of the 'Boston Three'. They were willing to offer a deal if I was willing to go to the United States and plead guilty. I said I would think about it and they returned home. As things turned out, the decision to plead guilty was taken out of my hands when I arrived in America. I was simply told by the Provisional officer in charge there to do so.

The following week, on 9 December, the High Court delivered its decision on my appeal. It upheld the verdict of the District Court – to extradite me – and I was once again at the disposal of the Minister for Justice. In the meantime I had decided not to appeal the verdict to the Supreme Court in case it ran against me. I was mentally prepared to go to America, but since it was so close to Christmas I wanted to remain in Ireland for that period and I did not tell the authorities until January that I was not going to appeal, after which time I was to be handed over to the US marshals. I was ready for whatever that would bring.

Chapter 3

Extradition to America

Spring is in the air during the month of February in Ireland. It holds a promise of things to come, although it's still frosty and cold. It was on such a morning that I was removed from my cell in Portlaoise prison and handed over to the police who took me at high speed to Shannon airport. There I was handed over to two United States marshals. This simple exchange meant that I was the first, and, as it turned out, the only Republican prisoner extradited to the US from the Republic of Ireland.

It was not a pleasant feeling to be given over to the security agents of another country by your own people. There was a sense of being alone and exposed. I remember once sitting on an old cannon looking out over Botany Bay wondering how those transportees felt so long ago. Now I had some idea. As the plane flew out against the sky, the feeling of isolation was compounded by the news that had been filtering through in recent days that I had been betrayed: the communication about my movements from the United States to South Africa had been dispatched on 10 December; allowing for the time difference, that was 11 December in Mozambique. As I had only decided to travel on the day I was arrested, the 13th, someone close to me who knew my intentions must have informed on me. This was a very bad feeling.

At Shannon the marshal handcuffed and placed leg-irons on me, which were connected by a foot-long chain. This was not the first time I was chained up – I had been handcuffed in Ireland and had experienced both handcuffs and leg-chains in South Africa – and I did not think it unusual in the context. It did, however, make walking very difficult. We sat in the last row of seats in an aeroplane that I had spent hours working on in the past. Now it was my prison ship, carrying me into exile. The US marshals, one on each side of me, removed the chains and the flight proceeded in the usual way. The other passengers were then loaded and were unaware that I was a prisoner. On the US side, the passengers were to be allowed off before I was removed. A marshal's job was to escort prisoners from a pick-up point to some destination. Usually the prisoner was in custody before being despatched, quite unlike the movies.

Essex County Jail, Boston

When we disembarked at Kennedy airport in New York an agent had made prior arrangements to move us quickly through the building to board a flight to Boston. It was interesting to hear this man speaking with an Irish accent – the perfect agent to disarm and 'suss-out' Irish people who were not quite kosher at the main arrival point in the US.

At Boston airport I was handed over to two other marshals who chained me up rather tightly and placed me in a van. They were unsettled as I remained silent when they spoke to me. I was taken to Essex County jail, northeast of Boston. The induction process was fixed and there was no deviation from the procedure: everything you possessed was taken away and you were given the standard US remand-prisoner clothing; then you had a shower, put on the boxer shorts, T-shirt, orange jumpsuit and plimsolls that had been supplied. Nobody told you that if you didn't have your property collected or posted to somebody it would be donated to a charitable organisation in a number of weeks.

I was led out into a courtyard in my flimsy clothes and cloth slippers. It was covered in snow and the wind was bitterly cold as we made our way to a cellblock where new arrivals were held for a few days to assess their behaviour. Passing through the security doors I entered an auditorium with cells on two levels around a rectangular space that contained some tables and chairs. A guard sat at a desk at one end. As I approached him he said, 'What the hell are you doing here, is it domestic?' I suspect he did not see many people of my age arrive there at 11.00pm. When I explained my position his attitude became quite friendly and he put me in a cell on my own. There was only a mattress on the bed and while he was away getting sheets and blankets I lay down and fell asleep because I had been travelling for twenty-one hours.

Five hours later I was on the move again. After a sandwich and a small carton of milk, I was led out through the snow to the federal marshal's office and prepared for removal to court to be charged. The orange jumpsuit was removed and my own clothes were returned for the court appearance. A chain was placed around my waist and secured with a padlock. There were two positions for your hands: each hand could be cuffed at your side or handcuffs were attached to the chain in front. In this position a box was placed on the cuffs between the hands so that your fingers could not touch. A foot-long chain attached the two leg-irons. Depending on the mood of the individual who was putting them on, the leg-irons could be very tight. The rules insisted that the iron ring be tightened around the bare ankle. As you moved your foot forward the chain caused the iron to rotate rearwards on that ankle and forwards on the static leg. This was repeated each time that you took a step. Hence there was a constant sawing on your ankles, which drew blood if you had to hobble any distance. I assume it is to prevent you running away.

Although it was only thirty miles' distance it took five hours to get from the cell to courthouse. As we drove down Highway 1 it was strange to hear my name on the local radio news. When the marshals realised the bulletin was about one of their prisoners they switched off the radio. Prisoners were taken into the courthouse in the centre of Boston through a submerged driveway with a tight security system. I was told that one man had made a breakaway when the van door opened before the automatic doors closed and slipped out into the street, leaving his handlers inside – following this incident the doors of the transport were kept secured until the automatic exit door was fully closed.

We were taken up out of the bowels of the earth by lift and placed in holding cells. Nobody asked questions about other people's reasons for being there. If it was volunteered that was fine, but never ask was the rule. However, my fellow prisoners had heard my details on the news. Terrorist! They kept their distance and did not speak to me.

I was able to speak to my lawyer, Richard Bachman, for the first time through a grille a few minutes before going into court. This hearing was an arraignment before federal judge David Mazzone with US attorney Alexandra Leake for the government. The charges were read out (I was familiar with them since my arrest in South Africa):

1 conspiracy to violate Arms Export Control Act

2 conspiracy to injure or destroy property

3 conspiracy to destroy helicopters located in Northern Ireland and belonging to the United Kingdom, a country with which the United States is at peace

4 possessing property in aid of foreign insurgents (this charge of aiding and abetting was dropped).

I replied not guilty to each item and was remanded for a further appearance in March, which gave me time to consider what the new prosecuting attorney was offering me if I were to plead guilty.

It is the practice of most justice systems to remove chains when prisoners enter a courtroom. I have thought about that: why bother? Whose dignity is being protected, the judge's? I had been wearing the same shirt to court on various occasions for three months and my lawyer asked the judge if I could have time to change it for one brought into the court. He was amused and said he had no problem with me wearing a dirty shirt in his court. I think he missed the point.

After appearing in court one had to remain in the holding cell until the entire court session had finished. Court closed at about 5.00pm and then the marshals had to complete their paperwork before preparing prisoners for their return journey to prison. This meant you returned between 7.00pm and 8.00pm. Fifteen or sixteen hours on two sandwiches and a half pint of milk or juice, and no further food that day! If a person had to attend each day on a long trial this procedure was performed day after day and the person being tried became listless and unable to follow what was happening in court.

After a few days in the induction wing I was moved to a unit on the fourth floor of the main prison block that was reserved for federal prisoners. There are three types of prisons in the United States: county, state and federal. County jails generally house local, low-level offenders. State prisons cater for people who commit more serious crimes within the confines of the state. The federal government in Washington administers the federal prisons, which are scattered across the country. These prisons house offenders who fall outside the control of county and state jurisdiction. This group includes foreigners, those who have committed offences that cross state lines or are committed on federal lands, and those guilty of organised crime. In such cases, the federal authorities will often step in when the state is unable to cope. Sometimes separate units within prisons, as in this case, catered for the various categories.

The cell I was placed in already had an occupant. He was a Cambridge University graduate of Indian-Italian origin. He was an extremely intelligent man and would recite in total every poem that I could think of, as well as all of George Bernard Shaw's work. He was a convicted con artist, and did not seem to have any financial support from outside the prison. He spent his time touching up people for cigarettes or conning newcomers into getting him something from the canteen. I didn't have a problem with that! The real problem for me was that he ground his teeth at night. It sounded like a horse trotting up and down and it was impossible to sleep. I requested, and was granted, a move to a different cell next day, but we remained friends, as I enjoyed the intellectual stimulation, a rare commodity in non-political prisons.

A section of the prisoners in the federal wing of Essex County jail had been expecting my arrival. Generally they could be termed the 'Irish Mafia', associated with James 'Whitey' Bulger, brother of William Bulger who was president of the Massachusetts Senate at the time and later head of the University of Massachusetts and a respected elder statesman. South Boston is populated mostly by people of Irish descent and there was a level of support for the struggle in the six counties. Whitey Bulger's organisation would have contained many sympathisers and word had been sent to Whitey's associates to look out for me. Most of these prisoners were here because they refused to answer questions before a grand jury about Whitey's activities. Others were serving sentences in federal prisons across the States and were brought here to appear before the grand jury. Strange how two brothers, each in their own way, wielded such power in Massachusetts. William dominated democratic politics in south Boston by supplying jobs, speeches and handshakes. Whitey ran the local rackets, gambling, loan-sharking and drugs. Before I would leave prison in the US all that would change. In 1997 the authorities revealed that Whitey had been an FBI informant for twenty years. I can well imagine how his associates who did time to protect him must have felt. While I was in federal prisons, there was a rumour there that he tipped off the FBI about the ill-fated IRA arms ship, *The Valhalla*, which was intercepted off the Kerry coast in 1984. In any case, Whitey Bulger and his companion Catherine Greig disappeared in 1995, with or without FBI assistance, and they are still missing.

In a short time I was asked to move into a cell with Howard 'Howie' Winter. He was on one side of the Winter–Hill gangland war in Boston in the 1960s when up to thirty people lost their lives. He was here to attend a grand jury sitting on Whitey Bulger. Howie was an intelligent individual in his late sixties, and he behaved like a gentleman. We did not discuss the reasons why we ended up in prison. Overall, I was respected by prisoners and guards alike for my behaviour and code of silence. I didn't engage in unnecessary conversation. I could be trusted, a good person to have in a cell with you. The American witness protection system, where the evidence of a co-defendant was accepted against his friend's, had its flaws.

And when a prisoner was facing thirty – or 130 – years in prison there was a temptation to beef-up the evidence against someone else in order to get off lightly. In the same way a prisoner serving time like that who found himself in a cell with a high-profile prisoner could be tempted to weave a story from tit-bits to get his time reduced.

Life went on as usual in prison: we got out of the cells for an hour in the morning and I exercised by jogging up and down the stairs and using the weight machine. In the evenings when we were out for the hour I walked around the unit, a distance of about a hundred a fifty yards. While in the cells we lay on our beds because the cells were cramped. There was little conversation of any kind.

Prisoners in the federal unit were a varied lot – drug-pushers and drug-barons, bank robbers, killers; they were Irish and Italian and Jewish Mafia, Puerto Rican nationalists and Cubans waiting for deportation to a country that would not have them back. The Latin American prisoners became extremely noisy when the cells were locked for the night: why they had to shout at each other in different cells at night I could never understand. They had about three hours to communicate when they were out during the day!

I wasn't in Boston long when I saw violence; by later standards it was quite mild. Two young prisoners had an argument about basketball. It escalated into a loud exchange of threats of violence and one individual said he would 'get' the other. The threatened man returned to his cell and prepared to defend himself. He fitted a razor blade into the handle of a toothbrush to slash his opponent's face when he approached,

Most of the prisoners were in their twenties; they came from a country of plenty yet there were still pockets of extreme poverty and crime. In Boston it was Charlestown. Two young boys from there were in for robbing a bank. They had almost finished their sentence in the federal prison system for a bank robbery when they were taken to this county jail to answer questions before a grand jury about a second bank robbery. After they had negotiated that inquisition successfully and were due to return to the federal prison system to finish the short time remaining, their behaviour became more erratic. When they were in the little library one afternoon they ran riot, pulling down the bookshelves and computer, and knocking an elderly guard over. Now they were in real trouble, but they didn't seem to care and they didn't listen to the older men from Charlestown telling them to behave themselves since they were so close to release.

I returned to court in Boston in March for a bail hearing, which was not successful. In April I returned to the same court to plead guilty to all three charges. That decision was taken out of my hands – I was requested to do so by our people in the United States to avoid the possibility of my co-defendants (the others who comprised the 'Boston Three') being put on the stand as state witnesses in my trial. I was remanded for sentencing on 15 June 1994 and returned to prison.

As June approached the snow melted and we were allowed outside once a week in the courtyard for two hours (still in the orange jumpsuits and plimsolls as we were still on remand). If you had the money, you could order a salad or ham roll. I was told that the county sheriff's daughter ran this business. At that time the sheriff who ran the prison was under investigation for fraud and the contract to house federal prisoners was being rescinded and given to a recently constructed county jail at Plymouth!

I returned to court for sentencing on 15 June. In the US there was a points system for sentencing and the guidelines for my length of sentence was 22 points, which gave about three years; however, the system also allowed for a departure from the guidelines and in my case I received an upward departure of six points – this was because of penalties for special skills, higher education, military service and severity of offence. This took me to a level of 28 which meant a possible sentence of six to seven years instead of three. Since all the charges were closely related, all sentences would be served concurrently. Judge Mazzone decided to give me the lower end, but double the guideline: six years in federal prison. I could live with that, no regrets. If I had been tried with my co-accused, the 'Boston Three', years before, I could have got twelve years.

Chapter 4

Touring the States – through Its Prisons

Weeks before my court appearance a process of moving federal remand prisoners from Essex County jail to Plymouth prison had begun, so when I left court on the evening of 15 June 1994 to serve my sentence I was headed for Plymouth. It was not federal marshals who escorted me this time. Plymouth transported their own prisoners and the vehicles used were not as kind to the body as those used by the marshals. It was a converted van with wooden benches running from front to back. When you were chained up you couldn't prevent yourself sliding forward when the vehicle braked and then rearwards when acceleration took place. If the benches were not tightly packed with bodies, you got thrown around and even bruised.

Plymouth

Plymouth prison was built to reduce contact with people outside your own housing unit – you never had to leave your unit except when going to the medical unit. Each unit held about eighty people, four to each cell. There was no formal provision for exercise, reading, education or other stimulation necessary to remain healthy in mind and body. Because the unit was so secure prisoners were allowed to spend more time out of their cells, but the area allowed was very small for eighty people and I found it far too crowded. This over-crowding caused all sorts of problems, with prisoners getting into dangerous squabbles over nothing. While the others were out I passed my time writing, doing press-ups or day-dreaming about the different countries where I had lived. Food was delivered to the units on a trolley by an outside firm and visits were conducted in a room entered through a door at one end of the unit. Reinforced glass windows looked out to another room where visitors accumulated to speak to prisoners by telephone. At the opposite end of the unit there was a high walled area, about thirty feet by twelve, where you could see the sky and get some fresh air.

After a claustrophobic six weeks here the cell door opened in the middle of the night and a voice called out, 'McGuire, get up, you are out of here.' In the US, prisoners were constantly moved from one jail to another, without notice. I had to walk away from the few things I had in the hope that they might catch up with me later, because I was not allowed to carry anything, absolutely nothing. I had, early on, adopted a strategy with regard to my writing: to avoid losing material I had written, I posted it to a friend every second day, and after I returned home years later it was posted to me. In this manner, I accumulated my writings in prison. Moving was a fixed procedure: the federal marshals arrived at 7.00am to chain you up and put you on the bus. For security reasons you were never told where or when you were going, and for the same reason you got moved on regularly.

My sense of location and direction anywhere on the earth is very good, and with the rising sun on my right I knew we were now heading north. We passed through Boston and into New Hampshire, picking up and setting down prisoners at various county jails before ending up in Hillsborough county jail outside Manchester city in New Hampshire. I would become accustomed to the harshness of being moved over the following four or five years as I 'toured the States' through their prisons.

On the way we had passed by Concord. I had visited it years before with one of my 'Boston Three' co-defendants, to see where 'the shot that was heard around the world' took place at the start of America's War of Independence against Britain. Strange, I reflected now, how the descendants of the people who fought that war for freedom were now dragging me in chains past that hallowed place at the behest of their old enemy and prolonging our oppression. But the wine of freedom when drunk for a long time tastes like water. The maintenance of the status quo is a factor when you become a world power, and in order to achieve this, misbehaviour of friendly regimes is ignored.

New Hampshire

New Hampshire is in the heart of New England. Most of the town names here are from Northern Ireland and England, and there was a strong dislike for people from the Boston area, who were largely descendants of southern Irish stock and, as such, seen as inferior to Ulster Scots. Their county jail was not very nice either. I was held in my cell twenty-three hours a day; the other hour I was allowed out on my own to have a shower. The cell in which I remained was one of a number used to house new arrivals until medical status and behavioural attitudes were evaluated. The high wall of another building backed on to it so that very little daylight entered through the small window, requiring the light to be switched on during the day. During my three months there I ran into difficulties by having to use prison-issue soap because my money never arrived from

Plymouth and I could not purchase the proper toiletries. The result of this was the slow spread of dandruff from my hair on to my face and eyebrows, causing eye irritation.

While I was held in this cell new arrivals came and moved on every couple of days. They were a varied lot, from all walks of life. Joe was a full-blood Indian who had a problem with his girlfriend's family because he drank too much alcohol and became abusive. John from New Orleans had moved to the cold north when the fish catches dropped off in the Gulf of Mexico. He was an alcoholic and had hit his alcoholic girlfriend while in a drunken stupor. Neither of these men had the required fifty dollars bail to get out. Another arrival was a well-to-do businessman who also had a drink problem. He was drunk while in control of a high-speed boat running too close to shore when he hit an obstacle, throwing his two nieces overboard and into the propeller and causing them horrific injuries. He was a broken man when he sobered up. People such as this often slept for many days and nights after arrival.

When I was moved from the holding cell I was able to communicate with the general prison population but the fact that I was allowed to do this was an indication that I would be moved on again within a few days. Most of the other prisoners were waiting for trial or had been convicted of organised crime, murder or drug trafficking. One individual was a biker from California who had been in a federal prison there and got into the regime's bad books. He was sent east on what is known as 'diesel therapy'. This tactic was used on a person who stayed reasonably within the rules but cleverly disrupted the running of the system, questioning everything, refusing to work and making booze. The therapy consisted of putting a person on a 'slow' bus across the country. Each evening they were placed in a county or city jail, and in a day or two they were picked up again, and so on. The bus in question did not have to be going exactly where they were heading, but they were moved anyhow. As you might imagine, their food consisted of sandwiches and a half-pint of milk or juice. They might or might not remain long enough in a jail to get a hot meal. Mail or money never caught up with them while they were on the road. This journey could last a year or more. I heard of a man having a sack of mail dumped into his cell when his travels came to an end.

Otisville, Pennsylvania

When I was moved on from New Hampshire it happened during the daytime and it was the first and only time this happened to me in the US. Federal marshals chained me up and drove me to the local airport. A Boeing 727 aircraft sat waiting on the tarmac surrounded by marshals, some at strategic points with automatic weapons. This was one of a number of aircraft operated by the federal prison system and referred to as 'Con Air'. With almost two million prisoners in the US, an airline was needed to move them around from prison to prison for various reasons, such as court attendance, punishment, change of level of security or a move back near home. When you arrived at the aircraft you were in chains and had been searched many times. On the plane you were searched in great detail again. I had a sliver of paper with a phone number between my fingers and it was confiscated. I did not know where I was going and did not believe I could remember a phone number to let the 'Boston Three' committee know where I ended up. The only thing allowed was a receipt for the possessions you had left behind and hoped to see again.

It was quite difficult to climb the rear stairs into the aircraft with leg irons on. With your arms tightly secured you could not hold the rail or extend your foot to achieve balance with the short chain. It was also difficult to get into the seat without the use of your hands and it was virtually impossible to get up out of the seat into a standing position. Most people had to be assisted by the guards. If an accident happened, few could hope to survive. The women prisoners who occupied the front seats in the aircraft fared no better. These federal prison aircraft flew around the country in great half circles such as the route I was on: from Oklahoma south through New Mexico and north into California; or from Oklahoma south in a sweep to Florida. There were many points along each leg where prisoners were picked up and set down. One of the key hubs was Oklahoma airport. Here, in recent times, they constructed a prison in the airport itself where the aircraft pulled up beside the prison and a finger came out to allow prisoners to walk to the reception area through many security doors.

I was removed with other prisoners from the aircraft at Otisville, a joint civilian–military airport, then bussed up to a prison in the hills. Otisville is a small town of about one thousand people on the Shawanguck river near the border between Pennsylvania, New York and New Jersey and about seventy miles northwest of New York city. Most federal prisons were located in small, poverty-stricken areas away from any major city.

Otisville prison was my first experience of federal prisons and it was quite a change from county jails. This was a medium- to high-security facility and it followed the same layout and security level of similar federal jails. Four housing blocks divided into eight housing units, each holding 180 prisoners. These housing blocks were arranged in a straight line or a horseshoe shape around the service facility, which included dining hall, medical unit, gym, school and factory. Backing on to those there was usually a field for baseball and football. Two razor-wire fences, separated by an area containing motion sensors and other detection devices, surrounded the whole complex. There were armed guards in towers at various intervals and a truck with armed guards drove continuously, day and night, around a road at the outer fence. I was told that some prisoners lose control and rush the fence, ending up shot or entangled in the razor wire. Then the occasional guard also committed suicide during their long, lonely vigil in those towers. I have never witnessed either of these events take place.

In federal prisons movement from one place to another was done ten minutes to the hour every hour, except during meal times. This meant that there was nobody moving about for fifty-minute intervals. If you were caught moving outside these times you were in trouble. Food in federal prisons was generally much better than in city, county and state jails. There was enough to eat, especially if you got in early, but the quality varied from place to place. In order to feed so many people in one hour there was strict control. People were allowed into the dining hall in rotation by housing unit, work place, disciplinary default or other requirements. To try and gain advantage by jumping up the line in front of other people was regarded as disrespectful, and retribution was swift and sometimes fatal. On one occasion when I was in the food line it happened – shortly after, he dropped out on to the ground. It seems he got a blow of the edge of a fibreglass tray over the ear. Naturally, nobody saw anything.

The freedom to go outside and walk or run around the football pitch after being locked up so long gave me a sense of well-being and allowed the various skin disorders to clear up, although the sun-damage would never rectify itself fully. Before you got a job or found one for yourself in this jail, you were free to go out to the recreational area between meals, but had to return to your unit for meals and were last to eat. Those that worked in the factories were served first. At 4.00pm everybody, except those who worked in the dining hall, returned to their cells and a head count was carried out; all bodies had to be accounted for. After the evening meal everybody was free to pursue their individual interests until 8.30pm, lock-up time. The main unit door was then locked from the inside and the outer door from the outside. After a further head-count at 9.00pm the keys of this door were taken to the duty office, perhaps a quarter of a mile away.

This routine did not apply to people in the 'hole', a special housing unit that was partially underground with subdued artificial lighting where prisoners who broke the rules were sent for punishment. This unit in Otisville looked rather foreboding from the outside. 'Sammy the Bull' Gravano, Mafia boss John Gotti's sidekick, spent eighteen months there before he cracked and turned government informant. Prisoners said that the cooling was turned off in summer and the heating turned off in winter, and it really gets cold up there.

Allenwood, Pennsylvania

In a short time I was in chains again and on my way to the airport. Moving could be quite uncomfortable and some people reacted badly to it. But there was no way that you could prevent it, so you could do it the hard way or the easy way. I disciplined myself, and let it all happen. This time I was removed from the aircraft at Harrisburg, the capital of Pennsylvania. From here we were taken by bus up the narrow and tortuous Route 15 along the Susquehanna river to Lewisburg where people were dropped off at the federal penitentiary.

A penitentiary is a fifth grade up in security rating. The layers of security rating are dictated by the crime: first comes open, then low, medium, high and penitentiary, and above that there are two further levels, which are generally partially or fully underground, such as Marion in Illinois and another in Colorado. Here the most violent prisoners are held alone in cells that may have a barred enclosure attached to the cell so that the prisoner can sit outside. In other locations there may not even be an enclosure and even the shower runs along to the cell door which is opened so that the prisoner can take a shower and then return to his cell. Dark, high brick walls characterise most penitentiaries, which are used to hold dangerous people. Our destination was Allenwood, about one hundred miles north of Harrisburg. There were four prisons in this five-by-three-mile complex. Three were close together, and one, the lowest security or open prison with no walls or fences, a few miles away. I was placed in the medium-security prison, which looked down on the low- and highest-security complexes. In all, there were about five thousand prisoners at Allenwood.

The journey from Otisville took twelve hours and once again I was faced with the induction procedures. Filling up forms, fingerprinting, photographs, ID card and a worthless interview with a physician's assistant (PA). Generally the PA was a person with limited medical training, or an emigrant waiting to sit medical exams. In some cases people who dropped out of medical school and failed to repay loans were made to work it off in a federal institution. I still had a serious skin problem due to sun damage in the tropics. This was brought to the PA's attention and duly noted, and I was placed in one of the housing units.

Crowding was so bad here that people often had to sleep in the common area. There were one or two beds available in cells but some people preferred to wait and get into a cell with one of their race. I did not care who I shared a cell with in terms of their race as long as they were easy to get along with, so I was happy to share with an Afro-American rather than be exposed to the open. Exhausted from travel, I went to bed as soon as I could and fell asleep. When you shared a cell with other people who were there when you arrived, you generally deferred to their routine and rules. As time passed you might suggest modifications that were more amenable to all concerned. If you found that the routine didn't suit you, you could always move to another cell when a vacancy came up and you were acceptable to the other occupants.

Next morning I was hungry and up at 6.00am for breakfast because I had had nothing to eat the previous day. As I waited to get into the dining hall I let my eyes drift over the faces of the other people in the line and was delighted to see one of the 'Boston Three', Richard Johnson, in the group. I had not seen him since the FBI taped our conversation in his apartment five years previously. I discovered that another of our group, Martin Quigley, who had been sentenced with Richard, was also here. Although there was a total of five engineers indicted, including myself, Gerard Hoy from Pennsylvania had finished his time in prison, as had Christina Reid, from California. The remaining three of us were now in Allenwood – for a short spell, as it turned out. It was good to see Martin and Richard again after five years, but I would have preferred to meet them under different circumstances. For the short time we were there it made the place feel a little friendlier. Prior to my arrival in the United States the FBI were interested in building a psychological profile of Irish political prisoners and tried to get some of them to cooperate, but they refused, unwilling to add to the FBI's understanding of how we thought or operated. For security reasons, we now spent little time together, except when we were in the open.

In my travels through the prison system in the US, I never met an Irish person except those associated with the republican movement. There were two other men in Allenwood who were connected with the struggle in Northern Ireland: one was Mickey McNought from Derry who had been convicted with Pat Nee and others on a failed Brinks armoured car robbery in Boston's South Shore in 1991. (Nee had also been convicted in 1984 for his part in exporting arms to Ireland aboard *The Valhalla*, which was arrested off the coast of County Kerry.) The second man was Sammy Miller from Belfast who was convicted in 1993 with Limerick-born priest, Father Pat Maloney, of handling stolen money.

Allenwood medium-security prison was perched on a hill and overlooked the high wall of the penitentiary and the razor wire of the low-security unit some distance away. This bleak location exposed the prison and prisoners to the worst extremes of weather. It got hot in the summer and extremely cold in winter. I have had to walk backwards here against a temperature of minus twenty-five with a wind-chill factor of minus twenty, which pained my exposed face as if it were on fire. The bunk beds were fixed against the window wall and the wind chill turned the glass into a freezer. The only escape was to tape blankets over the window at night and wear your tracksuit in bed. If you were in a cell at the end of the heating-system run, there was little heat from the vent.

A prisoner had two weeks to find employment or be detailed as the system saw fit. The factory here produced furniture components ready for assembly at other prisons. This was part of the prison factory system operated under the name of Unicore. In Manchester, Kentucky, they produced camouflage uniforms and tarps for trucks; at Leavenworth in Kansas, printing; Petersburg, Virginia, printing and cable looms for aircraft; Ray Brook, New York, protective work gloves; Lewisburg, Pennsylvania, metal lockers and beds; Lompoc penitentiary, California, silkscreen signs and decals architectural signs; Lexington, Kentucky, furniture; Fort Dix, New Jersey, signs; Texarkana, Texas, furniture; Talladega, Alabama, furniture. The list goes on, and with so many prisoners available Unicore must be the largest corporation in the US. Nearly one in every hundred people in the US was in prison at the time I was there. Even at twelve cents an hour, Unicore would not have labour shortages. Seventy percent of workers were Afro-American – black prisoners said that most black men between the ages of eighteen and twenty-five were in jail. This work set-up seemed like a form of slavery, though they did break the law to get here in the first place. Family ties were bad and there was little support from the ghetto outside. The twelve cents an hour allowed them to purchase essentials to survive in prison. They were conscious that it was a form of slavery, but life was also tough in the ghetto.

I did not wish to work in the furniture factory in Allenwood and decided to look for a job that might benefit the prisoners or myself. Richard Johnson worked in the school and introduced me to some of the teachers. There was a seventy-five-year-old Jew who was doing clerical work and he took me under his wing. I ended up doing clerical work too and brushing up on my Spanish language two nights a week. The Jewish prisoner had worked with the United Nations, fallen foul of the Americans in Africa – and ended up here. He ran a philosophy class at night and when he was moving on he roped me into continuing it. It was quite interesting because it was a focal point for the more intellectual prisoners. Eminent people such as Joseph Campbell had produced lectures on video; this was an ideal means of opening a subject for discussion.

In time I moved on to producing study notes on science, mathematics and English for the general US basic education certificate, the equivalent to the Irish junior certificate. That created its own problems. On occasions one had to appear in a classroom to defend these notes against argument. We had disruptive members of the Nation of Islam who would dispute such things as the composition of the centre of the earth. Their rationale stemmed from a religious viewpoint, and, regarding scientific issues, they would say, 'It is not so because nobody was there to see it.' I decided to try to work at something different when I was moved to another prison.

There were several interesting prisoners in Allenwood at that time. One of them was a Russian soldier who had defected to the US with the Russian communication codes. But after he was settled he got greedy and decided to reward himself further by robbing banks. He was scheduled for deportation back to Russia after finishing his time. I wonder if that ever happened. And by one of those strange quirks of life, an American called John Walker was there also. He was the son of a US Navy man who had been trading American codes to the Russians. After the father left the navy he recruited his son John to secure the information for him. It seems his wife was unhappy with her lot and, unaware that her son was involved, she shopped her husband, much to her regret later on. John was a polite, intelligent individual.

Tommy Collins was there also. He was one of the bloodthirsty Irish-American gangsters called the 'Westies'. This group was led by Jimmy Coonan and operated in 'Hell's Kitchen', a low-income area in Manhattan located roughly from West 34th St to West 57th St between 8th Avenue and the Hudson River. Collins operated a social club at 722 10th Avenue and was a Westie soldier. Prisoners who knew him well said that he was not directly involved in the 'murder for hire' operation – but there were many other elements in the gang's portfolio to be involved in, such as loan-sharking, labour racketeering, extortion and narcotics, or cooperating with Mafia boss Paul Castellano. The bloodletting continued between the mid-1960s and 1987. At that point one of the main operators, Mickey Featherstone, testified against his mates, many of them his childhood friends. Eight defendants, including Coonan's and Collins's wives, were convicted on conspiracy to commit murder, gambling, extortion, loan-sharking and counterfeiting charges. Coonan went to Leavenworth for seventy-five years, Billy Bokum sixty years in Lewisburg, Mugsy Ritter forty years at Terre Haute, Indiana, Collins forty years in Sing Sing. Johnny McElroy got sixty years in prison but turned state witness and entered the witness protection programme with Featherstone. Coonan's wife got fifteen years and Collins's six months.

Featherstone continued to give evidence against his old friends and members of the powerful Gambino family, including John Gotti. During the 1990s there was a rumour going the rounds of federal prisons that the Westies were involved in the disappearance of Teamster boss Jimmy Hoffa in 1977. Prisons abound in such stories. I suspect it was this type of breakdown in the gangland code of silence that put paid to the alliance between Irish and Italian gangsters established by Lucky Luciano and Owney Madden more than fifty years before.

Most prisons had racist groups and city gangs. Allenwood had Aryan white supremacists, black Muslim extremists and ghetto gangs from the large cities on the east coast. This provided tension and often led to violence. Huge light assemblies dotted the prison complex, and cameras on top of these kept watch for signs of trouble. If a group was observed to be gathering, you could expect to see prison guards arrive to disperse them. Because of this you could expect to be stopped and body-searched for 'shanks' or contraband. This was nothing more than an irritant for me, preventing me from getting to where I wanted on time.

After some months my cellmate decided to work in the Unicore factory. Many prisoners made this decision because of economic necessity. If they had no support from outside they had to earn enough to purchase cigarettes, soap, shaving equipment and other items in the commissary. This meant working six days a week and overtime in the evenings to get about fifty dollars a month. Unicore workers were housed together so that they could be treated differently than other prisoners. This made economic sense and it was also convenient. They did not disturb other people when getting up early on weekends and coming in late, and in return they were allowed to eat first, getting the best of what was available. My cellmate left for the Unicore housing unit and I was getting a new customer. Before that happened another prisoner asked me to move in with him. He was known to hold strong racist views but I decided to make the change rather than take potluck on a new person moving in with me.

It was a move made in haste and though I got on well enough with the individual I regarded him as one of the most evil men I had ever met. He was a member of a pagan biker group and seemed to respect my code of conduct – quiet, no questions, no contact with staff and not be a member of any group. He felt safe enough to discuss some of the behavioural aspects of his kind of life. Among the pagan bikers there was a culture of drugs, not so much cocaine or heroin, but things like speed and amphetamines. The clubs seemed to attract people who had 'a need to belong' and as such could fall a following of teenage girls who were infatuated by the biker image. It was easy to get them to go on outings, the location or destination of which was kept secret. There the young girls might be given drugs and gang-raped. When the local chapter was fed up with them they could be passed on to another group and so on. Some just disappeared forever, dying in the gutter or murdered. Before my time he did not like some of the people he shared a cell with and did obnoxious things to get them to move on. One of his favourite tactics was to piss in their beds, not too much, but enough to cause a stench.

It might be thought that prison authorities have total control, and this is true up to a point. But without the cooperation of the majority of prisoners it would be impossible to run most prisons and the powers that be tend to make efforts to retain that goodwill. If a guard gets too troublesome there are ways to get him to look for a transfer to other duties or have the authorities move him. This biker had a novel method of achieving this. He would remove the rear of an empty toothpaste tube, fill it with excrement and re-seal it. Now he could wash it, put the cap on and carry it around. Everything that the guard handled exclusively, such as phone, pens, office door-knob and radio would be repeatedly smeared until he got the message.

The biker had problems with his leg and was on light duties, which consisted of keeping the unit clean. He spent most of his time in the cell and I felt he was concerned about his safety because he had organised a warning system. This consisted of a couple of soft drinks cans sitting on a locker and tied by a string to the cell door-handle. This was put in place whenever he wanted to lie down on his bed or when the door was locked at night. When doors were unlocked at 6.00am it was possible for an assailant to be armed with a shank, catch someone in bed and stab him to death and return to his cell undetected, but in our cell the opening of the door caused the cans to crash on to the floor. Such a racket shocked the would-be intruder, taking advantage away from him. It also alerted the occupants and heightened the intruder's chances of getting caught. I felt uncomfortable with my cellmate and decided to move as soon as I could.

I spent most of my free time outside, walking or running and, after 8.30pm lock-up, walking around the unit. The circuit of the ground floor was about 60-70 yards and it was about the same on the landing. The landing was used around this time as a parade area for the usual collection of gays found in most federal prisons who dressed up in plimsolls, dyed, oversized T-shirts and make-up. They were not much 'in your face' because they generally had settled partners. The worst violence and death was associated with homosexual intrigue and unpaid debts for gambling or drugs.

Time was passing and I was having no success in getting my skin cancer attended to. The PAs kept blocking my efforts to see a doctor. Their attitude was: 'It is OK, all we would be doing would be cosmetic.' Eventually I got to the point where I said that I would have to contact the Irish embassy and request them through Washington to assist me to get medical attention. It may have been a coincidence, but shortly afterwards I was called to the unit office and told that I was being transferred to another prison. As it happens, my daughter was due to arrive from Europe at that time to visit me and I had given a date to the unit and was told that it was suitable. For security reasons you were not told where or what date you were to be moved. On the morning of the expected visit I was moved from my cell at 3.00am and chained up for the bus ride at 7.00am. My biker companion wished me luck and said I was the best person he had shared a cell with over the years. My daughter arrived for the visit but by then I was on a moving bus somewhere in the mountains. I had not seen her since my arrest two and a half years before and it was a great disappointment missing her, but the ordeal of the bus journey and the new prison kept my mind off the issue for forty-eight hours. My daughter, too, was used to all kinds of difficulties as she had lived in the Third World as a child; in any case, she was on a working trip to the US and she simply continued with her work. Talking to her since, she says that missing out on the visit did not upset her unduly. Contact with family was difficult – during my years in America I had four visits in total from family members. Normally I wrote a letter home or made a censored phone-call at a set time each week if I was not on the move and my money was following me to my new destination – though there is actually a credit-card system that allows you to purchase a limited range of items and make a five-minute call in such circumstances.

Cumberland, Maryland

In the Pennsylvanian mountains winter gives way slowly to spring which lasts until June. It was a bitterly cold April morning as we hobbled along in chains and leg irons to the bus outside the security perimeter. The cold wind blew through the flimsy T-shirt and trousers and I remembered the blanket men in Long Kesh and started to sing. The few Afro-Americans with me joined in, humming and jerking their bodies in time. We were soon silenced by threats of being taken back and placed in the hole from gun-toting, tobacco-chewing guards. Then the bus refused to start and we had to sit there in the freezing cold for over an hour while they tinkered with the motor. We got on our way about 8.00am. The route we took that day through the Pennsylvanian mountains is still a mystery to me. We were on the road for eight hours to cover a distance of approximately two hundred miles. We travelled on twisting roads through the high country and I was shocked by the poverty that I saw along parts of the route. Up there they lived in dilapidated mobile home sites or wooden shacks that were falling apart. One might imagine that these unfortunates were black; not so, there are few black people living in rural America.

The arrival and induction process at Cumberland federal prison in Maryland was less of an ordeal than at most other places I have been. It was a more detailed operation conducted by pleasant individuals and did not entail hanging around for long hours. Perhaps the reason for this was that it was a new prison with new staff who had not yet been exposed to the harsh realities of prison work. And we were 'pussycats', sent here to open the prison and check out its facilities – the hard cases would arrive later! There were about three hundred people there when I arrived; the capacity was for about fifteen hundred. This meant the budget provided for better food and medical attention. Over the following year the population would reach its full complement, increasing stress and leading to a gradual degradation in living conditions.

When I reached my housing unit I was placed in a cell with a young German-American who was six foot four inches tall and about twenty-three stone weight. He was quite a pleasant person who was a convicted con-man. As usual after a journey in chains, I climbed into the top bunk as soon as I got organised and went to sleep. Hours later, when my body had recovered somewhat, I was disturbed by the bed shaking. As I came out of deep sleep I became aware of the loud snoring that accompanied the shaking. The huge body on the cot below shook each time he exhaled. That put an end to sleeping for the rest of the night and I moved to a different cell the next day. The occupant there was a businessman of German-Irish extraction who was convicted of transporting chemicals to manufacture amphetamines in his private aircraft. We got along fine for the short time he was there.

The first week there was spent getting settled in. I arrived with nothing but three pieces of light clothing and slippers – and there was snow on the ground. The time was spent in the clothing store, laundry, at interviews with the case manager, unit manager, medical people and sociologist. The medical doctor was a lovely African–American lady who had time to see people because of the small number of prisoners there at the time. It would become very difficult for her when the facility became overcrowded later on. She was interested in my travels around the world and the time I had spent in Africa. My body language probably indicated that I was not a racist and we had an easy relationship where I respected her and she looked after my pressing medical problem, which she considered very serious. Even with the best effort it takes quite some time to arrange an appointment with a skin specialist outside prison. Security, transport, and the number of people on the list determine how soon one can be taken out. When I eventually saw a specialist he immediately operated on the most serious cell cancer and arranged further treatment. It would take twelve months of cutting, scraping and liquid nitrogen treatment to clear up my skin.

When I arrived in Cumberland the prison was like a university campus – if, like me, you could ignore the double razor-wire fences. For me these wire fences were effective but not as obtrusive as walls that blocked out the light. It was possible to look through and beyond them into the high, wooded countryside, and this gave me a sense of openness and freedom. Quite a few of the original trees had been left inside when the facility was constructed. Trees with many grey squirrel nests flanked the walkways to the various buildings. The recreational area also had trees, but these were removed for security reasons during my time there.

The prison was located on a small hill surrounded by higher hills covered with forest. As spring drifted into summer I was able to adjust mentally to appreciate the beauty of the countryside. The trees inside attracted the birds, and the wildflowers had not yet been cut to extinction, and one could find space to be alone. Though I was behind security fences I had a sense of freedom up there, perhaps greater than the tobacco-chewing guards who were forced to work there out of economic necessity. I also had a feeling of nostalgia, bringing to mind the verse by Mary Coleridge I had learned many years before:

On alien ground, breathing an alien air,
A Roman stood, far from his ancient home
And gazing, murmured, 'Ah, the hills are fare
But not the hills of Rome!'

Cumberland was once called 'Queen City' and was the capital of Maryland then. When the railways lost their importance, manufacturing and mining interests moved away and the area went into decline similar to what happened in the neighbouring Pennsylvanian coal-mining communities. Federal prisons, while not welcome at prosperous times, were invited now; this one was located on the site of an old glass factory. In the old days the Cumberland gap was one of the few ways through the mountains and a decision was made to construct the Chesapeake and Ohio canal from the coast through there. It was mostly immigrant labour that was employed to do the job and quite a large percentage of the workers were Irish.

It was said that it was cheaper than getting the slaves to do the work, as when a slave got ill or injured there was a responsibility to take care of them and there was no such obligation with these poor immigrants. Yet, there was no shortage of workers. The job proved very difficult and before it was completed the Baltimore and Ohio railroad overtook it, making it redundant before it was finished.

The area was a 'flash point' in the American Civil War and was considered a strategic military objective. Starting with the John Brown episode at Harper's Ferry in 1859 the state of the Union deteriorated until it tore itself apart in the spring of 1861. Stonewall Jackson would march up and down the valley fighting off the Union forces until he was put out of action at Chancellorsville. As I sat chained in prison buses travelling through that most beautiful countryside I speculated about the wisdom of the Confederate forces invading Union territory. Establishing a frontier and defending it may have been an option. Still, if the populations and industrial capacity is considered, a Union victory seemed inevitable.

I decided to work in the facilities department of Cumberland prison. A prison with sixteen hundred people is a sizeable village in most countries and requires all the normal utilities and support. There would be only a half-dozen skilled prison personnel there and prisoners were used to carry out all the work. Because of my technical background I wasn't allowed to work on anything sensitive. If there was a serious problem with a system I would be asked to check it out, otherwise I looked after the spares, wages and general administration. After systems were up and running, prisoners arrived at the rate of about one hundred per week and soon the unrest began. Fights were frequent and there was a constant stream to and from the hole. Naturally, you only saw a small number of these incidents because of the size of the place and different work areas. But it was difficult to avoid problems; even an accidental brush with another person could escalate into a life-or-death situation. Such an incident happened when a large group of people was hanging around outside the dining hall on the narrow walkway. Passing through the group, a prisoner scrubbed the toecap of another prisoner's boot; he immediately apologised for the accident. The offended person replied, 'Not good enough, get down and lick it.' Naturally there was a negative response, with a note of aggression. This escalated into a heated exchange, which left the 'Bootman' losing face when the offender walked away, dismissing him with colourful language. The stage was now set. Who would strike first? The man who walked away armed himself with a 'shank', a sharp, metal spike about six inches long. He soon dispatched his adversary. After such incidents the 'goon squad' would arrive to remove the body and we never knew if he lived or died. His attacker was sent to the hole then transferred elsewhere to face trial.

One morning in 1996 at about 11.00am we were all returned to our housing blocks and locked in our cells. This seemed unusual to me because the people who worked in the kitchen were included. Who was going to prepare the meals? After a short time news of what was afoot passed from cell to cell. There was widespread rioting and destruction in federal prisons across the States – prisons had been torched and people had lost their lives. We were locked down before the news arrived to prevent the same thing happening in Cumberland. Prisoners were being transferred from the damaged facilities to every available space, including the hole, in those prisons such as Cumberland that had escaped the general mayhem. It would be spam sandwiches and a half-pint of juice or milk pushed in through a hatch in the door for the foreseeable future. This confinement could go on for weeks, which was unpleasant when you had to share a cell with other people. The only escape was to climb up and lie on your bed for hours on end. I allowed my vivid imagination to carry me back through stored memories of people, places and experiences.

After a few weeks we were allowed out of our cells and the process of returning the prison to normality was set in motion. There was nothing happening for a few days and it was good to get out in the fresh air once more. When the order was given to return to work most people ignored it. So, we were back in our cells again. The authorities knew that most prisoners had little support from their families who lived in the ghettos, and that they depended on the few cents per hour that they earned to keep them in cigarettes and toiletries. To break the deadlock they leaned on those who were the most dependent – most of them worked in the factory and they were removed from their cells and taken to work. They numbered about half the population and this action collapsed the protest. The remainder returned to work when the order was posted a few days later.

* * *

I kept to myself while I was in prison in the US. If someone spoke to me, I answered, and left it at that. Most people were aware of who I was and why I was there. At work I was often the only white person in there and the black men talked freely as if I was also black. Occasionally one would be reflective and say, 'At least you are here for your country, I am only a drug dealer.'

One of these men in his mid-forties had been in and out of prison since he was seventeen. On his first conviction, for a barroom brawl, he was singled out for rape but was able to escape by stabbing his attacker. For this he received more time and a reputation for violence. On his excursions outside he sold drugs and lived life in the fast lane. He still held the view that it was his only way to get a chance to sample the good life as opposed to living all his life in poverty in the ghetto. To prolong his time outside he tended to deliver drugs to rich customers and avoided selling on the street. He had many unbelievable stories about his visits to private homes. He informed me that one rich man had his fix and while getting 'high' he lay on the floor underneath a glass top table with a young nude woman sitting on her hunkers defecating on top of it.

Here also we had two brothers who had served in Vietnam and robbed banks in Texas after they left the military. One of them worked with me and talked about their modus operandi. They visited banks hundreds of miles away from where they lived and observed the routine of staff and security. When the decision to rob was made, they parked a second car a few blocks away with a change of clothes. They then disguised themselves and entered the bank, one controlling the people and the other dealing with the bank staff. This proved successful until they broke the rules and entered a bank without doing their homework because their selected target had to be abandoned due to police activity in the vicinity. No security was noted during a cursory check and they returned shortly afterwards in disguise.

The oldest brother entered first and the younger man followed to cover the door and customers. As the first man reached the counter he heard a shot. Thinking his brother had discharged the gun he turned to shout at him and came under fire from a security guard behind a desk in the customer area. He took a round in the shoulder but was able to pin the guard down by rapid fire from two hand guns he carried and retreat out through the door. He told me that he could easily have killed the guard if he had wanted to. They were able to make a clean getaway, but the first shot had hit the younger man on the skull above the left ear, severing an artery and taking part of his ear away. I was shown the ear and the missing piece, so I expect the story was true. Loss of blood was so severe that the young man needed to be taken to hospital and that meant going to prison also.

John Riggi was in the cell below me in Cumberland federal prison. He was believed to be the boss of the DeCalvacante Mafia family across the Hudson River in New Jersey. On the morning of 16 December 1985 he had a meeting with Big Paul Castellano, the Godfather and boss of 'the family' in New York. They met in a diner in Staten Island before John and his driver Tommy Brilotti drove to Manhattan to meet an attorney and, most importantly, to keep an appointment with John Gotti, the *capo* from Queens. It was dark and wet on that December evening when Castellano's car halted outside Sparks Steak House at 210 east Forty-sixth Street. The hit squad went into action immediately and both men were killed in the fusillade. John Gotti replaced the slain Godfather and it is difficult to believe that such a position would be open to a man involved in Castellano's demise if there was no prior understanding among the bosses of other mafia families.

Liam Atkins – if that was his real name – was in Cumberland also. He claimed he was a special-forces man and a member of Oliver North's team. When the Iran Contra scandal broke, he was in possession of the secret bank account numbers. He was unwilling to divulge these numbers and brought the wrath of the authorities down on himself. In order to help him change his mind, they revoked his licence to carry a gun, and at a later date they arrested him for being in possession of a weapon without the licence. He was cooling his feet in Cumberland federal prison when I met him and he claimed that he went to the Irish embassy in Washington to collect a passport before proceeding on a clandestine mission. I had some reservations about this but when I considered that the group *did* pose as Irish businessmen when delivering arms to Iran I did not know what to think.

* * *

When I was in Allenwood prison in 1995, I applied to the Department of Justice in Washington to be transferred back to Ireland to complete the three remaining years of my sentence there. For this to happen, legislation had to be enacted in Ireland. It was not until two and a half years later, in the summer of 1997, that I was told – in the middle of the night – to pack my few items for storage and I was taken to security for processing. I was not told what was happening but as my pieces were being stored I expected to return. In order to get out of the US it was necessary to appear before a federal judge. In the southeast this process is usually carried out in Oakdale federal prison in Louisiana. I had no idea where I was going on that July morning but after we got on the road the sun indicated that we were moving north. By early afternoon the bus was sitting in the stifling heat on the tarmac at Harrisburg airport. The aircraft was delayed and it was unbearably hot chained in your seat in the bus. By not providing food and drink, toilet problems were reduced, but dehydration could be a problem. The summer sun beat down on the metal of the bus and I willed the day to pass. Sitting there I think that I began to understand what was meant by 'Joshua's sun standing still on Gideon'. Buses arrived from all the prisons in the surrounding mountains but I was still surprised when I was steered towards a bus rather than the aircraft. In the late afternoon I was again surprised to find the bus heading south on highway 85. We arrived in Baltimore City jail at 7.00pm, twelve hours after leaving Cumberland, which is located in the mountains to the west less than one hundred miles away.

Baltimore

Baltimore prison was the worst that I had ever been in, worse than any in Ireland or South Africa. Located in the city centre, it was built to a vertical plan. The ventilation in the underground part was poor and the place was very hot. The processing took four hours and afterwards we were finally issued with our first drink and a sandwich in sixteen hours. We then received our jumpsuit and bundle of bedclothes and were put in a bullpen with standing-room only. Later we were told that there were no cells available and we were there for the night. It was virtually impossible to push through the bodies to get to the toilet in the corner and there were cries of 'hit the flush' every time someone used it. At this point I had the feeling that my time here would be a journey through the valley of darkness.

At 5.00am we were removed from the pen and taken up from the bowels of the earth to units on the high-rise floors and placed in cells vacated by other prisoners that morning. I was put with a prisoner who was there for a week because he did not turn up for his drug counselling. I looked at the top bunk. No pillow and a rancid, dirty piece of foam rubber for a mattress. Untying my bedroll, I found a blanket and half of one sheet and no towel. I was tired, so I steeled myself; I pulled the foam up on the metal edge of the cot, placed my slippers underneath to form a pillow and put my folded half-sheet on it. Throwing the blanket across the filthy foam in such a way that half of it folded back across me, I hopped in with jumpsuit still on and fell asleep. In the evening we were allowed out for an hour to have a shower and walk around the unit. I used the federal T-shirt, which I had arrived in, as a towel, hoping that it would dry for use the next evening. I asked the guard about the missing bedclothes and towel. He said politely, 'Yes, sir, I will organise that right away.' They never arrived while I was there.

After a few days my cell companion was released and a new man arrived in the middle of the night. Next morning I woke up when the guard banged the door so that food could be pushed in through the slot. I was utterly engulfed by fumes from the bottom bunk that smelled like chicken shit. My fellow prisoner was obviously living rough on the streets of Baltimore. Worse was to follow as he came to after forty-eight hours' sleep. He would then sleep during the day and prowl around the cell at night, talking to himself. Apart from the noise there was no way of knowing if he might 'lose it' and attack me while I was asleep, but I considered the top bunk a defendable position.

There was a vicious culture of stealing clothes and shoes in Baltimore. This was a battlefield and you could lose your life just as quick as your shoes. The weaker were attacked or intimidated, and one man from eastern India, a gentle individual, just sat there as they robbed everything. That was not always the outcome. One bully who tried to force a fellow prisoner to hand over his runners picked on the wrong man and was stabbed to death. For a while, we were confined twenty-four hours a day in our dark, hot cells.

In August 1997 James K. Bredar, a federal public defender, came to see me and said that he had been appointed to represent me at a court hearing in the US district court in Baltimore. At 4.00am on 15 August I was removed from my cell and placed in one of the many bullpens in the basement of the building. The numbers involved were unbelievable: all the pens were filled up and the procedure of preparing paperwork and other requirements started so that people were ready for dispatch to court and other prisons by seven o'clock. I was lucky that I was very fit and always participated in athletic events in prison: on my sixtieth birthday I competed in the all-comer mile event and came fourth – most of the individuals competing were in their twenties or early thirties. This strength sustained me in the hot and humid conditions in the depths of Baltimore city jail on that August morning where men thirty years younger than I were struggling to breathe. The ordeal lasted about five hours before I was chained up for removal to court.

The court hearing was an immigration procedure to provide some protection to people due for removal from the US. It gave them the opportunity to plead their case against deportation to a country where they would be at risk of persecution or death. I could not see how this applied to me as I had been brought to the US against my will in the first place. But the law is the law, and Judge Daniel Cline went through the list of questions and signed the necessary papers for the journey back to Ireland. On my way back to jail a male and female prisoner accompanied me. The man had absconded from a halfway house in Cincinnati when he had only a few weeks left before he was free. He said that the supervisor there had made it impossible for him to finish his time. He was arrested in Hagerstown, Maryland, after six years on the loose. His ex-girlfriend turned him in. The woman prisoner who was of Afro-European extraction was on her way to a prison in Louisiana for drug offences. She was the only female prisoner I ever spoke to in the US although they were transported in the same buses and aircraft.

After the court appearance I remained in Baltimore for some weeks and my cellmate slowly adjusted to his confined living conditions, not an easy task for a person used to living rough outside. He decided to try and improve his lot by getting moved to the sickbay area. To make this move he decided to fake a collapse. I counselled against such a move, but he persisted and spread himself on the floor. I banged on the door and when the guard arrived he had the look of a man who had seen it all before. He looked at me and I guessed he could read my face – a sense of amusement rather than concern must have registered there. He gave the man five minutes to get up, otherwise he would be back with the 'goon squad' to take him to the hole. That soon put an end to his playacting and he was still in the cell when I was removed for my twelve-hour journey back to Cumberland federal prison. On this occasion, regardless of the chains, I was really happy to see the high country after my experience in the coastal city.

Cumberland, then Lewisburg

After a month in Cumberland I was again travelling north in the early-morning sunshine. I looked out, perhaps for the last time, on the beautiful hills and valleys as we passed through the Cumberland Gap into Pennsylvania. After picking up more bodies at Harrisburg airport we arrived at Lewisburg penitentiary at 7.00pm after a long, hot day.

From the outside this prison is the most foreboding I ever saw. It sits out on its own and the high walls and watchtowers are constructed in dark brown brick that adds to the gloom. For such a large complex the reception area is extremely small, narrow, and partially below ground. Our bus arrived shortly after another, overcrowding the area and, to make matters worse, word went around that the prison was on total lockdown. It seems that the white Aryan Brotherhood had killed two black Nation of Islam Muslims earlier in the day. We were accommodated within a crowded hospital ward that had rows of two-tier bunk beds that made it very stuffy and dark. High-security prisoners in a crowded open space such as this increased the danger level. There was quite a lot of bickering and heated confrontation, and I was glad to be on board another bus after only two weeks.

I knew at this point that I was heading back to Ireland, but I still did not know from what port of exit I would leave the US. By midday this bus, with its three passengers, crossed into New York State. I was going to New York city. Climbing up into the high country again we dropped off the other two men at Otisville federal prison. This operation was carried out by the contingent of heavily armed tobacco-chewing guards and the occasion was used to dump a sandwich and small carton of juice through the door to me, much in the same way you feed lions in a cage.

Manhattan

The sun was setting on the upper levels of the skyscrapers as the bus with its lone passenger laboriously made its way through the traffic to Park Row in Lower Manhattan. The vehicle was reversed into the Metropolitan Correctional Centre (MCC) before I was unchained and led into the reception area. Here I frequently asked for something to eat or drink as the usual formalities were slowly adhered to. The answer was always the same: 'We are arranging that for you, Sir.' Eventually I was led into a lift and taken to level five, but there was no food there either.

In this prison, it seemed that the level of security increased the more you went up and, with the lift system, security was simple to implement. In 1990 Sammy 'The Bull' Gravano and John Gotti, the Mafia Godfather, had been lodged in maximum security on the ninth floor on multiple charges. Here people were alone in their cells and they were shook down every time they came out for a shower or exercise. Co-defendants were never out at the same time. As in most city jails the ceilings were very low, which created a gloomy atmosphere. This was exasperated by the shortages of bed-clothes and towels. The deficiencies were eventually overcome by waiting for somebody who was due to move when you could negotiate or barter for his. The seventh floor was medium-security and we were allowed out during the day, except for an hour for lunch and evening meal. There were a couple of pieces of gym equipment for exercising and you could walk up and down the unit until you became dizzy. Joe Doherty from Belfast spent years in MCC fighting extradition to Northern Ireland – he has a nearby street named after him – but he was eventually returned to the British.

After I had spent a couple of weeks here, a New York lawyer, Sean Downes, the only person allowed to visit me, handed in civilian clothes, an indication that my departure wasn't far off. One morning, early in October 1997, I was removed from level seven and taken down to the reception area where I was given my civilian clothes and placed in a holding room. In mid-afternoon the door was unlocked and a prison officer from Portlaoise put his head in and asked if I was ready to go. That was the second contact I had with an Irish person in eighteen months. The other person was Éamon Ó Cuiv, the TD from Galway and grandson of Éamon De Valera, who took the trouble to visit me in Cumberland federal prison. For this he will always have my respect, although we did disagree on many aspects of his grandfather's political life.

When I was chained and ready to go to JFK airport, Manhattan evening traffic was at its peak. The operation to get me there took on gigantic proportions. The traffic along the avenues to

Queensboro bridge was stopped by flak-jacketed police leaning out of their car windows. The noise of federal marshals, police and FBI car sirens was deafening as the cavalcade careered at breakneck speed along the avenues and boulevards to the airport. When we arrived at the Aer Lingus departure entrance, there was a stampede of armed and bullet-proof jacketed individuals to surround the vehicle in which I sat. I still find it difficult to understand the necessity for such posturing. Then my leg-irons were removed so that I could walk normally into the building – I do not know whose dignity they were trying to protect, certainly not mine. The marshals tried to cover the chains and handcuffs on my waist and, much to their annoyance, I kept exposing them.

As we entered the building, two lovely Aer Lingus stewardesses came up, took me by the elbows and ushered me into a lift. In the confusion, I ended up in the lift separated from all the high security milling around outside. When the lift reached the upper level the armed contingent came charging up the stairs and across the departure area to grab me, much to the astonishment of the waiting passengers – an episode from the Keystone Cops!

I boarded first, the US marshals removed their chains and I was seated between two Portlaoise prison officers in the last row of seats at the rear of the aircraft. When the passengers had exited to the arrivals building at Dublin, I was taken down the service steps on to the tarmac. The usual contingent of police outriders, prison transport, police cars and military escort was waiting there in the early-morning darkness. For me it was returning to a strange land after almost ten years' absence. As the cavalcade rushed along the new motorways I was totally lost. It was not until we reached Newlands Cross that I started to recognise familiar landmarks, but further south other towns had been bypassed, adding to my confusion.

The men were still in their cells when I was placed in the political area in Portlaoise. I was tempted to go around and kick all the doors and annoy them, but things had changed here also. The ceasefire had been in operation for years, and many of the people who had been there when I was taken to America were long gone. Many volunteers who had had to leave for foreign shores in order to assist their local units were returning from across the world; it seemed like a giant octopus was pulling in its invisible tentacles. Constructed over the years and radiating from the centre, these volunteers had actually helped to stall a vast NATO army. Strange to hear the many and varied accents along those landings – many more arrived by helicopter each week as the English- and American-born volunteers opted for the transfer to their spiritual homeland before release. I hope they found what they were searching for there.

There were ten weeks left on my sentence when I arrived back and they passed very quickly. The camaraderie that one finds in a political prison is missing elsewhere and keeps your spirits high. The prison regime had also relaxed and the police were no longer in their cage in the unit. People were getting early release before Christmas in 1997, and I was allowed to go with them about ten days before I was due out.

* * *

It was dark at 7.00am on that December morning when we walked out the door into the glare of TV camera lights. I delayed my exit to avoid the cameras and as my bag was being placed in the boot of a friend's car, a reporter asked the driver who I was and he replied, 'I don't know.' The reporter looked at me again and decided to ask no questions.

I was dropped in Dublin city centre and as I walked along Grafton Street I was jostled by the Christmas shopping crowds like a cork in rough water. It was as if I had come out of a sterile hell into a crowded jungle. My senses had been stripped and were now overcome by the scent of perfume, the aroma of coffee and other stimulants that had vanished from my existence long ago.

I reflected on my situation: so this was where life's journey had brought me. The cost was high. Everything I had was gone except the dreams. The dream that I could still work and make a good living; that the ceasefire in the north of Ireland was the end of the first step to freedom; that the peace agreement would deliver civil and human rights for all our people and would be the final step.

While in prison I kept the hopelessness at bay by working, exercising, daydreaming and writing. I had had the privilege of living in many parts of the world, had experienced many different cultures and peoples, and all of this changed me and my attitudes. Being confined gave me a rare opportunity to reflect on how my thinking had changed and how I had come to form my most deeply held beliefs, especially my political beliefs, which were the underpinning of my life's activities for over twenty years.

What follows in this book is my reflection on my life, written over those years in prison – reflection on my work and commitments, on my growing political awareness and on the part I played in the struggle in the six counties.

PART II
EARLY YEARS IN THE NORTH OF IRELAND

Chapter 5

Early Life

I was told that I was born on a grim winter's day – Christmas market day in Castleblayney in 1936 made my birthday easy to remember. Perhaps Maggie Barry, that wandering minstrel, called to look at me that day as she made her way back to Crossmaglen after the fair. Yes, there was still a living for a bard then in this ancient Celtic area. They walked around to all the surrounding towns, where they sang on the streets and sold copies of their songs. This singer was not from Armagh, she was a native of Cork. When she passed our way she always called in to rest her weary feet and have her customary sandwich and tea. When I was old enough to understand, I recall her playing the banjo and singing her wild Irish songs, her long, dark hair moved in rhythm with the music, weaving a magic that could steal a young boy's heart away.

My parents' small farm was located east of Castleblayney, across Lough Muckno in a triangle of mid-Monaghan that jutted into County Armagh. This area has distinct boundaries and is one in history and culture with south Armagh.

There is an ancient boundary on the south and west called the Black Pig's Dyke. This two-thousand-year-old double ditch or embankment runs across south Ulster. As children we learned the stories of how it came into being. One of these stories tells of an unpleasant schoolteacher who lived near Slieve Gullion mountain in Armagh who had a magic wand. When he was upset with disobedient children he would use his magic wand to turn them into birds or animals. One father, waiting for his children to return home from school, was very upset when four little pigs ran up to him and called him father. In a rage he ran to the school, grabbed the teacher's magic wand and struck him with it, turning him into a huge black pig. He then chased him across south Ulster. The pig kept his nose to the ground and so threw up the double ditch!

The people who lived in this area of Monaghan had generosity and a sense of identity. They had often suffered reverses at the hands of nature, but after the country was partitioned in 1922 they were cut off from their natural hinterland and although they were industrious they suffered great deprivation, especially during the economic war in the 1930s. Through this harsh material existence they held a great love for the land – the rolling hills and deep valleys was their earth, their past, future, their love. A land made holy by the blood sacrifices of their Celtic ancestors.

The old ways die hard and people living at the mercy of nature's whims retain animistic beliefs – spirits guard mountains, trees and rivers must be pacified, omens are read from shooting stars. Many other superstitions existed and still do. There are omens in the black cat crossing the road, meeting a red-haired woman going to a fair, the number of magpies seen, the cry of the banshee or the mutterings of some local 'simpleton'.

When I was young, pagan rituals still survived – yes, they were now adapted as Christian and used saints' names, but they were pagan all the same. The holy wells were a big belief, and these went back to the god of healing fountains, Nemausus. People circled sun-wise around the well while saying prayers, though they didn't sprinkle the blood of some sacrifice as they once may have done. Then there was the wishing tree, and sun-wise circuits were made around it, then pins or coins put into it and a wish made. May Day was marked and this was from the Gaelic feast of Bealtaine (Fire of Belenos) called after the Celtic god Belenos. Samhain had become Halloween; 1 November was the start of the Celtic new year, a time of human sacrifice to ensure luck during the coming year. The belief still existed that the gateway between this world and the other opened for a brief period that night. It was a night of fear and danger when the dead returned as ghosts and demons – and you stayed in the house. The masks worn and the games played nowadays by children, and the food or cash offerings by householders to them, hark back to the ancient fear of evil spirits and the rites used to appease them or calm their anger.

There was no electricity and no machines in our area then and it could be extremely dark and silent at night. The older people made little distinction between the real and the unreal world. Their imagination was vividly alert and not checked by logic or reason. Strange noises were imagined to represent demons or ghosts, and people hurried away in the dark, too frightened to investigate. The Irish people were a superstitious people and most of them still carried a good luck charm to ward off evil or for luck when playing a game. They were familiar with things they considered bad luck: the meeting of two people on a stairs, the number thirteen – people would not go on a journey on the thirteenth, or if a party had thirteen people they would send out for another person or send one home. Magpies were unlucky, as was putting a shoe on the table; a crowing hen was unlucky, a rooster crowing before midnight, a strange hen arriving at your house. When a hen was going to hatch eggs, you put one extra in for luck and placed a horseshoe behind the nest to ward off evil. When you finished milking a cow you spat on her to guard against the evil eye. I remember people saying that if your neighbour put his eye on an animal it was better to let him have it because it would do you no good. On May Day, May flowers were put in your well, but if someone got there before you they could take all your luck for that year.

The supernatural has always had a place in the folklore of Ireland. And the Monaghan-south Armagh area is rich in stories of ghosts and banshees. The banshee was supposed to be heard '*ag caoineadh*' or crying for certain families. When people heard the banshee it was expected that someone would die in that family. She was supposed to be seen combing her hair. I never found anybody who had seen or heard one; it was always a person who knew somebody who knew somebody else who did.

Ghosts were more common and most of the people of my parents' age claimed that they had seen a ghost. I heard many stories about people getting a fright, but I felt that natural things always caused it. Men walking home late at night with drink taken often sat down for a rest and fell asleep, then woke up to see strange things. This happened to a man that I knew when I was very young. He was on his way home from a pub; he had a pound of sausages for his meals the next day and he sat down at the entrance to a house that was supposed to be haunted. He woke up with something pulling him along by the coat. He instantly thought of the ghost and he instinctively lashed out with his walking stick and heard the yap of a dog. Two large dogs were dragging him along trying to get the sausages out of his pocket!

Another incident happened when two young men were returning late at night to their home. They had decided to cut the journey short by passing through a graveyard. Normally this route was used only during the day. One of their friends overheard them, went in front of them and climbed into a freshly dug grave. When his two friends arrived he crawled out, moaning, and they got out of there as fast as their legs could carry them. They were telling the story for ages afterwards until their friend decided to divulge the truth.

We had a frequent visitor who used to come for a dance, a *céilí*, which was the main social activity in country areas then. On one occasion he arrived quite distressed, claiming that he had seen a coach with a headless driver coming down the little road that led up to a house that was supposed to be haunted. I spent many nights lying out waiting for the coach, but it never came. When I reached teenage years the house was then unoccupied so I decided to investigate. The house had a sealed room which people said was there to restrain a ghost. I gained entrance to the room but found nothing. In frustration I became the ghost instead. I wrapped myself in a bed sheet and went around frightening people until a local man decided to fire his shotgun at me.

My father was of the Catholic faith and he was born at Cappy near Crossmaglen in south Armagh. He was a farm hand, working in the surrounding counties. It was doing such work in my home area in the 1920s that he met my mother's family, Protestants called Bailey, who lived at Tullydonnell, south Armagh. They were descendants of a planter family that came to Ireland about 250 years ago. Mixed marriages were not common then but both families seemed to get on well together, perhaps because my mother's brothers came to our place to fish. It was my aunt Lilly who first became involved with my father, and when she emigrated to the United States at eighteen years of age she expected my father to join her there and she wrote many letters to him. For some reason, she sent the letters through Margaret, my mother, who delivered them. The regular contact with my father developed into a relationship and they married in the late 1920s.

With the passing of each generation the once-large estate had been divided into smaller lots. The family dispersed and married into different names until it almost vanished. I remember visiting relations at Inniskeen and watching them prepare for the hunt; the senior member of the family wore a 'stovepipe' hat and a long swallow-tailed coat, and servants assisted him on to his horse.

My mother inherited the home farm when her father died. But when she went to probate possession, the farm was totally in debt to the banks. The small amount of money remaining after the bills were paid was used to purchase a small farm in Monaghan, near the old homestead. This is where I was born and remained until I was sixteen.

* * *

Shortly before I was due to go to school, I got sick with rheumatic fever and this delayed my starting school until I was six years old. I attended Dromore School which was about three miles' walk each way. When I first arrived I had four older sisters there in various grades above me; one sister was two classes ahead of me. Both of us were in the lower level, which was taught by Miss Gangley, whilst Mr Connolly covered the older grades.

This was a time when corporal punishment was the accepted thing. Miss Gangley used a bamboo cane and Mr Connolly preferred the less flexible ash rod cut out of the hedge. The cane was used across the hands or legs if you did not complete your homework or failed to answer a question. My sister was two years older than me and sat in a class slightly removed from mine. After the teacher used a tactic to demean her by saying, 'You can't answer that, I bet your younger brother can', I deliberately began to answer her questions wrongly to avoid hurting my sister; some years later we found out that she had a hearing defect.

The male teacher would send a boy out to cut a new ash rod for him when the old one became weathered and dried out. On one occasion when the boy came back with the rod, the master said, 'Let me try it, hold out your hand', and proceeded to give him five slaps on each hand. They were hard times for children. I was able to cope with school and had no problems getting results so I got less slaps than most. When you were struck with the rod on your little hand by an adult it crushed the flesh of your fingers and thumbs against the bones and it remained painful for days after. The cane left blue welts across the backs of your legs. The only way you could react to this brutality was to look into the teacher's eyes and not show any indication of the pain inflicted. The learning of this discipline at such a young age would serve me well in later life.

Children can be very cruel, and my parents' mixed marriage meant that we were different; when the other children got bored, this was something to pick on. Being different meant that the rest could gang up on you. I soon learnt that 'a good run was better than a bad stand' and after striking out at the offenders I would take to my heels and run, often climbing the nearest tree and standing off the attackers until they got tired and moved away.

During those years we fished for pike, perch and trout in the summer and hunted and snared rabbits in the winter months. I would sell the rabbits for the equivalent of eighteen cent or twelve pence each, which helped with the purchase of schoolbooks and gave me some pocket money. One of the best areas for this was around the old graveyard and monastery of Mullandoi on the eastern shore of Lough Muckno. There was a large population of rabbits in the old cemetery, and at night they spread out into the surrounding fields. This was a time before the myxomatosis disease was introduced into the country to deplete the rabbit population, which put an end to the trade in rabbits. I placed snares in the fields and had a constant supply of rabbits for sale. If a rabbit got caught in a snare during the early part of the night usually a fox or badger consumed it. To prevent this, I would check them before midnight and again in the morning.

In the night it was a scary place to visit. As usual there were all kinds of stories about ghosts and strange happenings at the ancient graveyard. When I found my courage flagging and my imagination getting out of hand, I would occasionally go into the cemetery on my nightly rounds and sit, watching and listening. I never did find anything strange, but my family thought I was quite mad. The rabbits did create an eerie atmosphere there. On my rounds through the fields I disturbed all the rabbits who then returned to their burrows and proceeded to beat their hind paws in the burrows underground and a drumming sound rose up among the ancient headstones.

As we grew up we all had our allotted work to do each day before going to school or play, and after we returned home. This could be feeding the cattle and pigs, collecting the cattle for milking, cleaning out animal houses, and collecting firewood or turf. Seasonal jobs required a full day's work and during that period there was no spare time except on Sundays. Potato digging was carried out in October when it was very cold and wet. The wicker baskets we used became wet and picked up a coat of clay, which made them a heavy load to carry even before the potatoes were put in them. Your back became painful and your fingers became numb with the cold and you broke your fingernails. The potatoes were stored in pits in the field to keep them fresh and prevent them drying out; straw and rushes were then put on top of them and clay put over them to a depth of eighteen inches to prevent the frost getting to them. Later in the winter or early new year they were graded by size into sacks for sale or seed. This was done at the pit and it was very cold, body-cramping work – all for four pounds (six dollars) per ton.

I remember farming as backbreaking work. Even the horse-drawn reaper left the sheaves behind to be picked up and tied. Placing them in 'stukes' was heavy work: four or five sheaves were stood on their end and their heads tied so that they could dry out before being drawn by horse and cart and built into a stack or rick in the hay yard for thrashing. Often, when the weather was bad, the stukes rotted in the fields before they were dry enough to build in a stack.

There was very little artificial fertiliser available and farmyard manure was used. Spreading this over the fields or in potato drills was very heavy, dirty work. 'Dropping' or setting seed potatoes was also very hard work because you had to carry the seed with you as you moved along the drill. During the growing season, thinning turnips, weeding and removing thistles, hand-spraying potatoes and cutting hay left little time for other pursuits.

The most labour-intensive and detestable work was harvesting flax. This was a cash crop that provided much-needed money in what was called 'hungry July'. Flax had been cultivated in ancient Egypt, and the dry climate there was more suitable for this task than the wet Irish weather. But the end product, linen, was valuable.

In south Armagh and Monaghan we were told that the Huguenots first brought flax-growing and linen-production to Ireland. The Huguenots were French Protestants who fled persecution in the sixteenth and seventeenth centuries, and many settled in Ireland. The soil in south Armagh and Monaghan was heavy and low in lime and therefore suitable for flax growing. The industrious Huguenots settled in this area and prospered. Their descendants still live all through the counties and used to be referred to as 'breakies'. Although flax-growing stopped in the 1950s, you can still see the remains of many of flax mills and the communities that grew up around them. In our immediate area there were quite a few flax mills: Carville's, Hill's, Keenan's, Loughman's and Rountree's. In Crossmaglen there were once about ten mills.

We are unlikely ever again to see flax-growing in these counties, but the work left an indelible mark on my memory. It was sown in the same manner as corn or wheat and was allowed to grow for a total of fourteen or fifteen weeks. The seed was smooth and slightly greasy to the touch and would slide out between our fingers as we sowed, or picked up handfuls to eat. The Linaria plant grew in a single stem to a height of two or three feet and produced a carpet of flowers. The sky-blue, flowering flax field was a marvellous sight to behold. Over the growing season all the thistles had to be pulled out by hand, because when the flax was ready for pulling the ripe thistle penetrated the flax-pullers' hands.

This pulling of flax out by the root and other aspects of the harvesting made it really backbreaking. The outer skin of the stem when processed became linen, and to prevent damage to this skin it had to be pulled out of the ground rather than cut. Flax, unlike corn or wheat, was unsuitable for tying the sheaves or 'beets' as we called them, so it was necessary to make bands for tying out of rushes.

Farmers helped each other at the busiest times of the year; this was called 'swap' work. When one farmer was finished a tack, the group moved on to the next until the work was finished for all members of the group. Since flax harvesting was so labour intensive, this collective method was used. When the time arrived to harvest it, a group of thirty or forty men gathered in the field to begin pulling the flax out by the root. Each man pulled his own strip and the line of men moved slowly forward in a 'boon', leaving a row of 'buts' behind each one. Our job as children was to keep each puller supplied with rush bands for tying. While all this was happening, other men loaded the flax onto horse carts and removed it to what we called a flax hole. This was a specially constructed reservoir of water about thirty yards long and six or seven yards wide. Here the flax was 'retted'. This was the process where the inner stem was rotted so that when it dried it became brittle and could be knocked out during 'scutching' to leave the outer skin or fibres.

The flax was placed in the water hole and weighed down by placing stones on top of it. It was left for nine or ten days and occasionally it was tramped on with bare feet to ensure it remained immersed in water. Removing it from the water was very heavy work. The stones had to be lifted to the bank for future use and the heavy, water-laden sheaves had to be manhandled up on to the bank. This was often made more difficult by practical jokers who tied two 'beets' together when they were putting them into the water. It was almost impossible to lift this out and it often had to be divided in the water. This heavy mess had to be loaded on to carts and transported back to a grassy field where it was spread to dry.

When it dried it had a bleached colour, very lightweight and brittle. It was our job to pick it up and tie it into bundles, again using the dried-out rush bands. The sharp, brittle stems now stuck into the flesh of your legs and arms, making it a nasty job. We took our flax to Carville's Mill near Oram for scutching. Water from Sumerville's river, which flowed from Armagh to Lough Muckno, was used to power both this mill and the corn-grinding mill some distance downstream.

Despite all the hard work, flax was a good cash crop for farmers at the beginning of the twentieth century, especially during the First World War. The linen was used as fabric to cover the wings and fuselage of aircraft. When dope was painted on it, it became very taut and strong. Flax-growing picked up again at the beginning of the Second World War, but it declined when synthetic materials replaced it.

The water left over in the flax-hole after retting was poisonous and a dreadful odour emanated from it for the rest of the summer. Those who worked at it had great difficulty removing the odour from their bodies. If the water was released or found its way into rivers or lakes it killed the fish. When my eldest sister was in her early teens a neighbour had a crush for her and made a nuisance of himself hanging around her. He was there as usual one Sunday evening in his best clothes and my sister arranged for us younger ones to push him into the flax hole when she lured him close. We were a couple of nine- or ten-year-olds and we rushed and pushed, but he was able to prevent himself falling into the water by grabbing hold of some bushes. He was a man in his twenties and he was able to catch up with me and grab hold of my suspenders. The button gave way and my trousers, or 'breeches' as we called them, and they fell down around my ankles, making running impossible. I received a couple of good closed-fist thumps on the backside for my misbehaviour.

When the harvesting of the flax crop was over there were quite a few barn dances held around the area. I was too young to attend and they had stopped when I was old enough. I always remember one that my sisters attended in McCooey's barn at Drumlogher beside Lough Patrick in Armagh. On this occasion the floor gave way and the dancers ended up among the cattle in the byre below!

Even with this work, we still had time to be children and play the usual games, and some unusual ones. We played a type of hockey, using naturally shaped ash sticks cut out of the hedges and a small metal tin or box which became round after it was played with for a time. The game had an element of danger, but a small number in a confined area could play it because the metal ball was not very mobile and it was durable.

Another game we played was 'hang on to the steer's tail'. Looking back, it seems very unfair to the animal. We would take hold of the 'bullock' steer's tail and try to hang on as long as possible as the steer jumped and kicked and ran, trying to dislodge us. Leaving your shoes or boots off helped your mobility and your ability to keep your balance. Eventually you fell when the animal turned sharply at high speed when water or hedge was reached. The runner continued on straight, due to the momentum, and plunged into a ditch, river, or lake, or was impaled on a thorn hedge. On one occasion my brothers and I decided to play this game with our neighbour's bullock; the neighbour ambushed me as I flew out through the gateway of a field behind the animal. I took the full force of an adult's fist in the chest, which left me stunned on my back on the ground. But I knew I was wrong and I took my punishment in silence.

When I was about ten years old I decided that I wanted a pet crow. We often trapped them but I wanted a young, undamaged one so I figured I could catch one by hand. I climbed up into the trees about sixty feet where the young crows were located, waiting to be fed by their parents. Here I patiently stalked them until I was close enough to reach out to one, but in my excitement I lost my grip and fell. Fortunately I hit many branches on my way down which broke my fall. The last thing I hit with my legs was a wall. This turned me up head first to hit a gravel-paved driveway. When I regained consciousness I had large gashes on the top of my head. I went to a nearby lake and washed my head and stopped the bleeding. I returned home and said nothing to anybody. Next morning my mother was shocked at my condition: I was unable to get out of bed for school due to all the knocks I had received all over my body.

* * *

This place of my beginning was a harsh land where only basic medical attention was available to a rural people. It was a time before antibiotics and vaccinations were available. Many children did not survive into adulthood. A bad diet and poor clothing and housing left people prey to all kinds of disease. Tuberculosis was endemic, whooping cough, diphtheria and polio took their course, colds often developed into pneumonia, and injuries got infected, with catastrophic results.

Fortunately no children in our family died, but some families lost most of their children to tuberculosis. I remember that they got sick one after the other as they reached their late teens, they went to hospital and we never saw them again. This was heartbreaking and made people very fatalistic. Work was started 'in the name of God' and would be finished tomorrow 'God willing'.

In this transitional environment there was at least one stabilising influence, my mother. Being of a Protestant background she had a healthy disregard for superstition. She was the powerhouse of the family, working hard and instilling the work ethic into her children. After a hard day's work, when the children were asleep, she sat up late sewing Carrickmacross lace in the hissing, sniggering light of a 'tilly' (storm) lamp. She continued doing this to supplement the family income until her eyesight deteriorated to the point where she had to give up. I was the eldest boy and I was as close as it was possible to get to her. She passed on to me some of her ways and values. Understanding the need for education, she kept a close watch on what was happening at school and encouraged us to strive to accumulate knowledge for the sake of knowledge as well as passing exams. There was little time to spread among so many children and any transgressions were punished with a sally 'switch'.

My father was the opposite; he liked company, enjoyed telling stories and would sing a song at the drop of a hat. He was very popular at parties and celebrations where he would always sing. He often talked about his friends who had emigrated to the United States and other countries, expressing some regrets that he did not travel himself. I suspect that the 'want' was not strong enough and he was happy to stick to his task of supporting a family.

* * *

When our allotted tasks around the farm were completed we were allowed time to be alone, time to find our own space. My quiet times were spent on the high hills. I would collect whatever fruit was in season into a paper bag and climb a tall tree. There I would sit looking out on the countryside with the warm, pine-scented summer wind whispering around me and daydream of things past and impossible things I never thought would come to pass, cataclysmic things.

To the east the beautiful hills and valleys rolled out on both sides to the high land in County Armagh. As I began to get a little older I often thought about the nationalist people who lived there and the amount of injustice and frustration they endured. Accustomed to hostile surroundings and abused without even having the right to defend themselves, they came to regard everything with mistrust and an unconscious hatred. These psychological obstacles prevented them from feeling at home or connected with the state. It seemed that their soul had now retreated to wander in a misty borderland where its tormentor could not reach or perhaps it was waiting for a new direction in life's forces when it could come out of the shadows of time into the sunlight once more. I looked forward to that day. As a young person I felt that I would participate in a struggle to bring about change if there was ever a possibility of success. In our area, nationalists felt that the south had abandoned them. It claimed jurisdiction over the thirty-two counties yet it ignored the plight of the nationalist people isolated in the six-county one-party state, and most of its attitudes would indicate that it favoured partition.

Britain was not interested in its colonial leftovers and hoped that things would stay hidden or just disappear forever. The northern regime did not want any nationalist representatives sitting in Stormont. The prime minister, Lord Brookeborough, was supposed to have said that he would not have one there even to sweep the floor. It was said too that the only way for a Roman Catholic to get into Queen's University, Belfast, was to donate their body for research. The Protestant ruling elite believed that they had a God-given right to rule themselves exclusively in security and privilege, coupled with a belief that they were God's tutors with responsibility to rule, guide and convert a lesser culture with reformist zeal (this belief is an echo of their co-religious in the southern states of the United States where there is little use or regard for democracy when it does not suit their purpose).

When independence came in the south there was a kind of ethnic mobilisation in the north to defend the insular, inward-looking parochial way of life of those in power. They tended to follow the local leader and paid little attention to central authority. They were, and still are, deeply attached to the land and they want to be left alone. Their loyalty was conditional on maintaining the status quo. Decisions taken in London could be rejected as interference and the local Orange lodge would decide to defy the government. This attitude made cross-religious or ethnic solidarity impossible. To retain control and privilege, the Unionists were allowed to put in place many measures without too many objections from the British or the Irish Free State. They were a product of their reformist beliefs, shaped and exploited by a corrupt empire, allowed a free hand for centuries to hold down a troublesome part of the kingdom. Government policies and actions came out of a deep and historical insecurity. In the country as a whole, for centuries the British had held their position through repression and military solutions, but this had finally failed against a determined people's army in the 1920s. The leaders of the annexed six counties would try new methods of control. The machinery of state would be used to construct methods of exclusion through laws and regulations, backed up by an armed and biased police force. The Unionists chose the route they believed would best lead to security, but it has led them to the abyss.

At council level one had to be a property owner to have a vote. If you had property in different constituencies you had a vote in each. But most nationalists lived in rented accommodation and did not have a vote. Then, a nationalist going forward for election with a chance of gaining a seat could be rendered invalid by being arrested on some minor offence a short time before election day. Another method used was to rearrange an old constituent area, where the nationalist population had increased, by splitting it up and integrating the pieces into predominantly unionist wards. In this way unionist minorities controlled the councils. And councils allocated housing and jobs. Their biased allocation of these essential items led to the Civil Rights marches in the 1960s. Jobs were also used as weapons to promote Catholic emigration in the government's fight to keep down nationalist population numbers. A friend of my family worked in construction, which is not the most secure type of employment. When he was out of work he would sign on to draw benefits, but after a couple of weeks he would be told that there was no further allowance and would be handed a slip with an address to report for work in London.

The police were drawn almost exclusively from the loyalist community and were expected to serve and defend the privileged position of that community. This required the brutal suppression of all signs of discontent or unrest. Loyalist marches were forced through nationalist areas and there seemed to be no limit to the force that could be used by the police. In reality this marching was a show of power, claiming ground and reminding the people who was in control. It was an expression of group solidarity and the loyalist community's resistance to integration, which it viewed as its potential demise. This clubbing together with other like-minded people in small, exclusive groups gives people a profound psychological satisfaction, and secret rituals will intensify the pleasure further. It is no coincidence that the psychological pressure created by strict religious restraints drives participants to seek periodical emotional relief, often in violence and hatred. Perhaps this ritual marching season was a safety valve. It seems for most people that it is a psychological necessity. They are proud to celebrate the glories and triumphs of their past as if three hundred years was only a moment ago. If they were to look beyond their cocoon, they would realise that the rest of the world regards this drama as being of little concern and believes that the clock slowed and all but stopped there a long time ago.

The regular police were bad enough but their reserve force, the 'B Specials', were a law unto themselves. They were mostly farmers or farmers' sons and were allowed to take their arms home when off duty. This meant that there was a large paramilitary force scattered around the countryside that acted as the eyes and ears of the authorities. In their effort to control people's daily lives these people watched their neighbours' every move, and when a person passed by one of their houses they would phone their comrade-in-arms further up the road and ask them to watch. If the person took longer than seemed necessary to complete a journey, inquiries would be made to find out where they stopped and whom they spoke to. When they went on duty they behaved in a brutal manner to young nationalists.

Many of their members believed that the Sabbath as a day of rest should be strictly observed and tried to force other sections of the population to conform to their beliefs. This led to conflict with people who enjoyed leisure activities on Sunday afternoons or evenings. Most young nationalist men had an interest in Gaelic football or hurling, and these games were played exclusively on Sundays. These young people were a constant target for the police and the reserve. When travelling to catch a train or play a match they would be detained for hours so that they missed the session. They might even be assaulted and have their hurling sticks confiscated on the grounds that they were offensive weapons.

People were terrified of running into a B Special roadblock at night in the country. Sunday was even worse because of the religious bigotry involved. The only people on the road late on a Sunday night were young Catholics returning from movies and dances.

Often the roadblock would be unmarked and the first warning was that they would be surrounded by armed individuals kicking them, hitting them with rifle butts and screaming obscenities. On occasion, they opened fire on the unsuspecting travellers, sometimes killing or wounding them. The saying went: 'Kill the occasional "Taig" [Catholic] and they will keep their heads down.'

Over the years small groups of angry and frustrated individuals were prepared to take up arms against all of this, but that was no more than an irritant to the northern administration and gave credence to their argument that repressive measures were necessary. To have any hope, the nationalist people would have to rise up *en masse* against the system. I thought that that day might not come in my lifetime, but I would be patient.

* * *

Memories are all that remain of the past and lives that have been lived. When my parents died I felt that many others died with them, all those people whose story nobody else knew. Memory can be the bringer of endless aching and hold you against your will, a day that has been lived and gone doesn't make it better than today. I find my memories rather pleasant; they stimulate me and carry me along in the life search for sights and experiences that give the soul tranquillity. Especially here as I write in an American prison. My memories are food for my soul.

Some of my most vivid memories from my childhood are the stories that an old British soldier told me. They had a profound influence on my later life. He was a man who preferred to tread alone, a very tall, straight man whose presence gave something to silence. After his retirement he lived down the road from us in a cottage behind Annyart Orange Hall. My parents knew him very well. Often on his way home from Castleblayney he would walk with us children. He seemed to prefer our company; perhaps he was amused by the wonder in our eyes as we accepted his stories without question. He told colourful tales about his travels in distant lands: about his exploits and experiences during the Boer War in South Africa; about travelling through the vastness of India and seeing its beautiful people; about war in the Middle Eastern desert, with Arab warriors on camels charging across the sand; he told of the colours in the sky when evening fell in the Orient. These stories threw a pink veil across my vision of the world so that my eyes could see only the beauty and wonder of it all.

Africa was what excited me most and I decided at that early age that I would go there one day. In time my eyes would look upon all the things he talked about and they were more beautiful than I had imagined. He would recite poems which I later learned were by Rudyard Kipling and one of these remains fresh in my memory in prison today:

> By the old Moulmein Pagoda, lookin' eastward to the sea,
> There's a Burma girl a-settin', and I know she thinks o' me;
> For the wind is in the palm-trees, and the temple-bells they say:
> 'Come you back, you British soldier; come you back to Mandalay!'

When I started second-level education I was some months short of my thirteenth birthday. I went to school in Castleblayney, four miles from home, and cycled there and back. I received my lunch every day from a lady called Miss Lamb who lived in the Alms Houses. My mother knew her from childhood. She had a small flat, which was very comfortable considering that the building was erected in 1860 by the last of the Blayney family that resided in the town that bears their name. Lord Blayney also set up a trust to maintain the complex, which was administered by representatives from the three main religious groups in the area, and this continued to function up until the 1970s.

It was also at this time that I purchased my first book, a science fiction novel about travel and adventure on another planet. It was different from the books that I was exposed to previously and I have long ago forgotten its title but it widened my range of reading and expanded my vision of the universe and our position in the scheme of things. Not unlike most rural families at that time, there were not many books in our house, but we did have a newspaper delivered by the postman every day and we had one of those large radios powered by two lead acid batteries which connected us to the outside world.

I was fortunate while attending second-level school to have a couple of good teachers. Our English teacher, Miss Duffy, was a very energetic, immaculately groomed lady who pronounced her words perfectly. Like most good teachers she soon became aware that I was interested in her subject and she took every opportunity to advise and correct me. From that time forward I was able to make steady progress.

Our science teacher, Mr Sheeran, was a very young man, who had a natural flair for teaching and was up-to-date on current teaching ideas. He was the first to give me an understanding of electricity. This was a fascinating subject for me. One of our farming neighbours, Mr William Pollock, had a workshop for repairing farm machinery. He operated welders and other equipment from storage batteries that were charged by a windmill-driven generator. This was the only farmhouse in our area that had electric light and because of the way farmers assisted one another then, I had ample opportunity to visit the farm and marvel at the machines and the bright, odourless light that illuminated at the flick of a switch. By the time I finished second-level education that farmhouse held very few secrets and I hoped to find a way to continue my studies in that field.

Our Irish language and maths teacher, Mr Markey, was very much from the Gaelic tradition and as such transmitted some of his feelings to us. As I searched around for an opportunity to get into a technical job, I expressed an idea to him about joining the Royal Air Force to further my education, but he reminded me that part of that job would be to suppress other people by force and counselled against it. Although he offered no alternative, I put the idea out of my head even though it had a great attraction for a teenager. The Second World War was only over six or seven years and there was no aircraft technical training outside of the military. It would be another ten to fifteen years before airlines would set up their own training facilities after the surplus supply of personnel from the war years was used up.

While I considered my options, an opportunity to work with the Great Northern Railway (GNR) arrived. The GNR headquarters was located at Victoria Street in Belfast and I went there for an interview. I was employed to do clerical work and I started in the ticket office at Castleblayney station. From the beginning it was obvious that the railways were in decline as road transport and the number of private cars increased. Yet it was an opportunity to get work experience and use the concession travel facilities to visit towns and cities around the country. I also travelled to England and saw some of the reconstruction effort after the war.

In a short time I was transferred to Dundalk to work in the customs clearance department. Here all the goods travelling north and south across the border by rail had their documents checked and presented to the customs for clearance. This station was also used to ship McArdles beer and livestock. The livestock handling was a once-a-month occurrence when Dundalk fair day took place. It led to my first contact with 'the dealing men from Crossmaglen' – however, they did not 'put whiskeys in my tay' as the song goes, and I did not take alcohol until I was thirty-five years old.

A very unusual business practice had been established here for many years. The farmer paid the drover to take the animals to the station for loading into the wagons for movement to other locations in the country or in England. This left the bill outstanding until the next month when I would search for the dealers and collect the account. That was the only time we saw the owners. I soon became well known at the fair; people knew who I was looking for and there were always amusing remarks and good-natured banter about how difficult it was to get the dealing men separated from their money.

It was about this time that I became aware of girls, rather I became aware that they were finding reasons to be in my company. When I returned to Castleblayney on the train on Friday or Saturday some girls would be waiting around to accompany me down the town or perhaps out the country on bicycles. On Sunday afternoon a visit to Churchill and Mullandoi were a pleasant pastime and I could always be found in the general area. Having been brought up in the country I was very reserved in my teens and contact with the opposite sex had to be initiated by the girls. Relationships remained platonic but I enjoyed the experience and attention. It was an opportunity to understand their different values, how they handled friendships, and the deception, intrigue and undercurrents in a group of young females as they learned to cope with competition. It was also an occasion to learn something about myself – I decided I had a strong preference for girls with red, blonde or strawberry-blonde coloured hair!

After working a short time in custom clearance I was transferred to the parcel office at the passenger terminal on the Carrickmacross road. This was a very busy office at that time, as cartons of cigarettes from the PJ Carroll factory went to every station around the country. Very often, transport would arrive with up to one hundred pieces, a short time before the departure of the train on which they had to travel. The weighing and costing of carriage on all of these at short notice was a tedious job. Soon I had committed to memory the cost of various weights to most stations and this speeded up the handling and removed the stress from the job.

Working at various jobs in transport was good experience, but I was still searching for a technical job and an opportunity to return to education. The old idea of the air force kept returning. I hoped to stay in transport but of a more modern type, such as an airline.

Many young people who worked on the railway in Ireland were travelling out to Rhodesia (now Zimbabwe), where the railways were expanding. I believed that this was a short-term solution. African countries were looking for their freedom – there was a war of liberation being fought in next door Kenya at that time, would it spread to Rhodesia also? I wanted to follow a different dream.

At work I often discussed my needs and most of the older workers around me were looking out for an opening for me. Mr Lee, a ticket collector, arrived one morning with a cutting from a newspaper advertising a requirement for apprentices in the Irish Army Air Corps. It was strange that I had never considered the southern forces before; being from Ulster we were in the natural hinterland of northern towns and Belfast, and we looked north where we had relatives living. I decided to fill in the application form against my mother's wishes – she did not want me to join the military as her uncles and brothers had been in the First and Second World Wars, and she had bad memories of those times. When I went for the interview in the military barracks in Dundalk, she arrived there for one last effort to persuade me not to go. But when she saw that I had made up my mind she gave up. During the interview I found answers to most of my needs. I was assured that I would get every opportunity to avail of a technical education if I performed satisfactorily in the technical examinations that would confront me over the next couple of years.

I did not return to work. I said goodbye to my mother and that night I was in the Curragh military camp to start six weeks' basic training (boot camp), before going as an apprentice for training at Baldonnel airfield outside Dublin.

Chapter 6

Military Training

The Curragh camp was a sprawling military complex left by the British on a plain in County Kildare. Here a large number of British troops had been stationed over the years, far enough from the centre of power in London to be out of sight but near enough if ever required to be used there or elsewhere in the empire. We were stationed in McDonagh barracks, named after the executed 1916 leader Thomas McDonagh. This barracks was set aside for basic training or 'boot camp'. It was here that I got my military training, which has stood to me all my life, both physically and mentally.

When you collect so many physical and mentally fit young men and put them together, it is only natural that they probe the boundaries of military discipline. The officers and NCOs had their work cut out until the lines which could not be crossed were defined in everybody's mind. Most of the drilling was carried out on the square but we were taken on to the plains for long runs or field craft training. To save himself from one of the strenuous exercises the sergeant would stand and have us double in full kit and rifle up and down past him to the point where his voice carried. Early in our training a whisper came though the ranks to continue on and ignore the sergeant's order. When we reached the about-turn point we continued on until we reached a wooded area and dispersed. After the instructors had collected us all up, the sergeant taught us a lesson that afternoon.

We were made to double for ages holding the rifle in front of us with extended arms until they had lost all feeling. We were ordered to return to the same woods in skirmish line and when we were amongst the stinging nettles we got the order to get down into the firing position – there was no way we could save our hands and faces from getting stung. We had learned our lesson.

When we were sent to Baldonnel a few weeks later, to the air corps headquarters outside Dublin, it was late November and the winter was setting in. We were housed at the riverside in Nissen huts. We spent a cold winter there before moving to more permanent quarters. The toilets and wash facilities were outside and there was no warm water. One evening I was 'horsing around' with a friend and he fell against a frame of a window in our hut. Next morning his bed and pillow were covered with fine snow that had blown in through the slit! You just got used to that sort of thing.

By December we were settled into our technical classes. We were lucky to have some very fine instructors who later went on to highly prestigious jobs all over the world. I applied myself totally to studying so that I could get the best results possible in all my examinations. Our class was referred to as DEs (Direct Entrants). We had enlisted for six years' service and six on reserve. Running parallel to us was a further class of about thirty apprentices. This meant that there would be about eighty people graduating together, all in competition for what they considered the best technical position. For the moment we had to slowly grind our way through classes on the theory of flight, practical use of tools, theory and practical studies on propulsion units, hydraulics, electrics, instrumentation, flight controls, air conditioning and, among other things, understanding the different metals and materials.

* * *

When we arrived at Baldonnel Colonel P Quinn was commanding officer of the air corps and Colonel WJ Keane took over from him in 1960. These officers had started their careers back at the very beginning of the army air corps. Colonel Keane was one of the first group of nine cadets recruited into the newly formed Free State Army in 1926. They were our direct link with the history of aviation in Ireland which fascinated us.

Military aviation began in Ireland before independence in 1913 when a group of biplanes from the Royal Flying Corps arrived to carry out a support exercise with the British Army. When this mission was over they returned to Britain and there was no further Royal Flying Corps activity in Ireland until the First World War. When German submarines started attacking ships along the western approaches to the Irish Sea, the British opened facilities for airships in Malahide in Dublin and Johnstown Castle in county Wexford. British engineers were selecting suitable sites for land-based aircraft at this time and a decision was reached to construct airfields at Aldergrove, Belfast; Gormanstown, Co Meath; Collinstown, which is now Dublin airport; the Curragh military camp; Fermoy, County Cork and Oranmore outside Galway. In 1917 work started on the airfields and Tallaght was the first to come into operation.

When the United States entered the First World War they stationed flying boats along the south and south east coasts to combat the increasing activity of German U-boats along the western approaches. Their land-based aircraft were operated out of an airfield at Bangor, County Down. After the war, Baldonnel became the headquarters of the Irish wing of the Royal Air Force, but most of the airfields were closed and some became internment camps during the War of Independence.

When Michael Collins was selected as a member of the negotiating team to travel to London for peace talks in 1921 there was grave concern in the IRA for the safety of their intelligence chief should the talks break down and Collins be isolated in London. It was decided that the safest way to extract Collins from London would be by air. With this in mind, Emmet Dalton, director of training for the IRA, began inquiries around the various brigades for people with flying experience. He was put in touch with Jack McSweeney, who was an ex-RAF pilot. McSweeney knew a fellow RAF officer, Charlie Russell, who had spent some time in Canada. It was proposed that Russell would pose as a representative of the Canadian forestry department and purchase a suitable aircraft in England. He was able to purchase a *Martinsyde* biplane, which carried ten passengers. The aircraft was positioned outside London, but as it transpired it was an unnecessary precaution.

After the Treaty, in February 1922, a lieutenant in the recently established Free State Army arrived at Baldonnel and officially took over the airfield from group Captain Bonham-Carter, officer-in-command of number two squadron, Irish wing, RAF. A few months later Sergeant Johnny Curran, a volunteer who had served as a mechanic in the RAF, and a Private Hughes took up duty at Baldonnel. There were no air service personnel, or any aircraft there at that tine. They found the aerodrome derelict, with most of the unserviceable aircraft burnt by the departing British and equipment and fittings damaged to prevent them being used again.

When the Civil War began on Wednesday, 28 June 1922, Jack

McSweeney was in charge of an air service that had no aircraft, and they had to turn to the British for supplies. The British were quick to respond, perhaps happy to see their old enemy fighting among themselves. Charlie Russell flew in the first aircraft, a *Bristol* F2B, which was handed over in July by the RAF who were still in occupation at Collinstown, now Dublin airport. A second *Bristol* was flown in from England around the same time by McSweeney. Within a short time the machines were being used to observe the movements and positions of the republican forces in counties Wicklow, Carlow and Kildare. With the arrival of further aircraft a training programme was put in place for officers who were transferred from the regular army.

In September 1922, the former RAF station at Fermoy, Co Cork, was put into operation to support the Free State forces in the south-west. Captain Fitzmaurice was given command of this station. By November of that year the deficiency of aircraft had been worked out and the number of aircraft had risen to eight *Bristol* F2B fighters, four *Avro* 504Ks and four *Martinsyde* F4s. The *Avro* 504s were fitted with a gnome monosoupape rotary single-valve engine. The entire engine rotated around the crankshaft and I was told that it was a difficult motor to keep serviceable.

The air corps did not escape from the stresses of the Civil War in its early days. In March 1924 after the Civil War ended, many in the army who supported the treaty and Collins's doctrine found themselves without a leader and were unhappy with the direction of the government policies. On 7 March 1924 ninety-two army officers resigned and a total of 115 failed to report for duty. To resolve the problem the government allowed most absent officers to resign and others had their commissions withdrawn. For the air corps it was more serious. Major General McSweeney, OC of the air corps, and twelve other officers absconded, taking with them four Lewis machine-guns, twenty-five rifles and seven thousand rounds of ammunition.

The mutiny came to nothing and the arms were returned to the government through the intervention of mutual friends. McSweeney was one of the officers allowed to resign and another ex-RAF veteran, Major Maloney, was appointed OC. Unfortunately, he was killed in a crash shortly after and Colonel Charlie Russell was appointed OC in 1925 and held this position until 1927, at which time Major J Fitzmaurice was appointed to the position.

* * *

I believe that my interest in aircraft was created when I was very young. German bombers in World War Two that lost their way due to British interference with their navigation aids, often flew over Ulster. When they got low on fuel and could not return home they jettisoned their bomb load so that they could crash-land. People from my area were quite frightened when they heard the distinctive sound of the German aircraft engines and at night the lights in the houses were extinguished. Visiting the string of bomb craters across the countryside was a form of social outing. As I got older this interest in aircraft stayed with me and every time I saw a plane I remembered the darkness until the sound of the engines faded. When I reached teenage years I read books about the early days of flying and I suspect that this was what influenced my decision to seek training in this field.

Of course, there was a great romance surrounding these pioneers and as a young man I fed avidly on that romance. The First World War produced a crop of young fliers who had a foot-loose, devil-may-care attitude to life, an attitude born out of the terrible high casualty rate endured by airmen. The aircraft had no refinements, no brakes and open cockpits, and engine failures were common. There were no parachutes and when an aircraft was on fire you had the choice of jumping or burning alive.

In the 1950s we were still fascinated by those early fliers, both men and women. Even now, as I write here in the confinement of the prison walls, I love to recall their exploits and daring. They were intent on pushing back the limits of aviation by setting new records for the duration on long flights between continents and across oceans. The flight across the north Atlantic, of course, had a fatal attraction and many people lost their lives attempting the crossing in the early days of aviation. I wrote it all out for myself to keep alive in me that excitement that flying can have, but I will spare you the details.

By the time I had entered the air corps Aer Lingus had introduced the *Vickers Viscount* aircraft on their routes. This very successful machine revolutionised air travel. It was pressurised for passenger comfort and could fly above bad weather. Its Rolls Royce Dart engine was ahead of its time and was a smooth, reliable propulsion unit with thousands of hours between overhauls, unlike the piston engines it replaced. With the growth in passenger traffic the Anglo-Irish agreement was changed to allow British European Airways (BEA) to fly passengers in and out of Ireland. This was a prelude to the explosion in air travel that followed in the 1960s.

* * *

When I arrived at Baldonnel I encountered a man called Gunner Tracy who had participated in the IRA ambush at Knocklong railway station during the War of Independence and was a direct link with the past. In June 1921 two of his comrades, Edward Foley and

Patrick Maher, were hanged in Mountjoy for their part in the action. This opportunity to hear stories in the 1950s from a person who had taken part in the struggle for freedom in the early part of the twentieth century made me think further about the nationalist position in the six counties. He was in a position to know what state the rebel forces were in in the early twenties and the lack of arms to counter the British threat of all-out war if the terms of the treaty were not agreed to. I reluctantly accepted that there was no viable alternative to taking what was on offer in the treaty, even though it left the nationalists exposed to loyalist discrimination and regular pogroms. After all this time, I still cannot see any alternative. The British who now lecture us about democracy within the six counties refused at that time to honour the democratic wish of the majority of Irish people expressed in the 1919 British election. Seventy-five percent of the electorate had voted to opt out of the union, but the response of the British was to use force to prevent this. Since Ireland was always a single electoral area, the annexing of the six counties then would be like the west counties of England opting out of Westminster today. I do not believe that would be allowed. The worst part was the establishment of a state in the north without any safeguards for the minority.

It is said that war is politics by another means and the major powers often use it to achieve their objectives. Would it be morally correct for nationalists to rise up against such an undemocratic state? I felt it would, but nationalism makes an uncertain fire and it could consume a whole generation. I remember reading that a Zulu king once said, 'War was a lion on whose back you fell, never to get off again.' War was a major decision for the people and they were held in such an iron grip that it would take a cataclysmic event to set them in motion. In the fifties the leadership of the IRA had moved in the direction of left-wing parliamentary politics, with most volunteers concerned about links with communists and the possibility of the Dublin and Stormont governments being officially recognised. As a result many people drifted away and the organisation was no longer active in many parts of the country. I assumed that it was gone for good, consigned to the history books. I set the issue aside and continued to focus on my studies, hoping to try to get to the Africa that my old soldier friend had talked about.

* * *

In the mid-1950s the air corps was retiring its wartime aircraft and moving into the jet age. The *Miles Master* and *Magister*, *Hawker Hector* and *Hurricane* had gone out of service. They had been replaced in the late forties and early fifties by *Seafires* and *Spitfire* T9s. The basic trainer was a *DH Chipmunk* T20 and the advanced trainer was the *Hunting Provost* T51. In general-purpose flights a couple of *Avro Ansons* remained from the war years together with *DeHavilland Doves* and *Miles Martinet*, a target towing machine. In 1954 work started on the laying of concrete runways and they were completed in 1956.

As our group of technical trainees moved through our various courses in mechanics, electrics and instrumentation during 1956-57 we had to take examinations at the end of each stage. I retained my determination to do well in all the exams and I put in many hours of study. Coming towards the end of our training one of the most interesting projects was to strip down the *Spitfire*'s Merlin engine and re-assemble it again. It was then fitted into the aircraft and each of us had to get in and carry out a ground power run. When the throttle was open full the engine produced an enormous amount of power – seventeen hundred horsepower for the small airframe. With full power in the static position it rocked and swayed and lifted up on its wheels. To prevent the aircraft tipping over it had a tail-wheel undercarriage, yet it was necessary to have four men lie across the tail plane with their backs to the slipstream to hold it down.

In September 1957 our class graduated together with the nine-year class that was running parallel to us. I was placed first in our class. I now had a choice of what I wanted to do and I opted for electrical aircraft work. This part of aircraft technology was in its infancy then. I was posted to a maintenance and overhaul unit in the Air Corps and I decided to enrol in a four-year night course in maths and electrical engineering at Kevin Street College of Technology, Dublin, which commenced in October 1957. There was no such thing as electronics then. William Shockely, John Bardeen and Walter Brattain had only discovered transistor action a few years previously at the Bell Telephone Laboratory, which started the solid-state electronics revolution in the 1960s. Termonic valves with their low current capacity were generally restricted to radio communications and television at that time.

I was still in the army, of course, and based in Baldonnel, about fourteen miles from Kevin Street. Keeping up attendance at the course would prove very difficult. When your duty fell on a class night you had to find someone willing to switch with you. Normally the only swap that you could find was in exchange for doing that person's weekend duty. This meant you attended classes during the week and were on duty at weekends. The course fees and travel costs consumed all your wages. Social life was practically non-existent between October and June when examinations were held.

During the summer months I tried to make up for the loss and I went to all the dances around the city with fellow airmen, and on special occasions we went further afield when Kenny Ball or Aker-bilk were playing. In most dance halls we had a group of girls that knew us and expected us to dance with them; it was all good, light-hearted fun. To overcome the transport problems we all had a standing arrangement to meet at a little confectionery store, The Mullingar on Parnell Street, that remained open late, and here we hired taxis and returned to the airfield.

We had a chaplain who could be counted on to remind us of our priorities, Father Bill O'Riordan. He was a man of his time. His sermons were always direct: 'Stay away from the nurses in the local hospitals'; 'Stay out of the Happy Brigg', this was a pub at Cleary's Cross on the Newcastle-Lucan road; 'Do not get involved in long and serious relationships until you are older and established in life.' He made quite a lot of sense to me at the time, for I had my mind set on travelling to Africa.

During my time in the military I returned home at regular intervals and found that nothing had changed. On many occasions I was stopped at night when returning from dances and the same abuse was dealt out, particularly on Sundays.

After a year in maintenance and overhaul I was posted to the general-purpose flight. This flight was involved in target towing, sea search and coastal patrol, aerial photography and transport, calibration of instrument landing systems and approach radar. Now that I was attached to a flight wing there was more involvement in flying. The most exciting, of course, was a trip in the famous *Spitfire*. There was a real feeling of flying and you were very conscious of acceleration when the throttle was opened in the air; at dusk the fiery exhausts of the Merlin engine were spectacular as they passed by each side of the cockpit.

I went to Shannon when college permitted as part of the

technical crew during the stints of instrument calibration and radar training. The *Dove* aircraft gave me a close call in the hangar there. Its Gypsy Queen engines had six inverted incline cylinders which had to be checked for hydraulic lock after overnight stop. This lock occurred when oil drained down into the cylinder head with its inlet and the exhaust valve closed to form an incompressible mass in the cylinder. It was checked by turning over the engine by hand using the propeller. Unfortunately the magneto switches were placed in the cockpit where a person leaving the pilot's seat could accidentally knock them on with their knee. This was a well-known problem, but I forgot to check their position that morning. When I turned the propeller, the motor started. To make matters worse, the throttle was almost full open and the chocks were at the rear of the wheels. The engine surged into high power, moving the aircraft forward towards the rear wall. When you are twenty-two your reactions are swift and, lucky for me, I heard the first cylinder firing and moved out of the way of the propeller until another crew member scrambled inside and switched the ignition off.

From the beginning, we were taught to respect propellers, moving or static, and to always walk around them. We were also trained how to safely swing-start an engine using the propeller. Two people were involved: the swinger synchronises his leg movement with his swinging arm so that he was stepping away from the propeller as he swung it, the second person held his other hand and assisted him through the moving away motion.

Some time later I had another run-in with a propeller that left a scar on my head – lest I should forget. I was refuelling on top of a wing when the flight sergeant decided to move the fuel tanker so that the other wing could be loaded at the same time. He neglected to tell me and the action of taking up the slack in my hose left me with its full weight, which pulled me off the wing, hitting my head on the propeller blade on my way to the concrete below. I was given the luxury of using some colourful language while I lay there that would otherwise not be permitted.

That same flight sergeant was a kind gentleman from County Cavan. When I first arrived at the base he was obviously checking the new arrivals to see if there were any from his area. He was familiar with where I came from and called out: 'Where is McGuire, that renegade from the border?' Later he was a father figure to me and encouraged me in all my endeavours. He also possessed a dry humour. On his rounds one night he called out, 'Put out that light', and some wise guy replied, 'It's the moon'. 'I am ordering you to put out the moon,' came his reply.

Baldonnel airfield was located in a beautiful part of the country. In the east and south the foothills of the Dublin Mountains started rising, and to the west and north west the land sloped away as far as the eye could see to the rich plains of counties Kildare and Meath. When our money was exhausted we often went for long walks through the surrounding countryside and villages, some of which date back a thousand years.

On a beautiful June evening in 1960 myself and Myles McHugh set out on a walk through Rathcoole and Newcastle. Myles attended college with me and had a very pleasant temperament, born perhaps out of the security of his six-foot three-inch frame; whatever the reason, he was very good company.

When we reached Rathcoole we decided to stop at a little store to purchase ice-cream cones. We entered the store through a group of young girls without focusing on anybody, which was our normal approach in places where we were strangers. On my way through I felt a jab in my ribs. I did not react to the blow but continued on to the counter where I stood waiting for my ice-cream and wondered whether it was an accident or deliberate. As I turned to leave, my question was answered. The answer lay in the blue sapphire eyes of the beautiful girl that stood looking at me – an Ophelia, or perhaps Dante's Beatrice? The shape of her face was a little too round, perhaps, and her nose maybe a little too large with a band of gold freckles extending below both eyes. For me, her chief allure lay in the folds of red-gold hair that framed her face in glory. I stared, astonished at the informal way she burst into my world, which was no more suited to her than to a brightly hued butterfly, my threadbare world tailored to pursue other dreams.

As she stepped out into the sunlight her long, shimmering copper hair covered her shoulders and I felt my well-ordered life under siege. I was under a spell, speechless at the feet of a young girl whose voice calmed my mutinous spirit. Caroline Kelly, the name kept returning into my head as Myles and I continued our walk. Perhaps our paths might not cross again.

During the winter months of 1960 to 1961 I met Caroline again. She had enrolled in evening classes in Dublin city and we travelled home on the same bus. This presented an opportunity to meet in a casual way during those months. By the following summer we were meeting by arrangement and a relaxed, easy-going relationship had developed. However wonderful this relationship was, I still had things to do that were time-consuming. When my final exams in college were completed in June I started to study for my Department of Transport civil aviation engineer's license. This took longer than I expected, almost eighteen months.

When I walked through the gate of the air base for the last time it was with a mixture of excitement and apprehension. I stood and looked back for a few moments, letting it sink in. I had no need to return here again, free at last, the time period that I was restrained by my word of honour was over. Those days may well have been the best days of my life but one should not believe that days you remember are better because they are gone. I had to leave them in the past where they belong, for memory can hold you in a place against your will.

Institution life – army life – with all its red tape and obstructions made life simple. You did not have to worry about food, clothing or a place to sleep. That was all changed now; I would have to learn to take care of myself in the world outside again.

What were my feelings about this place where I spent six of my young years? Perhaps gratitude would be the best word for it; gratitude for the opportunity to further my education, for the exposure to many complex personalities my own age, for the discipline and emotional education and most of all for the friendships formed there that lasted a lifetime.

Finding employment would have to be my top priority before my military gratuity ran out. Caroline and I still enjoyed an idyllic relationship that enriched my life without demanding a lot of emotional energy.

After obtaining my Irish Department of Transport civil aviation license I was offered a job with Ghana Airways in Accra. Ghana is located in the Gulf of Guinea in west Africa. It had achieved independence from Britain five years previously in 1957 and was formed by uniting the Gold Coast with the territory of Togoland. President Nkrumah led the drive for Ghana's independence. He was one of a group of African nationalist leaders who emerged after the Second World War and he enjoyed widespread respect.

When I reported to the Ghana Airways office in London I received quite a shock. The Irish civil aviation license was not acceptable. Ghana's civil aviation office was still administered by the British Airworthiness Authority, The Air Registration Board, or ARB as it was commonly referred to, and it accepted only British licenses.

The trip to Ghana was off. But I was still determined to work in Africa. The only way I could obtain a British license was to work for six months on British-registered aircraft and sit for their examinations. I had no alternative but to take employment with British European Airways at Heathrow airport.

During those months I worked in the 'line', which meant I was on arrivals and departures in front of terminals one and two at Heathrow. Caroline joined me in London, which was a very pleasant place in the early 1960s. It was the flower-power era and London was setting the trend for young people, with Carnaby Street the centre of fashion and British rock 'n' roll groups enjoying worldwide popularity.

Where I worked gave me a front-seat view of the crowds that collected at Heathrow to see the Beatles off on tour and welcome them back again. Enormous crowds of young people would begin to gather early in the day and they spent their time hanging over the spectators' balconies which were then in use – it was a more gentle time than now. Of course, the downside was the way they snarled up the traffic for hours, making it impossible to get home from work.

In total I spent eight months in London. I took advantage of these few months to extend my knowledge of the navigation, autoflight and instrument fields and when my six months were up I sat examinations for these and received the British license.

I had received an offer of a job with East African Airline in Nairobi and prepared to go out there at the beginning of November. This time I hoped that there would be no unforeseen obstacles.

PART III
TASTING THE EMPIRE

Chapter 7

Living the Colonial Lifestyle – KENYA

When I set out for Africa little did I know that during the next fifteen years of my travels I would see the end of the world that was described to me by an old British soldier so long before. I would personally observe the British Empire retreat, often reluctantly, from Africa, Asia and the Middle East. This meant that the problems of my home area were never too far from my thoughts as I observed the colonial system operate, and become dismantled, in other countries.

Working in various countries that once formed part of the British Empire gave me great insight into how that empire functioned and into the mind-set of those who governed and those who were governed. The empire was starting to retreat under pressure, but it was still functioning well in some parts of the world. I found enough evidence to convince me that the issues I had experienced at home in Northern Ireland in my early life were all part of the experience of a worldwide domination. I began to think that the empire would never relinquish its control unless it was uneconomical to remain in a place or it was pushed out – and then it would hold the line militarily until it found politicians friendly to its economic purpose after it departed. These were formative years for me, and later, when the people were ready and the time was right, my political activity was undertaken in this context. But as I reflect on those years now in prison, where life is monotonous and grey, I also remember them as years full of colour, variety, pleasures and curiosity. These places where I lived provided me not only with political conviction, but also with energy and a fascination for life in all its manifestations.

* * *

Sitting in the Skylon Restaurant in London's Heathrow Airport waiting to board a flight to Nairobi, it seemed that all my life I had dreamed of going to Africa. I had carried the dream from when I was a small boy living on a farm in Ireland near the Armagh-Monaghan border. There the old soldier told his stories about the music of the cicadas by day and the crickets by night, and about fighting in the Boer War. Stories of scorching days and freezing nights sleeping on the ground under a blanket and waking up to the lion's roar in the pre-dawn stillness. About finding a snake coiled up on top of his blanket enjoying the heat of his body, and, for the wide-eyed boy's benefit, telling how he grabbed it by the throat with his bare hands and choked it to death.

Twenty years had passed since those days. I was lucky. The apparent futility of life, service in the military, working by day, attending college by night and studying for endless exams had failed to drive the dream out of me, as it had with many others. Life had taught me that only grim determination would enable a traveller to reach his destination.

I had signed a three-year contract with East African Airways in Nairobi with the possibility of extension. I would not be an emigrant with permission to remain there; Ireland would remain my base. At this stage of my life I was filled with the wild hope of youth. I did not stop to think beyond the fact that I had employment that would enable me to see Africa. The idea that there existed an elite ruling class in a colonial environment, which I would become part of, did not occur to me.

In Africa I hoped to find a different world to live in for a time, away from the ordered routine of the west, a place where the strange and unexpected would prevent my days sliding away without my really living them. A place that would heighten my senses and my awareness. There were reminders of the road that I had travelled to reach this point in time; Caroline, whom I had recently married, was now part of the dream.

We departed London on a cold, grey November day aboard an East African Airways *Comet* 4C aircraft. This aircraft was the successor to the ill-fated *DeHavilland Comet* 1, the first jet airliner ever built. Designed in the late 1940s and built in the early 1950s, it had been a step into the unknown. Prior to this it took twenty hours of flying to reach Nairobi, now it took nine. The little-understood problem of metal fatigue led to the *Comet* 1 aircraft disintegrating in mid-air in the late fifties, and by the time the problems were resolved the American Boeing aircraft company had passed the British manufacturers out with their more advanced B720 and B707 aircraft. Nevertheless, I still feel that, visually, the *Comet* 4C aircraft was a most beautiful machine. Like a silver bird, its body had the right shape and proportions, the wings swept back cleanly, its four engines mounted inside the wing roots – and even on the ground it looked as if destined to fly. I had endorsements on my civil aviation engineer's license covering the electrical, instrumentation and autopilot systems on this aircraft, and over the next decade I would come to know all its idiosyncrasies.

We landed at Embakasi airport at nine o'clock on a summer's

morning in November, in what was then the British crown colony of Kenya. I felt the warm sun strike my head and shoulders as I stepped out into a world of diamond-bright light under a piercingly blue sky. As I looked around, my heart dilated with joy – I had finally arrived in Africa.

Norman Wilkinson, a gentle, smiling Englishman, met us at the bottom of the steps. He would be my boss in East Africa Airways over the next few years, and we would remain friends for a long time. While walking out to the carpark I felt elated in the rare, six-thousand foot atmosphere and the bright sunlight.

As we drove down the road from the airport to Nairobi, the wind buffeted through the open car windows and played games with the tips of Caroline's hair, causing the copper and gold to dance and sparkle in the sunlight. She looked more beautiful than ever in the extraordinary African light, and I wondered what chemistry, what combination of time and chance, what trick had Aphrodite played to make her, an extrovert bubbling over with laughter and love of life, choose an engineer – dull, serious and introverted. Was it possible that opposite characters could remain compatible for any length of time?

When we reached the motorway we were greeted by a visual experience never matched in any other country we visited – remembering it now thirty-five years later in this dull prison context, it still has the power to lift my spirits. The median and verges were covered with flowering bougainvillea, creepers and orange flame vine; the road stretched out in front of us as if on fire – a blaze of red, purple and blue, pink and orange, running for miles down to the city. We walked into our hotel through a canopy of flowering trees and a carpet of perfume-scented, lilac-coloured jacaranda flowers. They had fallen after being pollinated by nectar-loving insects and birds the night before. Later we went for a walk in the tropical, scented evening air, and watched the sun's fiery orb drop behind the Kikuyu hills – and we knew that we had entered a world that would change us utterly, and forever. In time, each of us would find our own Africa, an Africa agreeing with no one else's.

* * *

Like the railways and post office, East African Airways had its headquarters in Nairobi, and operated a regional service throughout the British East African territories of Kenya, Uganda and Tanganyika, along with an international service to London. It operated *DeHavilland Comet* 4C, *Fokker* F27 and DC3 aircraft. At the time it was considering placing an order for the BAC VC10 aircraft that were being developed by the British Aircraft Corporation. On reporting to head office at Embakasi airport on the day after our arrival, I learned that I would be stationed at Nairobi. My job was to supervise heavy-check maintenance, inspecting and testing systems and components for serviceability and integrity at timed intervals laid down by the aircraft manufacturers and agreed by the airworthiness authority.

After spending some weeks in a hotel, we agreed to be housed in an apartment on Riverside Drive called Elrich Court. The building consisted of six apartments located on a country road outside the city. This was near to the Parklands roundabout where we did our shopping and on Sundays attended the little Italian church built by prisoners of war in the 1940s. Here we learned to speak a bit of Swahili, and got used to the *shamba* (gardener) and *ayah* (child's nurse) calling us 'Bwana' and 'Memsahib'. The words basically mean 'Boss' and 'Madam'. I took an interest in the language and in time could communicate with the people we met when we were out in bush country.

The apartments were surrounded on three sides by tall trees, and when the light faded creatures of the day quickly disappeared and were replaced by creatures and sounds of the night. Flowers like the baobab opened, and scented the night air; bush babies hunted in the trees for insects and it took a long time to get used to their child-like cries in the darkness.

When we became acquainted with the other residents, most of whom had been born in Kenya, Joy Adamson figured frequently in their conversation. Her book *Born Free* had been published, and the stories about her and her husband George were fresh in people's memories. Peter Bally, her second husband, lived a short distance up Riverside Drive from us.

Nairobi was still a gossip-ridden town in the 1960s and within the ranks of the very rich there was an undercurrent of backbiting, petty dislikes and jealousy, which kept things on the boil. The Muthaiga country club in Nairobi was the meeting place for the estate owners of the highlands and their rich and titled friends living in the city. This exclusive gathering was presided over by the ruling elite, and provided the stage for the bizarre behaviour and outlandish entertainment of people far removed from the social norms of Europe at that time. Here husbands and wives attended parties and formed liaisons – remarriage within the group was an ongoing process. It was rumoured that older members of this group had belonged to the Happy Valley set, a notorious group of upper-class people who frequented parties at a house near Gilgil and another house called D'jinn Palace, a Moorish building located on a five-thousand-acre farm on the shores of Lake Naivasha, north of Nairobi. There, the story goes, the guests had unlimited access to drink and drugs, and participated in mass sexual activities. But that was during the 1930s and 1940s, twenty years before our arrival; nevertheless, the old saying 'Are you married or do you live in Nairobi?' still had some truth in it. Wife-swapping still existed across the white population, and it was not unusual to see a fellow worker's wife dance the night through with another man – nor would you be surprised to meet them downtown, arm in arm.

As I settled into the job we began exploring Nairobi. It was difficult to imagine that, only sixty years before, this modern city, the commercial centre of three territories, with its tree-lined boulevards and mini-skyscrapers, was no more than a railroad station on the small Athi river where the Masai warriors watered their cattle. In the 1880s British interest in East Africa was restricted to Zanzibar, but after the Berlin conference in 1885 the British, French, Germans and Italians went full steam ahead with their imperial ambitions. Germany ended up with Tanganyika in East Africa, and the British held a protectorate in Uganda and the area later to be called Kenya.

The aggressive colonial activities of the Germans, and the British policy of retaining control over the source of the Nile, prompted a reluctant British government to authorise the building of a railroad from Mombasa, on the coast, to Uganda. Unfortunately, it had to be built through low productive regions with no traffic potential, and when it was completed in 1901 it operated with a large loss. The government, wishing to generate economic growth and increase traffic, decided the best way to do this was to attract European settlers to Kenya. In 1901 the crown issued an order in council which took government control of large tracts of land in Kenya, and offered them free or on very favourable terms to 'suitable' people willing to settle there. This offer attracted a group of British and

European people from wealthy families. Some were prodigal sons or 'black sheep', and most were sophisticated and well educated. Most of them settled in what was called the White Highlands, an area close to the Equator with a monthly mean temperature of 70°F, and ranging in altitude from five to eight thousand feet. This area stretched from the neighbourhood of Nairobi to the edge of the Rift Valley and the foothills of Mount Kenya. In this equatorial region the high altitude removed its most annoying feature – excessive temperature – and the rich murram (red volcanic soil) was well suited to European-style farming.

So here, especially in the area east of the Rift Valley, was gathered the largest colony of Europeans on the African continent north of the Zambezi river. These first arrivals and their children enjoyed a privileged position, living close to the sun in a beautiful but untamed land. When I arrived very little had changed; the descendants of the titled class lived a life of opulence, and most Europeans had servants to wait on them hand and foot. Many could be abusive and hit their servants. I witnessed a white motorist kick an African who was filling his car with fuel; he must have seen disapproval on my face because he uttered defensively, 'Lazy bugger.'

In the 1920s the white settlers, led by Lord Delamere, promoted home rule and ran a feudal-style state presided over by ex-army officers and aristocrats. This was a similar type of system in some ways to that being set up in Northern Ireland at the same time, and when implemented would lead to violence in both cases. This movement was led by a group of Europeans with influence in London and they blocked the rights of the majority when they threatened what the settlers regarded as their exclusive right. Soldiers returning from the First World War, particularly those who had served in British East Africa, were encouraged by Britain to settle in Kenya, and the government offered them land on very reasonable terms. This policy provided needed customers for the railroad and increased the white population with loyal and trusted people who could be depended upon to control the African and keep the Asian from rising above their perceived station. An old Goan, whose son worked with me in the airline, told me he remembered good land going to Europeans for a few East African shillings per acre, but his family was not allowed to purchase. This was a great injustice to the Indian people who were very hard-working – I doubt if the country could function without them even today.

I began to have a problem with the colonial system here. Before the British arrived, the areas where the white farmers settled were farmed by the Kikuyu, Meru and Emba tribes, and they made excellent use of the land. But heavy taxes were imposed on the Africans to force them to leave their tribal land and work for the white settlers at subsistence wages. To make sure that there was no incentive to remain, they were not allowed to grow coffee, tea or other cash crops. This reminded me of what took place in Ireland during the various plantations, although here it was not as extreme as the 'to hell or Connaught' Cromwellian period in Ireland in the seventeenth-century, when thousands were driven off their lands and forced to go west of the Shannon river where the land is less fertile. Although I had no emotional involvement in Kenya, I found it unsettling. But there was a comforting element there also: the natives had fought a war, and independence was due in three years' time.

* * *

Aviation is, of course, of enormous interest to me and I could indulge this in Kenya. The older employees of the airline had started their working life in the 1920s, when flying was in its infancy, and they talked to me about all the colourful characters involved in that pioneering era. The east African territories covered a vast area; there were few roads and no communications, so the coming of the flying machine contributed in large measure to the area's rapid development between the First and Second World Wars. Many of the new arrivals had had experience flying on the western front during the war, and they were quick to see the advantage that aircraft offered for commuting from outlying plantations to Nairobi and other towns, where they frequented the country clubs and socialised with friends. Civil aviation developed from the military, and it formed a worldwide 'old tie' network where stories and gossip travelled fast. Even in the late fifties and early sixties, with the advent of jet aircraft, people from the Irish Army air corps were flying with airlines scattered from the United Kingdom across the Middle East, Far East and down to Australia. They arrived at regular intervals and called to see me, with all the latest news about friends and acquaintances stationed around the world.

In Kenya the older mechanics enjoyed telling and retelling stories from their youth, about the early days at Wilson airfield, about the barnstorming and enigmatic early aviators. There was frequent mention, of course, of Beryl Markham – the first person to fly solo from England to America. Another flier frequently remembered was John Carberry, an Irish peer. He had inherited the title Baron Carberry, and served in the Royal Naval Air Service during the First World War. He had a coffee estate north of Nyeri and kept a beach house at Malindi on the coast. His wife, Maia, was also an enthusiastic flyer, but she and her pupil were killed in a training accident at Dagoretti in 1928. He married a third time – to June Mosley, a native of South Africa.

Another more colourful and enigmatic flier in East Africa also lost his life in an aircraft near Voi – everybody in the airline had a story to tell about Dennis Finch Hatton. He too came from an Irish family and purchased land in Kenya before the First World War. People who worked at Wilson airfield remembered him as a very tall, bald, handsome man. He was quiet and pleasant, but could become caustic when work on his aircraft was behind schedule.

People outside East Africa may have a vision of Finch Hatton as a romantic 'white hunter'. This he was, but he was also a shrewd businessman, with a farm and *dukas* (shops), and also operated a lucrative safari business, collaborating with Baron Bror Blixen, a Swedish white hunter. They catered to the very rich who wanted to shoot lions and elephants, and counted the King of England's sons, the Prince of Wales and Prince Henry, among their customers in the late 1920s.

His friend, Baron Blixen, had married Karen Christentz Dineson and they decided to try farming in East Africa. He arrived first and obtained land at Ngong, near Nairobi. Karen arrived later, before the First World War. The baron was a philanderer and preferred the life of a white hunter to the struggle of trying to grow coffee on the Ngong hills where the altitude was too high for coffee. He drifted into full-time hunting, and in time his womanising prompted his wife to ask him to move out of the house. In that type of society it could be expected that Karen Blixen would not remain alone for long. It caused a stir when she entered a relationship with Dennis Finch Hatton, the most eligible and sought-after bachelor in the Muthaiga set, and friend of her husband. They never married, although the relationship lasted until his death at Voi. Karen then returned to Europe and lived out the remainder of her life there. Her book *Out of Africa* became very well known.

* * *

I was told many stories about the struggle for independence from the British as this had occurred only a few years before I came to Kenya. Dark clouds were gathering over Kikuyu land in the late 1940s. For the African, nothing had changed since the 1920s. The land question had become more explosive with the increase in the African population and the return of African soldiers who fought in Europe and elsewhere during the war. Jomo Kenyatta had journeyed to London in 1929 to present the grievances of his tribe, the Kikuyu, directly to the British government. Failing to secure redress, he remained there to continue his work, returning in the forties to re-involve himself in Kenyan politics.

World War Two served to mark the beginning of the end of European predominance in East Africa. Relations between the colonial rulers and the new African generation deteriorated as the colonial government continued to turn down African demands for reform. By 1950 intelligence reports confirmed the existence of a new subversive organisation called the Mau Mau. They were quietly recruiting men and women who were administered a blood oath. Animals were sacrificed, and the recruits faced their sacred Mount Kenya; drinking the blood, they pledged to drive the *mzungu* (whites) into the sea. A great deal of emotion centred around the blood oath in the press, yet the Masai drank blood from their cattle every day of their lives, just as Europeans drink wine.

The inevitable violence finally arrived in 1952 and white settlers and their families came under attack; some were chopped to death with *pangas* (machetes). Most of the fighting took place in the Kenyan forests. The two main hot spots were Mount Kenya, where General Qina was in charge, and the Aberdares, where Dedan Kimathi had control.

I learned a lot from hearing about this war. Frank Kitson, who would figure later in the conflict in the six counties of Northern Ireland, was a major in the army during this campaign. He was joined by Ian Henderson, a native-born white Kenyan attached to police intelligence. They used psychology and other brainwashing methods to 'turn' captured Mau Mau 'players'. These turned insurgents were formed into gangs and returned to the forests, led by disguised white officers to hunt their former comrades. This tactic, combined with leaflets dropped from aircraft and messages broadcast from loudspeakers carried on helicopters encouraging surrender, proved very successful. By the mid-fifties the insurrection was over, apart from sporadic activity by a group in the Aberdare mountains. Talking to white and black Kenyans who had been involved in the conflict taught me a lot about the tactics used by the British. Later I was able to read Ian Henderson's *The Hunt for Kamathi* and Frank Kitson's *Low Intensity Operations*, books that gave me further insight into British thinking, which I found very useful.

The Africans were gradually allowed on to the legislative council until they formed a majority in the early 1960s. After Harold Macmillan made his famous 'winds of change' speech to both houses of parliament in Cape Town, South Africa, in February 1960, a new cry was heard over Kikuyu land: *Uhuru!* (freedom). Governor Malcolm McDonald handed over power to Jomo Kenyatta in 1962, and elections held in 1963 gave the Kenyan African National Union (KANU) a majority. '*Harambee*' (pulling together) became the national slogan. Caroline and I attended the celebrations in December 1964 when Kenya was declared a republic and Jomo Kenyatta made president. It was exhilarating to witness this moment in the ending of the British empire. Very soon, however, tribal issues raised their heads. Oginga Odinga, from the Luo tribe, became vice president, and he immediately became unhappy with the composition of the government. His relationship with the Kikuyu-dominated cabinet became very hostile and he resigned in 1966. In recent years these issues have dominated Kenya, but I was not there to witness it.

* * *

It was in 1956 after the hostilities died down that George Adamson shot a lioness and later found that she had three cubs, which he took home. Two were sent to zoos in Europe and his wife, Joy, kept one, which she named Elsa. Elsa was released in what is now Meru National Park on a tributary of the Tana river. Joy later wrote an account of rearing this cub and of her release to the wild in her book, *Born Free*.

In 1964 a contract was signed for the production of the *Born Free* film. When the movie was being made in 1965 it attracted quite a few famous visitors to Kenya, and we often sat at the Thorn Tree open-air café at the New Stanley hotel to see people like Bill Travers and Virginia McKenna, who had the lead roles. The film opened in March 1966 with a royal command performance in London. It was a great success; it promoted tourism in East Africa and also helped gain support for the Adamsons in their campaign to have more land set aside for the protection of wildlife in Kenya. This was a very difficult issue as, in the early days of independence, the government had to meet the heightened expectations of the local population for land and food, if necessary at the expense of wildlife.

* * *

Kenya had incredible beauty and incredible suffering; it was a savage land even in the 1960s. Death came swiftly to man and beast, young and old. All the tropical killers were there – many kinds of malaria, sleeping sickness, elephantiasis, leprosy, tick-borne fever, cholera, yellow fever, 'Nairobi throat', and countless other viruses carried in the red dust. Another ailment was called 'Nairobi eye', and was caused by a small yellow and black striped insect that always made for the eye. When one attempted to brush it away it secreted a fluid which inflamed the eye.

Drought was a constant killer, and in some areas it lasted for years, killing thousands of people and millions of animals. Before independence, I remember the Royal Air Force delivering food and famine relief on a daily basis, long before the media or the pop culture concerned themselves about the ever-present famine in Africa.

Wildlife was abundant and widespread throughout the country. Apart from the normal danger from wild animals, it was very simple to lose one's life when an animal charged across a dirt road in front of a car, especially at night. The airline's chief engineer died in this manner on the road to Mombasa.

Families of monkeys and baboons seemed to appear as if by magic when an automobile stopped. We learned a timely lesson on one such occasion, having stopped to watch a fish eagle eat its catch while our eighteen-month-old daughter remained beside the car eating an apple. As I looked back at Kelly, I was shocked to see a blue-balled vervet monkey make straight for her. Before I could reach her, the monkey simply held her wrist while he removed the apple, then quickly returned to the bush. In delayed reaction, Kelly beat the grass with a little stick held in her other hand – fortunately, she had not resisted the monkey, or the outcome would have been different.

We had many adventures in Kenya and I remember them now with gratitude, glad to have them fill my mind. After I had completed a particular weekend on late shift, we decided to head for Amboseli National Park for a few days' trekking across vast areas of Africa still undisturbed by man, a peaceful, primeval land possessing incredible beauty. This was what I had come to Africa for. I was not interested or rich enough to be with the 'upper class', and most of my spare time was spent roaming through the country, seeing the wild life and fishing.

The park is located on the Tanzania-Kenya border near Kilimanjaro. To travel there I got the loan of a Volkswagen van from our next-door neighbour at Elrich Court. Each year he entered the East African car safari race, a three-day-and-night ordeal; he also competed in motor-cycle racing, scrambling events and managed a garage across the street from Nairobi University. The van was fitted out with sleeping bunks, very convenient as hotel accommodation wasn't available then.

We departed Nairobi at ten o'clock on a Monday morning. It was the dry season and it was very hot as we drove across the tawny Kapiti plain, a wasted landscape that rolled away into emptiness along the Tanzanian border; even the Masai with their emaciated herds find it difficult to survive here. As we drove along the murram track towards Namanga, the Volkswagen swayed ominously from side to side as the tyres tried to retain a grip on the loose, sandy soil. The seasonal downpour would soon drench this plain and run-offs had been scooped out at intervals along the side of the road to allow water to dissipate without turning the road into a river. I must have dozed off – the thump of the van hitting the water drain brought me back to my senses. I saw the sky and the sun turning slowly as we rotated through the air, nose-up. I reached out my left arm and pinned Kelly in her seat where she sat between Caroline and myself. The van struck the ground on the left-hand corner of the windscreen, and the engine, rear axle and wheel assembly parted from the body and rolled to a stop some distance away. The van was a total wreck. The last thing I could remember before the accident was a Masai man standing on one leg and resting on his spear, like an icon from the past. He was gone now, unwilling to involve himself in the affairs of the crazy *mzungu*. The rack containing the bunk beds had moved forward and struck me in the back, pinning me against the steering wheel, and bottles of drinks had left their cool box and broken. As we rolled, my head smashed into the broken glass on the upturned roof, cutting gashes in my scalp. Fortunately, Caroline and Kelly came off lightly, each receiving a small cut on the head. I lost a lot of blood. But our greatest problem was finding shelter from the midday sun. Also, all our water and drinks had spilt. In a country with so few people it was possible that nobody else would travel that road on that day, or for several days. In those circumstances people had learned to assist one another: if you met someone in trouble you stopped and helped. Another day they might have to stop for you. You just had to hope somebody would come along. After four tortuous hours, a dust cloud appeared on the horizon, and we waited patiently as the cloud slowly approached. After an hour the huge plumes of red dust were close enough for us to see the car that was causing them. Fortunately, an American couple in their seventies were returning after a weekend of religious celebrations in a remote village and they were kind enough to take us back to a hospital in Nairobi.

It was returning from one such visit to Tsavo that the opportunity of returning their service arose. In those days it was a murram road – loose sand and clay. Hard corrugations covered the surface – they seemed to have been cut into it by vehicle tyres as they bounced at the natural rhythm of the shock absorbers travelling at forty miles an hour. To avoid the tortuous hammering at this speed, it was necessary to travel at a speed below or above that of the absorbers – but not too fast, otherwise the steering became unstable when you hit the loose areas. In these circumstances driving was a challenge.

A few miles north of Simba we were driving behind a truck at about fifty miles an hour when an open-top military landrover passed at high speed. As it was about to pass the truck, the truck pulled out and shunted the landrover into a water drainage ditch – and drove on. Remembering our ordeal on the Amboseli road I stopped to help. Cans of fuel strapped to the sides of the landrover had ruptured, and fumes engulfed the wreck, overpowering the two soldiers. When we dragged them out of the ditch, one was quite seriously injured and the other was functional. He decided to remain there while we carried his companion back to a hospital in Nairobi and reported the accident to army headquarters. In solitary moments I remember, and wonder if the two young men recovered. They were British soldiers fighting in the war in Aden who had come to East Africa for a rest.

* * *

One thing I particularly remember about Kenya is its wonderful colour. Remembering it now provides a huge contrast to my current circumstances. The largest lake in Kenya is Naivasha; here I spent some of my days off fishing with my family. The lake had a great variety of birdlife, including storks, pelicans, herons, ibis, fish eagles and duck. We often hired a boat and fished among the islands of floating papyrus for black bass and tilapia, the latter being fish of the same genus as the nest-building fish in Lake Victoria. The lake was an ideal place to view the many famous farms that dotted its shoreline and ran up to the escarpment behind.

Lake Nakuru, located further north along the valley, provided one of the most spectacular bird shows on earth. I recall its vivid colours with the greatest pleasure. The eight-mile-wide Menegai crater overlooks this brackish lake, which is a habitat favoured by flamingos. Its foul-smelling, grey soda mudflats provide a desolate home shunned by many other creatures. This lake, like others in the Rift Valley, has no outlet and forms an evaporating pan where saline water is concentrated into a stronger and stronger solution where algae and other organisms provide food for the birds. Lesser flamingos gather at Lake Nakuru in incredible numbers. Their black tipped, pink-blotched wings, red feet and black-tipped red beaks fill the air with fire as wave after wave race across the shallow water and lift into the air. The flamingos live and nest in these soda lakes where the temperature reaches one hundred degrees Fahrenheit. The stench is overpowering and the glare of the soda crust is blinding. Their nests consist of soda collected into mounds. Far from the shore they are inaccessible to humans and predators.

A pleasant alternative to fishing at Naivasha was to take the one-hour drive to Thika on a Sunday afternoon. It is famous for its flame trees which formed a scarlet ribbon along the murram road and gave a red hew to the countryside. Then when we visited the coast we stayed at Nyali beach, a beautiful area a short distance north of Mombasa with sand beaches so white that they looked like a strip of eternal snow running between the blue sea and the green, tropical vegetation.

We also visited the lovely island of Tanga where Caroline's cousin, Eugene McArthurs from Keady, County Armagh, was Catholic Bishop. The settlements along the coast, with their minarets, white walls, carved doors, people in flowing kanzus and turbans, reflect their ancient Arab origins. The islands of Lamu, Pate, Kilwa, Mombasa and Zanzibar saw many empires come and go since the first century AD. The Indians, Arabians, Portuguese,

Dutch, French and finally the British all occupied these islands during the last two thousand years, but it was the Arabs who remained, mixing their language with the local dialects to produce Swahili.

* * *

In the September of 1965 I returned to London to receive training on the avionic system of the British Corporation's VC10 aircraft. The courses took eight weeks and were conducted at the BOAC training establishment at Hatton Cross, Heathrow Airport. BOAC already operated this type of aircraft on its worldwide services, which included the South African routes. East African Airways, being an associated company, handled their flights as they passed through on their way to and from southern Africa. The aircraft was introduced into EAA in the late 1960s, after I had left East Africa. In the early 1970s one of them had an accident while taking off from Addis Ababa. It struck a piece of equipment on the runway and failed to get off. When a ditch filled with fuel from the aircraft's ruptured tanks ignited, some of our friends lost their lives in a sea of fire that day.

We returned to Kenya where the prophets of doom had been busy sowing the seeds of unrest within the European community. Jomo Kenyatta, once the great nemesis of the white settlers, was now perceived as their only hope in a sea of Africans ready for revenge. The presence of Bruce McKenzie as Minister for Agriculture in an otherwise native government, did give some comfort to the white farmers, but there was still a large exodus. For others, in jobs that could readily be Africanised, the future seemed bleak. My contract with East African Airways was up and I had to make a decision whether to stay if it was renewed or to move on and see some other part of the world that the old soldier had told me about long ago.

From 1965 *shifta* (bandits) were causing serious security problems; stories of attacks were told and retold and gained in ferocity with each telling. Things had changed. The mentality of people had changed. There was no one thing I could point to for this, but as well as the stories, there were issues with identification cards and new taxes. I did not regret the passing of the colonial era, only the change that prevented me from roaming freely through the wilderness. The thought of watching all this slowly vanish as the native people rushed into the twentieth century did not appeal to me. Better to remember this primordial Eden the way we had found it, with its immortal ways, breathtaking sights, its incredible light and a people never in a hurry – if something is not done today, then tomorrow will do, except they never quite focused on tomorrow. It is not difficult to imagine that the gods stopped here on Mount Kenya for a while on their journey to Greece. I have not returned to East Africa for forty years now but I still carry a vivid picture in my head of another time, never to be experienced again.

I decided to move on and see some more of the world. We said goodbye to Kenya in June 1966. I was offered a position with Malaysia–Singapore Airlines. Its headquarters were in Singapore, and it had been set up after the separation of Singapore from Malaysia ten months previously.

Chapter 8

Early Post-Colonial Life in South East Asia

I returned and saw under the sun that
the race is not to the swift,
nor the battle to the strong,
nor bread to the wise,
nor riches to men of understanding,
nor favour to men of skill,
But time and chance happens to them all.

Ecclesiastics 9-11

South East Asia/Indochina is the meeting place of Indian and Chinese culture, a society very different from Europe's and very ancient, perhaps older than the Middle East.

These thoughts started to take root in my head when we returned to Ireland for a short break before setting out for Singapore. I decided to do some reading to gain some appreciation of their culture since I would have to work with the people. I learned something about the ancient history of these countries – Burma, Laos, Vietnam, Malaysia. I also learned that the colonising of these areas by Europeans had a profound affect on the lives of people in these regions. I found out that it all began in the fifteenth century.

The Portuguese had been trying to reach the Orient for a century before they finally made it around the Cape at the end of the fifteenth century. Over the next ten years they made their way to Malacca, on the Malay peninsula, and on their way established defensive and trading posts in West Africa, Cape Town, Mozambique, East Africa, Muskat in the Oman and Goa in India. They used their superior technology to capture Malacca and hold it for the next hundred years until the Dutch arrive to expel them. The Dutch main base was in Java and as they were more interested in the Archipelago to the south, where great profits were available, Malacca fell into decline. Over a hundred years later the British East India Company arrived in the Malacca straits and pushed the Dutch out. Malacca was an ideal entry point to South East Asia because of its position on the straits: eight or nine major air streams advance and retreat with the monsoons and assisted navigation, allowing the sailing ships to hug the Indochina coast on their voyages to Macao, Canton and other cities in Cathay. The British would retain control of this strategic area for almost two hundred years.

In the sixteenth century the European trading companies were more interested in trade than in acquiring territory, but their arrival in South East Asia opened a chapter of European dominance in the area that would last for four hundred years – I would experience the tail-end of it. Colonialism developed differently here than in Ireland or Kenya, and to some degree in South Africa, where military intervention was used to displace the native to make room for the colonial power's own subjects. In South East Asia it started with economic colonialism, but as the economic order changed and the mother country needed the products the traders were supplying, colonial powers intervened to protect supplies.

The British East India Company, for example, was a huge organisation and had its own forces to protect outposts and ships. They moved east along the trade routes, using force where necessary, and taking advantage of squabbles between rulers in India and South East Asia to establish a foothold wherever they could. When they bit off more than they could chew, they had powerful politicians and bankers in London to lean on the government to 'send in the marines', much in the same way that money and big business in America today influences decisions in Washington. Generally, powerful countries start out with a benign economic agenda, but as the economy of the world shifts it often happens that they feel the need to intervene militarily to protect vested interests.

To a large extent it was the industrial revolution in Europe that triggered full-blown colonialism in South East Asia. During the last half of the nineteenth century, competition between the European powers spurred on the military occupation of countries to protect established supplies.

The British had control of the tin and rubber in Malaya when they placed the Straits of Malacca trading centres under the direct rule of the Crown. Later they forced 'advisers' on the Malay states and formed a federation. This federation was supposed to be governed by agreement, but in reality the rulers had lost their power and a system was in place for government along standard colonial lines.

When the crunch came, the strong and wise King Mongkut of Thailand – the ruler portrayed in *The King and I* – and King Mindon of Burma were willing to compromise with the aggressive Europeans, but the others tried to resist and were subdued by military force. Emperor Tu Due in Vietnam was defeated by the French, who by the end of the nineteenth century controlled all

Vietnamese territories including Cambodia and Laos, basing their claims on those of the Vietnamese emperor who was now their lackey. These three countries were then referred to as French Indo-china. When King Mindon's son, Thibaw, came to power in Burma he refused to compromise with the British, and Burma became a province of India under British rule. The Dutch controlled the old Majapahit Empire in what is now Indonesia, and it became known as the Netherlands East Indies.

* * *

Nothing could prepare us for the culture and physical shock that we encountered when we stepped out of the aircraft at Paya Lebar air-port in Singapore. We had been travelling for over thirty hours in cramped conditions, quite unlike the relatively spacious comfort of non-stop present-day aircraft. The aircraft then were very noisy and the air-conditioning systems were poor, at a time when nearly everybody smoked. The narrow body allowed only three seats in a row with a narrow isle. These were slow, inefficient machines, requiring refuelling every seven hours. We had arrived during the south-west monsoon period when heavy rains fell and temperatures and humidity were in the nineties. These conditions can be debilitat-ing; your body and clothes are never free of perspiration, day or night.

I carried Kelly across the steaming tarmac and Caroline had her own problems because she was expecting our other child in a couple of months. Fortunately we were met by an official from Malaysia–Singapore Airlines (MSA) who handled our passage through customs and immigration. As he drove us through the throbbing streets of Singapore, the incredible noise of the traffic and the mass of humanity jostling on the sidewalks and overflow-ing on to the streets shocked me. Having been reared on a farm where our next-door neighbour was half a mile away, and after living in the wide-open, empty spaces of Africa, the crowded cities of the east were quite new to me. Our hotel, The Ambassador, was located downtown near the waterfront and had no air conditioning, only ceiling fans which circulated warm, humid air that drifted in off the ocean.

It was difficult to adjust to the humidity and I slept very little before I reported to Paya Lebar airport the next morning. Malaysian–Singapore Airlines had largely operated in the past with DC3 and F27 aircraft, but after the Borneo provinces of Sarawak in North Borneo (now Sabah) joined the Malaysian Federation in 1963 there was a requirement for larger aircraft to link these outlying states with the capital, Kuala Lumpur. My first job was to cover twelve-hour day or night shifts on the ramp or tarmac where the aircraft arrived and were prepared for departure. There were two of us on this job; I rotated between days and nights with my opposite number, Stewart Johns. This meant that I had no rest days during the first months.

* * *

The first weeks in Singapore were very difficult and taxed my resolve. But I knew things could only get better and I decided to take it all and continue. After night duty, it was difficult to sleep during the day in a hotel. To relax I often took a stroll in a little park located on the waterfront across the road from the hotel. It was pleasant there before the tropical sun climbed high into the sky. I had visited it early in the morning a few times before I realised that the grass was littered with condoms. Like other open spaces in the city it was used by young lovers after darkness fell.

The purchasing of a car and getting accommodation had to be

EARLY YEARS

Growing up on a farm in Ulster in the 1940s and 1950s was a simple life that involved hard work. Going to school meant walking three miles in the early morning and three miles back, and when you got home you had to do your share of difficult farming tasks – with no machinery available, human and horse had to bear the load. I had a growing sense of awareness of the divisions and injustices within our society and a sense of hopelessness that nothing would be done about it. During quiet moments I would think about how society came to be like that and whether there was any solution.

Top to bottom: Me (behind) with some of my siblings in the 1950s; the rural landscape of my childhood; my father in his early twenties; my mother as a young woman; my sister and me.

MILITARY TRAINING

I was very interested in aircraft and drawn to the military lifestyle. I received my basic military training at the Curragh camp before being assigned to technical training in the Air Corps in Baldonnel.

Top to bottom: an Irish Air Corps aircraft from the 'General Purpose Flight' and some of the ground crews. I am at the bottom, right; my group of Air Corps trainees in the Curragh in 1956. I am seated at the extreme right, second row from the rear.

SUNNY DAYS IN THE COLONIES

About twenty years of my working life was spent in former British colonies and I have many memories of those sunny times stored away in my head. The colour and wide open spaces of Africa, the crowded, intense human life of the Far East, the hot deserts of the Middle East, the joys of life of the Bahamas and Trinidad are with me in my memory and helped me to survive my years in jail.

Above: with my future wife, Caroline, outside the Shelbourne hotel, Dublin, in 1961 before we left for Kenya; the family in Singapore 1967; an Arab dhow used for fishing trips in the Persian Gulf; snorkelling in the Bahamas with my son; the memorable junkanoo festival in the Bahamas.

TAKING ACTION

As the repression of the nationalist Civil Rights marchers grew more violent in the 1970s, events such as these shown here moved me to become involved in the military struggle to bring about political change in the six counties.

Below: British troops search for volunteers and weapons during the Falls Road curfew in 1970; local people stand at the body of an innocent civilian shot dead in Derry on Bloody Sunday.

Opposite: Civilians being rounded up by British soldiers after thirteen civilians were killed by the Parachute Regiment in Derry on Bloody Sunday 1972; a Loyalist march being forced through a nationalist area in 1985 – little had changed ten years later!

Colman Doyle

Colman Doyle

Colman Doyle

Brendan Murphy

ON THE RUN – ARREST

Working while on the run in Nigeria was an unusual experience.

TOP TO BOTTOM: Standing on the tarmac at Calabar in Nigeria with an aircraft belonging to the company that I worked for; with one of the medical staff at a leper colony in Nigeria where I sometimes helped out by repairing analytical equipment on my days off; this is the the veranda of the budget car-hire cabin at Nelspruit airfield in South Africa where I was arrested. The airfield has been updated from a grass track to an international airport in recent years, but the cabin still remains; Nelspruit police station where I was held during court appearances; my first prison in the United States was Essex County Jail, next to the sheriff's headquarters.

The Trial and Conviction of Irish Activists at the Behest of the British Government.

uly 12, 1989, marked the end of a seven-year investigation conducted by the ·BI, and the beginning of a nightmare for five Irish activists. On this day ?ichard Johnson left work early and came upon the FBI attaching a listening levice inside his car.

'or seven years the FBI attempted to prove ıat Richard Johnson, Martin Quigley, amon McGuire, Christina Reid, Gerard loy were exporting weapons to, and in the rocess of building a missile system for, the ·ish Republican Army. Saturation FBI sur- eillance included opening their mail, bug- ing their cars and homes, and bugging undreds of pay phones just to intercept one hone call. And yet the FBI could not gather nough evidence to justify an arrest.

ecause of the botched attempt to bug ?ichard Johnson's car, the FBI was forced ıto a premature arrest and the need to nanufacture a case. Ultimately the govern- ıent had to dredge up an eighty-year old tatute never before used in American ourts — possession of pro... oreign insurgents... Λazzo...

...publican newspapers thrown in as evidence as guilt!

The jury deliberated only a few hours before finding the defendants guilty on all counts. Then Judge Mazzone's antagonism to the defense took on a new level of vindictiveness when he almost doubled sentencing guidelines because he considered the defendants a "threat to national security." Guidelines in the case of Richard Johnson and Martin Quigley called for... fifty-one...

[FISA] has the power to approve surveillance of suspected "terrorists" for as long as is deemed ...cessary by the ...vernment, ...hout need to ...fy the reason ...rpose...

ment, and FBI agent, Brendan Cleary visitec Richard Johnson in prison, without notifying his attorney — a clear abuse of the law!

The law that allows such a travesty of justic is the Foreign Intelligence Surveillance Act (FISA). FISA is designed to protect U.S. national security against foreign agents, and has never before been invoked agains an American citizen. The FISA court sits secretly and continuously, FISA judges are secretly appointed for seven year terms, surveillance can be secretly authorized for indefinite periods, and no outside review of reason or purpose is allowed. Well might the famed Alan Dershowitz opine, "The Act is a serious threat to the civil liberties of all citizens."

When Dershowitz appealed Richard Johnson's conviction he argued, "Whether or not you believe in Mr. Johnson's innocence, I hope that you will agree with me that like any American citizen, he is entitled to the fundo mental protections afforded by the Constitution: to be free from unreasonable searches and seizures, to confront his accusers and not to be deprived of his liberty without due process of law. The Foreign Intelligence Surveillance Act has stripped hin of those fundamental protections... I would now like to ask for your assistance... to do what you can to inform the public about the grave injustices that Mr. Johnson has suffered at the hands of our governmer with the hope that one day soon, the interests of justice will finally be served in this case."

...no Are ...e Defendants?

Richard Johnson, a Radar engineer with the highest security clearance, has made significant contributions to both the space program and to national defense. Richard's prison evaluation should entitle him to a minimum security facility, but the government refuses to transfer him, citing national security as its reason. He is serving ten years.

Martin Quigley, a computer engineer, was born in County Louth, Ireland, near the infamous border which divides the country. He had only been in the U.S. a few months at the time of his arrest. Martin was sentenced to eight years.

Eamon McGuire, a native of County Monaghan, Ireland is an electronics engineer. Indicted with the others in 1989, no effort was made to try him, although he lived openly in Ireland and Africa. He was finally extradited to the U.S. in 1994 and sentenced to six years.

Christina Reid, an engineer from California was just released after serving three years and six months.

Gerard Hoy, a Pennsylvania native and computer science research assistant served two years.

The incarceration of these innocent people has exacted a heavy toll on their families also. Because the government makes no attempt to place prisoners near their homes, elderly parents and grandparents have been forced to travel thousands of miles to visit their children. For Irish nationalists, even this comfort is denied.

Richard Johnson's parents travel over a thousand miles in one day to visit him. Christina Reid's mother saved vacation time to travel from Chicago to California as often as she could. Martin Quigley and Eamon McGuire can only receive annual visits from their families.

What You Can Do:

Over $250,000 in trial costs and expenses have been incurred since July 12, 1989. The extreme financial hardship on the prisoners and their families is overwhelming, especially in light of their present situations. Please help. Show your support and protest this travesty of justice by making a donation to the BOSTON 3 DEFENSE FUND. Thank you.

Donations can be made to:
BOSTON 3 DEFENSE FUND
c/o Larry Downes
319 Broadway, 3rd floor
New York, NY 10007
(212) 587-3300

I would like more information about The BOSTON 3.
Name:
Address:
Phone:

The Boston Three Defense Fund

Richard Johnson

Martin Quigley

Eamon McGuire

OUTSIDE SUPPORT

A montage of some of the support efforts for the 'Boston Three', of whom I was one, and other Irish prisoners in the United States.

SOUTH ARMAGH

Crossmaglen is the most feared part of the South Armagh IRA brigade area, to which I belonged. Signs such as: 'WELCOME TO CROSSMAGLEN – SNIPERS' ALLEY', 'SNIPER AT WORK', and, on ceasfire 'ON HOLD', after a ceasefire 'I AM BACK' were nailed to telegraph poles. Morale is said to have collapsed in some British army units here. By the early 1990s, with all the knowledge we had accumulated over the years, the Mark 15 Buster was developed and it proved very successful against helicopters when they were coming in to land.

Here a helicopter uses a match at the Crossmaglen Ranger pitch to shield it from attack during descent. The military still occupy part of the GAA grounds.

Brendan Murphy

organised after I had a few hours' rest before noon. To do this I had to take public transport or walk, which pushed me to mix with the local people and get to know the city. Singapore of the 1960s was a city quite unlike modern-day Singapore. It still retained many characteristics of a nineteenth-century city of the east. There were no skyscrapers; the four- or five-floor buildings in Raffles were the tallest. Most of the employment was generated by the British presence in the area. There was no industry or manufacturing infrastructure. It was an overcrowded city with high unemployment, where often twelve people lived to a room.

Sir Stamford Raffles had stepped ashore on the north side of the Singapore estuary in 1819 and put in place the principles for the city's development as a free port. When he set up Singapore the prospects of British expansion in the area looked bleak. The British East India Company still controlled Penang, but there were constant attempts by the company to reduce their presence there. The Dutch were annoyed by Raffles and had they pressed home their objection to Singapore in the beginning, it is likely that the settlement would have been closed down.

When negotiations took place five years later, the port was a proven economic success and the British retained possession when the Anglo-Dutch agreement was signed that year. The same treaty allowed the British to take possession of Malacca in exchange for Bencoolen, which put an end to Dutch political connections with the Malay Peninsula and left the British in control of the important trade route to China.

Moving around on foot was the best way to explore the ethnic areas with their many cultures, and appreciate the atmosphere of old Singapore. The city, like most Malaysian cities, had a predominantly Chinese character, but there were many other races living here too, all in their own quarters of the city.

Chinatown was a maze of small streets where you could discover all kinds of Chinese merchants, craftsmen, shrines and temples, some dating from the mid-nineteenth century. During my first few days wandering around Chinatown I encountered my first Chinese funeral. A man carrying a special flag for calling the spirit of the deceased led the procession – this was an essential duty performed by the dead man's son. A spectacular funeral was important, and a ceremony which did not meet the expectations of the neighbours would bring disapproval on the family. Proper dress was required, and special characters, weeping and wailing, were supposed to be heard above the clash of cymbals and other noise. All this was accompanied by the burning of the possessions and of artificial money made out of paper for the deceased to use in the afterworld.

The passing port trade fuelled business in Singapore's Chinatown; anything you wished to purchase could be obtained or produced in twenty-four hours. This was especially true for Change Alley, which runs between Collyer Quay and Raffles Place. You could change any money in the world to the currency of your choice. Here also you could be measured up for suits, jackets or shirts, which you could collect the next day.

Numerically the Malays, the original inhabitants of the region, were the second largest ethnic group; they were called '*bumiputra*' or 'sons of the soil'. This was an appropriate name. Their lifestyle was based on strict Islamic teachings and traditional values, and they preferred to live by agriculture and fishing. On Singapore Island in the 1960s there were still Malay '*kampongs*', or villages of wooden houses built on stilts to avoid the monsoon flooding. Here people wore traditional dress: for women, a loose long-sleeved tunic called '*baju kurong*' over a tight-fitting costume called a '*kebaya*'; men wore a '*kain songket*', a cloth with a border which was tied around the waist to hang like a dress.

The Indians settled in an area that became known as 'Little India'. Here they established a thriving community. Some of the houses still retained beautiful Indian facades and shops specialised in saris, garlands, spices, dried vegetables and fruit. South-east of Little India and adjoining it was the old Arab, or, more precisely, the Muslim quarter. This was where early Arab immigrants settled and followed their professions and religion. Like most immigrants they named streets after places in their homelands – Arab Street, Baghdad Street, Muscat Street, Jeddah Street and Haji Lane. In the 1960s no particular area was exclusive to any race of people and you could find all races living throughout the city. However, the old quarters still retained an atmosphere reminiscent of the people's homelands.

A large number of Europeans lived in Singapore at the time. Their numbers were inflated by the presence of the huge military bases on the island. Singapore was one of those postings where families accompanied military personnel. This presence and the port activity formed the commercial life of the island. With independence in 1959, many Europeans had taken Singapore citizenship or, like myself, were expatriates on contract.

Unlike Africa with its colour and emptiness, what most immediately comes to mind from the East now, in the closed, dull environment of an American jail, is crowds and noise. I find it wonderfully exciting to contemplate; even though it was difficult to experience at first, I am delighted now to have those memories. After three weeks of wandering on foot I finally purchased a car from a Chinese vendor. This enabled Caroline and Kelly to accompany me to view living accommodations. The traffic was terrifying;

it must have been the worst in the world. The thundering lines of cars never gave way to allow you to filter in, you had to barge your way in and hope for the best. There was a continuous clamour from hooting vehicles, and taxis crossed your lane to reach prospective customers or stopped dead in front of you without warning.

Traffic lights were not considered applicable to cyclists, trishaw operators or motorcycles. Trishaws, with their terrified passengers, and motorcycles almost hidden under father, mother and several children, dashed out of side streets across traffic, oblivious to the danger and the angry blare of horns. Pedal cyclists, with boxes of fruit stacked over their heads and on rear fenders or carriers, sailed into traffic junctions to become entangled in lines of traffic, unbalancing and spilling fruit across the hot asphalt.

We decided to rent a house on Frankel Avenue. Most of the houses here were detached. The East Coast Road, where the house was, ran along what was then the seafront from Mountbatten Road, where sea-planes had arrived in the 1930s and 40s. When we made a return visit to Singapore in 1974, land was being reclaimed from the sea all along the East Coast Road and I expect it is now some distance inland. The British Far East Air Force base was also nearby.

Because of our proximity to the air force base, quite a few military personnel and their families lived in that area and I often had conversations with soldiers involved in the war there. They seemed to have a rather cavalier attitude to it. They described the action as flying over the jungle in helicopters waiting for an individual to sprint across a clearing like a gazelle and hoping that they could down him with a burst from their machine gun mounted in the doorway. In contrast to that, and at the other extreme, were the secretive operations of the SAS. The covert ops of the SAS were the best and often the only way to control the borders on the island of

Kilimantan during 'confrontation' with Indonesia. When the British announced their intention to withdraw their forces from east of Suez in 1968 they were the dominant power in the near east and South East Asia. (After that, I believe, they started to lose all their former influence and became a secondary player to the United States.) There was a residue of goodwill towards them in the areas still and I believe that this was sustained by the ruler's reliance on the covert ops of the SAS to keep them in power. Coping with this new role of retaining British influence below the surface caused a radical change in the way the SAS behaved. They were rarely seen in uniform any more, operating instead with total anonymity at home or overseas. This was fortuitous for them because the uprising in the six counties of Northern Ireland would require similar services shortly after. They would welcome this opportunity of having a proving ground so close to home.

I was at home one afternoon arranging furniture and other requirements before moving in when the local grocery store delivery man arrived to say he would take any orders I had and would have them filled and delivered the same day. Since I had no need of supplies that day, he said he would return when I moved in – and assuming I was living alone asked me if I required an '*amah*' 'for housework or for bed' – everything I needed, he could supply! The traders in Singapore were sharp businessmen. They had an eye for new arrivals and zeroed in to grab their custom. There was an array of mobile food vendors who operated miniature kitchens from bicycles and travelled around the residential areas. They were called 'Tick-Tock men' because they used various instruments to make a distinctive sound to announce their arrival outside your home. Some used a miniature hide drum on a stick, like a lollipop, and it had a ball tied to it with a length of twine; as they rotated the stick, the ball played a distinctive rhythm on the drum. You soon got to recognise it – that would be the Indian vendor selling samosas. The click-clock of two sticks held between the fingers – that would be the Chinese man selling noodles.

The landlord of the house that we rented asked us if we would like to retain an *amah* (for housework!) that the previous occupier had. Since the previous people were Europeans, we decided that this might be a good idea because she would be familiar with the European lifestyle and requirements.

As luck would have it, she was a beautiful, gentle Chinese woman. Her name was Sai Keo; she was in her late thirties, married with eight children. She became a good friend of our family. Her own family lived in Dakota Crescent in one of the first apartment blocks built by the government after independence. Her two-bedroomed apartment accommodated mother and father, eight children and grandmother. She insisted in calling me 'Master' and Caroline 'Missy'. I did not like it, but I could not get her to change; she would always revert to the term after a few days.

In August 1966, Caroline entered hospital to give birth to our son, Glenn. The birth was normal and everything was fine when I visited them on my way to work that night. On my way home next morning I called to see them again. I was shocked, to say the least. The window of Caroline's room had been left partially open during the night and mosquitoes had entered and attacked Caroline's arms and face. In her exhausted condition she could not feel the bites and her face was so badly bitten that she could barely open her eyes. Standing there, disguising my outrage, I resolved that, mosquitoes or not, this was the end. She would not be put through the ordeal of giving birth again.

When Glenn arrived home Sai Keo was delighted, and went

around fussing about him. In her spare time you would find her sitting on the veranda with the baby across her knee, gently massaging his back or stroking him with the fringe of his blanket. This was a habit which he retained into his teens. She provided a gentle buffer between the children and parents and allowed time for me to get experience in how to handle children. After a few months Kelly started calling her 'Mammy', and Caroline told the child that *she* was the mammy; the child explained quite clearly that she was the mother but that Sai Keo was her mammy. When my days off work coincided with Sai Keo's, I often took the children down to her ground floor apartment so that they could play with her children. Her husband's name was Lim. Of course, in the Chinese tradition she used her maiden name during marriage; only when she died would her husband's name be bestowed on her.

He was a bus driver and her parents, who were Hokeins, had arranged their marriage, as an unmarried girl at the advanced age of sixteen was considered a liability. It was normal for parents to organise a husband for their daughters without telling her about it until a few days before the event. For financial gain they might even have decided that she would become a concubine. A concubine was a kind of institutionalised mistress, acquired and discarded at will. They could acquire considerable power but their social status was different from that of a wife. Wives were not for pleasure – that was what a concubine was for. The Chinese believed that a man in a high position should have as many as possible – they showed a man's status.

To question parents' decision was considered impossible. Even if the girl refused to consent to their wishes, she would not have been taken seriously. The only way to object and be taken seriously was to commit suicide. This did occur, usually in a young lovers' pact with a secret boyfriend. Some Chinese family rules were not rigidly applied in Singapore, but in a Chinese household the younger generation was definitely subservient to the older, with suitable decorum to mark their relative positions.

Sai Keo's mother had arrived in Singapore before the First World War, and she did not speak English, but I talked to her using her granddaughter as an interpreter. Her feet were bound – when she was a child her toes had been bent back under her feet, bound and crushed. This horrific mutilation was to make a woman walk like a 'young doe' and was allegedly introduced a thousand years before by a concubine of an emperor. She said that she experienced constant pain, and that the toenails were forever growing into the soles of her feet. When I asked her why she did not unwrap them, she said she did when she first arrived in Singapore but they were more painful unwrapped so she reverted to the bandages. She still grieved for her only son, Sai Keo's brother, who was taken away by the Japanese in 1942 and never seen again.

Since 1937 the Japanese had been at war with mainland China and showed the Chinese no mercy. Because of this and other excesses, western countries had applied trade sanctions against Japan. These sanctions were very effective because Japan depended on raw materials from outside. To ensure these supplies she turned her attention to Indochina. To reach the desperately needed rubber and oil in Malaya and Netherlands East India she would have to deal with the large British naval base in Singapore. She invaded Malaya on 8 December and raced on to Singapore. General AE Percival surrendered Singapore to the Japanese on 15 January 1942.

During the War of Independence in Ireland in 1919-1921, it was the same General Percival who declared a state of emergency that allowed some British forces to burn and kill at will. I realised that the links between various colonised countries, through British army personnel, continued to crop up as I moved around the world. The defeat at Singapore was the greatest disaster the British had experienced in two hundred years, losing approximately 150,000 men to a Japanese loss of 15,000. The defeat of the European power had a profound affect on the local population. They thought the British were invincible and would always be there to protect them. Their defeat exposed the Chinese population to the same harsh treatment that their countrymen were receiving back home and things would never be the same again.

The older Chinese valued the opportunities the British colonial system gave them to escape the unending wars and famine at home and live a reasonable life in Malaya. Sai Keo's mother still had great respect for them. On one visit, as I got up to go I decided to leave some money to pay for the soft drinks the children had consumed. Reaching into my pocket I pulled out Singapore dollars and a British five pound note fell out on the floor. When the grandmother saw the Queen's head she became all excited and asked for the note, not to spend but to keep as a memento. After 150 years the British were preparing to leave the area in 1973. She was unhappy about that and she was unhappy that her eldest grandson had received his call-up papers for the new Singapore defence force. Perhaps she had seen him as a substitute for the son she lost to the Japanese.

* * *

In the 1960s it was difficult to imagine Singapore entering a golden age. It was still a dirty city. Trash was thrown out on the sidewalk and street, a bucket of dirty water could be emptied out of a shop door on to your shoes. Unemployment was very high. Families still lived in overcrowded conditions. The people were uneasy about the future and conversation would always return to the possibility of obtaining a visa to emigrate to Australia, Europe or the United States.

The entry of Singapore into the Malaysian Federation caused internal stresses and disagreements. The majority Malay people felt that their political supremacy was under threat and civil war was not far off. Finally, in August 1965, Singapore was voted out of the union. They had no option but to go it alone and Singapore became an independent republic. Indonesian confrontation collapsed. When we arrived in Singapore there were two Indonesian agents awaiting execution for blowing up a bank in Singapore. They were executed some years later although the threat had long passed.

Lee Kuan Yew's government believed that Singapore could survive alone, even enter a new golden age. The greatest effort would be directed at attracting tourists to the island or making it an attractive stop-off point. Most visitors were businessmen or people on a break from the monotony of small outlying areas of the region. The continuing build-up of American forces in Vietnam was stimulating the tourist industry in Hong Kong and Taiwan but very few soldiers on rest and recreation were coming to Singapore, although some of the special forces' families lived there. In 1968 we were asked to handle one of these 'rest and recreation' flights per week in addition to our normal flights, and later the frequency was increased. On one occasion I was standing near the long line of soldiers as they embarked for the return journey to Vietnam and a young man, nineteen or twenty years old, left the line and went to a Chinese girl who was waving to him from the perimeter fence. He put his hand in his pocket and handed her a fistful of notes. As he rejoined the line I commented about him giving his money away and his reply was, 'I have no need of it, I probably won't make it back out of the jungle this time.'

Singapore was not very interested in promoting a 'sex for sale' image. It had unique attractions because of its history and multinational and cultural make-up, and wanted to attract more up-market tourists. The government introduced a blitz in schools and community centres, on radio and television, to educate the population and promote a cleaner, quieter, friendlier Singapore. When the promotion ended they introduced harsh penalties for the breach of new anti-social laws prohibiting car horn-blowing in designated areas at a certain time of day or night; rubbish bins were provided along all the streets for depositing trash, cigarette ends and chewing gum. Breaches of any of these regulations meant a stiff fine on the spot. By 1970, the laws were having the desired effect and Singapore was on its way to becoming the pride of Asia.

* * *

Sai Keo was very experienced and enjoyed taking care of the children together with the housework. This left very little for Caroline to do and she decided that she would like to find employment. She preferred to be involved in modelling and show business rather than work a regular nine-to-five job. After taking a refresher course in modelling she joined a modelling agency and beauty academy and after a short time she had established herself in business and was involved most days in fashion shows, seeking sponsorship for shows or stage productions and the occasional movie.

There was a certain amount of social activity surrounding Caroline's work and, with my job settling back to near normal working hours, we started taking more interest in Singapore night life. Like most cities in Asia, Singapore never slept. In the 1960s movies seemed to be the most popular entertainment. Dancing was also very popular then and music was often provided by all-girl rock groups from Korea and the Philippines. There were places like the Tropicana that provided upmarket entertainment and other establishments that provided dancers for hire, hostess bars, or strip shows – something to satisfy everybody's taste.

In the early morning after a show we would visit Buges Street. After dark this street was filled with food stalls, tables and chairs. Hawkers furiously stirred ingredients in steaming woks, producing inexpensive, mouth-watering food for night clubbers. Buges Street had another attraction. It was also a place for the more exotic people to parade up and down to see and be seen. Due to the lack of facial hair on most Asian men, it was not difficult for them to dress up as women. I have met newcomers to Singapore who invited one of the beautiful 'ladies' home before they realised the lady was a young men.

* * *

My life had become more organised and had settled into a predictable routine, so I was able to get a few days off. We decided to cross the three-quarter mile long causeway to the Malay Peninsula and spend some time sightseeing.

During my time in South East Asia, Malay rubber production employed about a million people and produced 45 percent of the world's supply of natural rubber. It all started with the rapid industrialisation in the west at the turn of the century, which provided a boom in prices. With great profits to be made in rubber, financial houses in Britain started to provide funds to clear the jungle and establish plantations. The industry was labour intensive and it attracted a flood of labourers from the Indian subcontinent into

Malaya. Most of the Indians in Malaysia today are descendants of this group of migrants.

It was easy to distinguish where the jungle ended and the rubber began. Apart from the regular rows, rubber trees are tall and slender, there are no branches on the trunks and the foliage spreads out at the top, joining each other to form a canopy. This provides an inviting shade from the tropical sun.

On day visits to the Jahor district, I saw tappers working among the rubber trees. I was curious to know why they wore so much clothing in the scorching heat. Their bodies were completely covered, with only a small slit to see through. My curiosity got the better of me one afternoon. We decided to leave the hot car for the cool shade of the rubber trees and see how the latex was collected.

We had just about finished examining the spiral track cut in the bark of the trees and the metal spout fixed at the end of the track so that the blobs of latex could drip into the cup-like container, when Caroline started complaining about insect bites. For some reason insects preferred my wife, and when she was with me I did not have to worry about bites. When we looked around, a cloud of mosquitoes had surrounded us. They obviously thrived in the cool shade of the rubber trees and were the more aggressive type with stripes, called 'tiger mosquitoes'. We made a dash for the car, but some were able to enter before we managed to close the door. Caroline eliminated them with frantic swipes of a towel.

On our way north we paid a visit to Malacca. It is rich in history and much of Malaysia's early story lies within its boundaries. Malay, Indian, Arab, Portuguese, Dutch, Chinese and British, all had left their mark there. Walking through the colourful Portuguese quarter on the seafront in the 1960s, I had a feeling that they were the hardiest European colonisers. They have a darker skin now and speak a language called Papia Kristang, derived from Malay and Portuguese. I could not help thinking about how hard life must have been four hundred years ago. The Portuguese seem to have withstood the ravages of this tropical land better than the others. Albuquerque descendants were still there, regardless of defeat, disease and all the political upheavals that have taken place since.

As we moved closer to Kuala Lumpur, the capital, we became more conscious of another major economic activity in Malaysia, the production of tin. Like rubber, more tin is produced in Malaysia than any other place in the world and on the outskirts of Kuala Lumpur we saw the Kinta Valley operation, the largest open-cast tin mine in the world. It is difficult to miss it. In contrast to the green jungle vegetation elsewhere, this valley is a desert. Here thousands of acres of mine tailings stretch across the valley and huge dredges drag tin from the earth twenty-four hours a day, seven days a week. In the 1860s the tin trade was dominated by rich Chinese living in the straits; settlements which were often backed by capital from British banks and traders. Disputes between rival Chinese factions and Malay chiefs spread to the streets of the straits, particularly Penang, and threatened the peace. These led to a call from merchants to Britain for protection and gave the British the opportunity to place the settlements under the direct rule of the Crown.

The Cameron Highlands are north of Kuala Lumpur, which rises five thousand feet above the steaming jungle. As we made our way up the winding road we could feel the lessening of the oppressive heat and humidity of the plains below. By the time we reached the plateau I realised that my body and clothes were dry for the first time since we arrived in Malaysia the previous year. I was told that this is the only place in Malaysia where tea is grown. On our way up I had my first glimpse of a Sakaris, a negrito aborigine people that inhabit the north-west jungle of the peninsula. As he walked along the road I was surprised by how much he resembled the Australian aboriginal. The British ignored these jungle people until after the Second World War when they were used by the communist insurgents as porters, cultivators and guides. They did not like being cooped up in jungle compounds as they were semi-nomads, but they were won over by social and medical services that were provided there.

On our return to Singapore after journeying to Malaya, I was again very aware of the mass of people and the endless noise. Familiarity and living on top of each other can be a destructive thing and there were times when I instinctively yearned for privacy and space. When I had my rest days during the week it was possible to visit quiet places such as Changi beach, the Botanical gardens, Canning Fort or Tiger Balm gardens. Our daughter, Kelly, was old enough to communicate, so I took her along, usually sitting on my shoulders.

* * *

Singapore, with its kaleidoscope of people, had an endless round of festivals and the new year was celebrated four times in twelve months. Every month, with the exception of March and July, had more than two festivals in progress. The Thaipusam festival took place in early February and honoured Lord Subramanian. This was an Indian affair where penitents pierced their bodies, cheeks and tongues with sharp lances on weighted hooks. They shed no blood and felt no pain as they paraded in a trance-like state accompanied by the image of Lord Subramanian.

The festival of the hungry ghosts was held during the seventh lunar month, or the first weeks of September, when the Chinese believed that the spirits of the departed wandered the earth. Some communities pooled their resources and held celebrations, which included a Chinese opera troop or *wayang*. At the beginning of the seventh lunar month a *wayang* would arrive and set up its outdoor stage on Coal Stream street, which was quite close to Frankel avenue where we lived. Sai Keo always looked forward to this celebration and in the evening you would find her there with our two children. These marathon dramas, with their high-pitched music, songs, and puppeteers, performed ancient plays of Chinese mythology. Today, forty years later, when I hear Chinese music it lifts my spirit. Somehow during those years my western ear learned to appreciate the music of the Orient.

The mooncake festival was also held in September, on the fifteenth day of the eighth moon. It celebrated the overthrow of the Mongol dynasty. According to Chinese legend, secret messages of rebellion had been smuggled inside mooncakes as part of the uprising that led to the end of the Mongol Empire.

In October the Thimithi, or fire-walking festival, was held. Here devotees walked over a five-yard pit of burning coals without any apparent ill effect. Deepavali was held on the first of November. It was a joyous Hindu festival of lights which celebrated the victory of light over dark, good over evil. The most important celebration of the year was the Chinese New Year. On the eve of the New Year, family relationships were reinforced with a get-together and all debts had to be settled before the New Year arrived, even if it was necessary to take another loan afterwards. The Chingay parade was held in conjunction with the New Year lunar celebrations. The parade moved through the narrow street led by stilt-walkers and acrobats who added a festive atmosphere to the celebrations. The mythological lion, symbol of power and goodness, was an integral part of any Chinese celebration. The dragon danced through the streets on the legs of men. This man-powered creature of red and gold silk and *papier-mâché* advanced towards each flash of fireworks amidst a deafening noise of gongs and drums.

* * *

I had recently obtained certification cover on the Rolls Royce Dart turbo-prop engine and I was asked to go to the Borneo states where Malaysia–Singapore Airways had taken over the routes operated by Borneo Airways. Soon I was flying across the fabled South China Sea. It was the inter-monsoon period and I was able to see the countless islands scattered like emeralds across this once pirate-infested sea. I was going to Kuching, the capital of Sarawak, home of the original 'wild man of Borneo' and once the possession of the White Rajah.

Sarawak and Sabah, two British possessions located on the northern part of the island of Borneo, had joined the independent Malaysian Federation six years previously. Borneo is the third largest island in the world. In the 1960s, seventy percent of the island was still covered by virgin rainforest that had never been felled. Under this unbroken canopy, bands of nomadic punas hunted with poisoned darts. They were timid and rarely came out into the sunlight. Living in small groups, they ranged over very large areas of jungle, living on wild sago and the game they shot with hardwood blowpipes.

Flying across Borneo I got the impression that it was a land of mighty rivers crashing down mountainsides and meandering through jungle vegetation and swamps – a wild, thinly populated island, where travel was mostly by riverboat. Sarawak state had an area of almost fifty thousand square miles and in the 1960s there were only about two hundred miles of useable roads. When I was in Kuching it was a small river town still locked in the nineteenth century. Although it was twenty-two years since the last rajah had left Sarawak, their palace, the Astana, remained and the traditional cannon boomed every night at eight o'clock. This seemed to be the signal for people to clear the streets and return to their houses – people went to bed early each night for there was little else to do.

Living in Kuching, it is difficult to avoid expatriates. It is also difficult to avoid some long-time expatriate telling you the story about how an Englishman, James Brooke, whom the then Sultan of Brunei befriended, slowly robbed the sultan of a large part of his kingdom. In the first half of the nineteenth century the thirty-six-year-old came ashore near Cape Datuk in the north west tip of Borneo and during his lifetime he would carve out a personal kingdom and change the map of Borneo.

The story, as related to me, conjured up a vision of a man struggling ashore from a shipwreck or following an attack by pirates. Later I learned that this was far from the true story. He was a former military officer in the East India Company and was no stranger to the east. When Brooke left England he had plans to establish a colony in north east Borneo. When he reached Singapore, he was invited by a group of Singapore merchants to switch his attentions to west Borneo where the Dyak people were in revolt against the Sultan of Brunei. The Singapore merchants were attempting to take advantage of Brunei's misfortune. Brooke agreed to help the regime in Brunei in return for the title of rajah and the right to trade and govern the area where the revolt was taking place. Brooke was the first of three white rajahs, all Brookes, who were absolute rulers of Sarawak for one hundred years. The British recognised Brooke's title about twenty years after it was conferred on him and Sarawak became independent of Brunei.

Regardless of how Brooke got Sarawak, one has to admire how he tamed this wild and primitive land. He suppressed the murderous pirates who preyed on offshore traffic and built forts on the turbulent rivers to prevent the Iban from head-hunting. As the savage Iban were brought under control in the area surrounding the river, the white rajah moved on to the next river. Successive rajahs followed this policy until Sarawak had five divisions that extended from the west to the present border with Brunei.

I saw my first 'wild man of Borneo' in Sibu. His delicate features surprised me. He was very short, like a child that had failed to grow. He had rings in his ears and his tattooed skin hung loosely on his body. He did not seem troubled by his surroundings. He looked proud and self confident, with his hard black eyes. His *parang* (machete) dangling from a cord on his waist, stirred memories of childhood stories about these one-time head-hunters. Did this man ever take a human head with that all-purpose *parang*? He was old enough to have been in his twenties when the British unleashed them on the Japanese during the Second World War.

When I was in Sibu on a working visit I arranged for a boat to take me on a day trip up the Rajan river. I did not realise how intimidating the river could be. The water was very turbulent and the boat was forever dodging to avoid floating debris and limbs of trees. In the past you could encounter an Iban war party on this river, many warriors to a canoe, slicing through the water on a head-hunting expedition.

Upstream from Kanowit we got out of the boat and took to a jungle path to visit a longhouse where relatives of the boat owner lived. The forest in this region was very ancient. Inside, it was bathed in a dim green light, and smooth, straight trunks of trees passed upwards into the canopy that blocked out direct sunlight.

There was little vegetation to impede movement, except where there was a break in the canopy.

After twenty minutes or so we emerged from the jungle into a small clearing where small plots of rice were growing. In the trees across the clearing a longhouse stood on stilts. Curious children gathered on a balcony, their laughter and chatter becoming excited, presumably at the sight of me. The people seemed to be overjoyed to have one of their own visiting them. The residents left their private rooms and gathered in a communal area where the floor was completely covered with a large handwoven mat. Here the women, bare to the waist like the men, mixed freely with the men, unlike the people on the plains.

We were offered rice cakes and fish; and a locally brewed alcoholic drink was also available but I declined, as I had never taken alcohol. I did not see anybody with body fat; their diet seemed to consist of rice, fish and whatever else they could kill. Most of the conversation consisted of questions directed at their relative, and although they seemed a very hospitable people I felt uneasy. Sitting on the mat surrounded by these people, I could see the human skulls in roughly made baskets hanging from rafters. Most of these heads belonged to Japanese soldiers who had occupied Sarawak during the Second World War. The end of these gruesome relics was in sight. During the 1960s the Japanese authorities put a programme in place to purchase any of these skulls that came on the market.

We had spent so much time in Kanowit and the longhouse that it was getting late in the day. Here the night arrives before you realise that the day has ended. The constant humidity causes a mist to rise in the jungle when the sun goes down. With my inexperience I did not relish travelling on the river after dark, so we decided to go downriver instead and over the border into Brunei.

The British had placed Brunei under its protection at the end of the nineteenth century and so it remains today. Whenever you mention Brunei most people think of oil. In the 1960s it was receiving thirty-five million dollars a year in oil revenue, a large amount of money for a population of less than 100,000. About half of the population were Malays, most of them living in the stilted village in the Brunei river – the old Brunei water village, Kampong Ayer, probably existed a thousand years before Magellan's fleet sailed into the river nearly 450 years ago. Despite the country's wealth, there was not much evidence of money here in the 1960s. A mosque built ten years previously was the only new building in town.

When the British decided to withdraw from east of Suez they prevailed on the current sultan's father to hold some form of democratic elections in 1962. The opposition party, led by the pro-Indonesian Sheikh Azahari, won thirty-five out of the thirty-six legislative seats. This was not the democracy the British had in mind when they proposed elections as they did not wish to see Brunei's oil and currency reserves removed from their own sphere of influence. The British sent in a Gurka battalion, and after a sharp, bloody encounter Sheikh Azahari's supporters were crushed. About thirty of the elected representatives were arrested and were still in prison when we left Malaysia. The outcome of the elections and the resulting rebellion probably influenced the sultan's decision to remain outside the new Malaysian Federation and under British protection. To ensure that there would be no repeat of the 1962 uprising, British expatriates were placed in key positions in the government and security forces. Entertainment in Brunei revolved around these expatriates when I was there. It was difficult to avoid regurgitated local stories in such a small community and after a few days I would be ready to move on.

* * *

My next port of call was North Borneo, or as it is now called, Sabah, 'the land below the wind'. It continued to be administered by the British-based Royal Charted Company until it was taken over by the Crown after the Second World War. Our main base of operations was the capital, called Jesselton until it was changed some years ago to Kota Kinabalu. In the 1960s it was a modern town of about twenty thousand people. It was occupied by the Japanese during the Second World War and was almost completely destroyed by allied bombers.

In the 1960s travelling by air was the only safe way to get from one part of the state to another. Regional flights from west Malaysia arrived and departed each day, and local flights operated to Victoria, Bandau, Sandakan, Lahad Datu and Tawau. Piracy was endemic in the waters surrounding North Borneo; often the tradition was handed down from father to son for hundreds of years. If you wanted to travel by sea you had to take your chances of avoiding the pirates who generally murdered everybody on board leaving nobody to tell what happened. Their primary targets were small craft plying the waters between North Borneo and the islands of the Sulu and Celebes Sea.

The Royal Navy has been involved in operations against pirates in these waters for over a hundred years, but still they flourished. When I was there in the 1960s, British troops still operated coastal patrols with the North Borneo police and their presence prevented the pirates from raiding onshore villages.

While I was in North Borneo we had a problem with one of our *Fokker* F27 aircraft at Lahad Datu on the Celebes sea coast. The defect was eventually traced to a defective sensor harness and we were delayed well into the night. While it was being taken care of I went for a stroll along the airstrip which was cut out of the rain forest. Night here was as black as the darkness that falls on the African savannah, but the jungle is deep and rarely silent. The persistent insects and strange sounds caused my thoughts to reflect on a time when Europeans first arrived here.

What manner of men made the long journey here in sailing ships five hundred years ago? Perhaps the tropical islands with all their dangers were preferable to the smelly, disease-ridden cities of Europe of that time. Whatever the reasons, perhaps they were poorer, tougher men than those who exist in Britain today. (Then as I stood there my thoughts turned to the SAS who were at that time operating three-month tours in the very jungle I was looking into and I had second thoughts about the men of today!)

One of the reasons they made that perilous journey lies southeast from here across the Celebes sea – the Moluccas, better known as the 'spice islands'. European powers once fought wars over these remote islands where cloves, mace, pepper, ginger and nutmeg once existed in abundance; now these islands support subsistence farming. Before refrigeration was available, these spices were highly prized because they were the only means of making rancid meat palatable.

The Dutch used Ambon in the south Moluccas as the administrative centre of the spice islands. After the Second World War an independent republic of Indonesia was declared. The Dutch allowed the spice islands to join the Indonesian Federation, which included Sulawesi and the island of Timor. In 1960 President Sukarno abolished the elected parliament and formed a new republic claiming jurisdiction over the whole archipelago. The spice islands and Sulawesi (Celebes) went to war, which resulted in about thirty-five thousand people from the spice islands moving to Holland where they remain to this day. Their plight came to international attention when some young expatriate spice islanders hijacked a train in the 1970s which led to the death of one hostage and a couple of hijackers. Timor's continuing struggle against the government in Jakarta attracted world attention in the 1990s. The extent to which the problems return home with the coloniser never ceased to amaze me.

When I was in Borneo in 1968 reports were being received that a tribe in the central highlands called the Yali had killed and feasted on two missionaries who had destroyed village fetishes. Even then it was still one of the wildest, most isolated frontiers on earth. The outside world knew little about the real life of this primitive, sweltering land where tropical glaciers existed in the cloud-covered central mountains, where Stone Age tribes still practised cannibalism, where ferns grew to giant size and a tribe called the Korowai lived in houses built in the forest canopy one hundred feet above the ground.

It was truly another time and place, yet here in prison in the United States a change of light, or perhaps a smell, triggers my memory and my thoughts return to Borneo. Was it the lack of red tape and the simplicity of life that made so many expatriates spend most of their lives out there? In any case, I was not allowed to remain in Borneo for very long. I had to return to the frantic world that was Singapore.

* * *

The airline's new *Boeing* 737s were due to arrive and staff were being sent to the United States for training. This left us with a shortage of technical people again. The introduction of the *Boeing* 737 made the technical end of the job more interesting. It introduced many new concepts at the time. Electronics, developed for space flight, were widely used for the first time in all systems. The hydraulics, flight controls, electric power, and avionic systems were centralised and constructed in modular form wherever possible. Previously you could find bits and pieces of these systems scattered through the aircraft as their installation was an afterthought. This new approach made maintenance much easier.

As an expatriate on contract I had to study to update myself on this aircraft and obtain the Air Registration Board certification cover. This took about two hundred hours of study. When most of the technical problems were taken care of at night, I used to spend some time studying in the office or on the aircraft. One morning while I was doing this a day-shift supervisor arrived and on his way to the office he checked to see if the aircraft was prepared for upcoming flights. If the technical log was not on the aircraft, the normal procedure was to check in the office. He did not do this; instead he requested the refuellers to uplift a normal load while he checked in the office. What he did not know was that there were two men working in one of the fuel tanks. They had to frantically retreat backwards through the tank baffles and wing ribs as fuel gushed in on them, washing them out through an access panel in the undercarriage bay. It was just another reminder of how careful you have to be around aricraft.

The American Embassy staff in Jakarta flew into Singapore regularly in a DC3 aircraft because at that time President Sukarno of Indonesia was following a pro-Moscow policy which impoverished the country. Food was scarce, and rice and frogs' legs were a luxury. Singapore was their source of supplies. One afternoon I was sitting in the office which looked out on the runway where the DC3 was taking off. A couple of seconds after lift-off the port engine failed and the aircraft swung left into the ground. It took me a second to realise that I was not dreaming, by which time the gasoline on board had caught fire. It quickly consumed the aircraft and everybody on board lost their lives.

The airline continued its relentless expansion. With the arrival of the *Boeing* 737s services were planned for Hong Kong, Phnom Penh, Bangkok and Taipei in Taiwan. A Chinese ex-Qantas man, called Loy, was scheduled to go to Taipei station. Before going he decided to get married and Caroline and I were invited to the reception, our first Chinese wedding. Each dish was placed in the centre of the table and you selected as much as you wanted. Being inexperienced I ate my fill of the first few dishes and ended up watching as further mouth-watering dishes continued to arrive, in all fifteen courses. The bridegroom had to follow the customs, one of which was to visit each table, about twenty, and drink a toast. This was a glass of brandy, the preferred Chinese drink on these occasions, which had to be downed in one go to the collective roar of '*Yam seng*'. It seemed that a man would lose face if he was not able for it. By the time it was over I felt sorry for Loy.

After the wedding we went to Bangkok. While we were there *Time* magazine featured the famous article of an American soldier on rest and recreation from the Vietnam War in the bathtub with a couple of girls in a Taipei hotel. Due to the outcry in America about the practice, the hotel in question was closed for the duration of our stay there.

Approaching Bangkok by air I had the impression that it was built on swampland. The land on the outskirts of the city was given over to rice fields, which were all flooded. The only dry areas were the perimeters of the fields where palm and banana trees grew. The city was laced with canals instead of streets; all connecting to the mighty Chao Phraya River which flowed through the heart of the city. Canalboats and riverboats were the main mode of transport then, although twenty years before they had started to fill in the canals to cater for the ever-increasing numbers of cars that clogged the existing streets and spewed noxious fumes into the humid, shimmering air.

Bangkok, or as the Thais call it, Krung Thep, 'the City of Angels', was booming in the sixties, but it was a mess. The economic development was fuelled by the influx of large amounts of cash from the United States who were using Thailand as a forward base as they became more deeply involved in the Vietnam War.

There was a great deal of construction being carried out and the streets were inadequate for the traffic that crawled along at one mile per hour. Badly maintained vehicles pumped smoke and noxious fumes into the hot, shimmering air. Despite these drawbacks, Bangkok was an extraordinary city of shining temples and happy-go-lucky people. One rarely encountered unpleasantness, even in the endless traffic jams, and drivers seldom ever sounded their car horns or showed any other sign of impatience.

This serenity was a product of Buddhism, Thailand's major religion. During their lifetime most men donned monk's robes for a period of time. Here they learned to forgive and not allow life's unalterable whims to upset the smooth passage of life. This ability not to dwell upon transient irritants gave rise to Thailand's unusual hospitality, which made an outsider feel at home.

When we were there thirty years ago the area occupied by Patpong streets was no more remarkable than the other collection of small streets, yet in recent years these few streets have become famous around the world as the city's red-light district. The east-coast resorts south of Bangkok, including Bang Seng, Si Racha and

Pattaya, were quiet fishing villages. Bangkok citizens used these villages as seaside districts until they became tourist resorts.

There were very few tourists in Bangkok in the 1960s. I remember visiting the Grand Palace complex with Caroline and the children one afternoon when there was only one other western woman there with her children. It was a great privilege to be able to see some of the world's great architectural spectacles before commercialism arrived.

Out of all the places I have visited in Thailand, the Grand Palace complex on Rattanakosin island in the heart of Bangkok had a stunning affect on my visual senses that lasts to this day. I have found nothing that compares with its magnificence. Wat Phra Kaew, 'the temple of the Emerald Buddha', serves as the royal chapel, grand palace and government building. Perhaps I should mention here that a temple in Thailand is not a single building. Generally it is a walled compound within which stands a collection of buildings, ornaments and statues. The buildings are a riot of colour, adorned with gold leaf, Chinese porcelain fragments, decorative stucco, woodcarvings and murals. They are topped with soaring spires or elaborate multi-tiered roofs that are often drenched with images and carvings of mythical life forms such as the sacred Naga, a fierce-looking bird. Giant demons, called Yack, guard most of the buildings from evil spirits. The Kinnaree, a mythical half-bird half-woman, or half-monkey half-woman, statues are regulars at most temples. Observing that most demons were depicted as half-women I asked some of the people that I worked with at the airport about it and they said that the tradition came down from a time when Ayutthaya was the capital. It seems that there was a practice then of ritually putting women to death by slowly crushing them in the city gates so that they became demons to protect the city from enemies and evil spirits. Strange logic, I thought; I would have expected them to destroy the city rather than protect it after their experience.

The Bilauktaung mountains run almost half way down the Malay peninsula. In the 1960s it was a wild region with forests, crevices and wild surging rivers. The Asian elephant, the Sumatran rhinoceros and the tiger roamed these mountains which rose to an average of 3,500 feet. They formed a natural barrier between Burma and Thailand, but they had one weak spot. This is a pass called the 'Three Pagodas Pass'. Burmese soldiers and elephant cavalry used this pass centuries ago to attack Siam (Thailand). This pass was of great interest to me. The bridge over the River Kwai is located here, west of Kanchanaburi town. It was made famous a few years previously by the movie made from Pierre Boulle's novel about the Japanese efforts to link the rail systems of Burma and Thailand. It seems that the Japanese also found that the Three Pagodas Pass was the most convenient route for their war effort. They were in a hurry to consolidate their gains and wished to cut the required time to build the link from a few years to twelve months. To achieve this they used livestock rail cars to move hundreds of thousands of Asian labourers and tens of thousands of allied prisoners-of-war into the mountains. The civilians were mostly from Malaysia and Indonesia, the allied soldiers were mostly British, Australians and Dutch.

In 1942-3 these labourers were kept in unsanitary, disease-ridden camps, poorly fed and overworked, and they died in their thousands. It is estimated that one hundred thousand Asians and sixteen thousand Europeans died. As I stood looking at that railway I wondered if the remains of Sai Keo's brother lay hereabouts. In Kanchanaburi town there are two grim reminders of the horrors surrounding the construction of this rail link. About nine thousand allied servicemen lie buried in the Kanchanaburi and Chong-Kai war cemeteries. The Kanchanaburi cemetery was kept in impeccable condition and the little white headstones stretched out as far as the eye could see. Kelly, then four years old, amused herself by running and hiding behind the headstones, too young to understand the significance of the place.

When we visited the bridge in the 1960s, we were the only ones there; it was silent except for the singing of the birds in the forest. It was difficult to imagine that so many people had died such horrible deaths in that beautiful high country. The bridge itself was an anticlimax. It was of metal construction and spanned a broad, slow flowing river flanked not with jungle but semi-deciduous forest.

Thailand, that fragrant land of another time, is locked into my memory. Almost forty years ago Thailand was a place of great beauty. It was a serene land with beautiful women and monks in saffron robes, a land of religious, cultural and historical festivals. A land of architectural splendour from the centre of Bangkok to the ancient temples of Chiang Mai in the north from where great rivers flowed south to the sea. Thailand was different, not just different from the West, but different in the way its people viewed life and conducted relationships with other people. For over two hundred years it had remained culturally and politically undivided in a region of conflict. It avoided colonisation by the European powers when all its neighbours went under. When the Japanese pushed the Europeans into the sea or prisoner-of-war camps, the Thais did not resist and came to an accommodation with them. In the 1960s communism stopped at its borders.

* * *

My three-year contract was due to end in a few months but I agreed to stay on for a further six months. The airline was becoming large and the structures within the maintenance department were more specialised and less flexible. In any case, I had made up my mind to look for a contract closer to home because my mother had suffered a heart attack the previous year.

My remaining nine months in Singapore proved eventful. Our daughter, Kelly, started attending kindergarten; she went to Bethseida School on Frankel Avenue. It was about this time that she had a problem with two of her teeth. The dentist decided to put her to sleep and extract them. Everything went well and there didn't seem to be a problem when she was put to bed that night. Caroline and I decided to go out on the town and we left Sai Keo to take care of the house. When we arrived back at about three o'clock in the morning and looked in on the children, Kelly's pillow and bed sheet were soaked with blood. We rushed her to the general hospital where it was decided to stitch her gums to help stop the bleeding. I was asked to restrain her while the doctor stitched inside her mouth. This was probably the most distressing thing I had to do during my life; but it did solve the problem.

I was back again working on the twelve-hour day and twelve-hour night shift. Going to work I frequently took a short route to Paya Lebar airport, using a very narrow, one lane road. This passed through a Malay village where the houses were built in a swampy area, on raised mounds or stilts, and access to them was by wooden planks from pathways. If you met another vehicle on this road you had to slow down and pull over to the edge to allow it passage. On the evening of 13 May 1969, I took the Jaban Ubi route and came across a man lying in the road. When overseas, airline staff were always told not to stop at an incident but to drive to the nearest police station to report it. The road was too narrow to pass or turn back and I couldn't drive over the body so I got out and pulled the man out of the way. The body looked as if it had severe head injuries. I did not stop to check if he was alive; I got out of there as fast as I could.

When I reached the airport I was told that racial strife had broken out in Malaysia and was spreading to Singapore. The local workers were from various Asian races and they were quite concerned about their families and their own safety. The authorities in Singapore moved quickly and were able to prevent violence spreading. But the atmosphere of uneasiness prevailed for some time and prompted some of the Malay and Indian workers on my shift to ask me to pick them up and leave them home. One man, an Indian of Tamil extraction, even insisted on travelling in the boot of my car. He adopted this approach because there was a rumour, one of many at the time, that a European's car had been stopped in Kuala Lumpur and the Chinese lady passenger was taken out and killed.

The Malaysian general election held on 13 May 1969 triggered these events. Fearing that minority racial groups were going to take control of the government, Malays started gathering in the streets of Kuala Lumpur after four in the evening. The crowd eventually attacked a Chinese vehicle and killed the occupants. This sparked off general violence that killed hundreds of people and left much of Kuala Lumpur in flames. It was ironic that this should have happened when I was here in a country that had inherited these problems from the British colonial system. From a distance it seemed that the people in the six counties of Northern Ireland were facing similar problems created by the British at that time

The Malays did not like the idea of giving up political control, but they were still in a position of economic disadvantage in their own country. The Malaya government had put in place a programme called the 'Bumiputra Policy', or native assistance policy, after independence. Unfortunately this policy deprived many young Chinese of jobs and affordable housing and caused bitterness and racial antagonism. The government had to walk a tightrope. It tried not to upset the rich Chinese who controlled the country's finances by moving too fast with the 'Bumiputra Policy' and at the same time implement the policy at a rate that did not anger the Malays, or cause them to rise up in revolt. The elections were abandoned in the Borneo states and a national operations council was set up to run the country until order was restored. It was still in control when we left Malaysia in early 1970.

Chapter 9

Changes in Ireland

We decided to return home for a vacation in August 1969. I was allowed seven weeks' leave per year. It seems that this odd figure was arrived at in early colonial times to allow for the slow sea journey to Europe and back, and give two or three weeks at home. It had been some time since we had made the long journey home. We had used the previous vacations to visit Hong Kong, Taiwan, and to travel around Australia. I found that things had changed quite a bit in Ireland. This vacation was spent with Caroline's parents in Dublin and at my parents' home on the border of Monaghan and Armagh. The children, now five and three years old, enjoyed being on the farm and went with their grandfather to attend to animals and do other chores. This was very exciting for them because they had never been on a farm. At that time of year it was normal to go out to the potato fields each day and dig up what was required for dinner. When the children saw their grandfather dig up the potatoes, in their innocence they wanted to know who had put them in the ground.

Since we were last at home the Northern Ireland Civil Rights movement had been formed to obtain local voting rights, equality in public housing and employment. As I viewed events from far away I wondered if indeed I was watching things unfold that I had daydreamed about when I was a young boy sitting on a treetop. Had the people's soul decided to return from its misty lair to confront its tormentors? If that were the case then some cataclysmic event which would push things over the top would follow as night follows day because the system would resist change to the very end. After all, the northern state had been set up out of a deep and historical insecurity. It was believed that this route would lead to security, but instead it led to the abyss. Loyalism could be defined in terms of its history, Protestant traditions, location, stern Calvinism and a mission of separateness which was almost taken to be an expression of God's will. If you looked at it that way, then cross-ethnic solidarity or integration was death.

The British reform of the educational system in the six counties in 1948 opened up higher education to working-class nationalists for the first time. By the 1960s there was a sizeable group of people who had passed through the system and were emerging as potential leaders in the nationalist community. When Captain Terence O'Neill became Prime Minister in the early sixties he was considered a liberal politician and he raised the hope for reform among the nationalists. But that was not to be the case. In 1966 O'Neill met the then southern premier Sean Lemass, the first such meeting since the country was divided in 1921. This gesture was too liberal for lower-middle and working-class loyalists steeped in an intolerant brand of religion similar to that practised in the southern states of America.

Confronted with a party that would never countenance change or reform, O'Neill was confined to empty rhetoric that created a climate of dissatisfaction on the nationalist side too. The loyalists responded in the age-old way by joining the Ulster Volunteer Force (UVF), a citizen army created in 1912 by Edward Carson to ward off the effort of the Liberal government in London to introduce home rule for the whole island of Ireland. These loyalist murder gangs combed the Catholic streets looking for easy targets and in June 1966, long before nationalists looked for their rights, they killed twenty-eight-year-old Patrick Scullion. A few weeks later they attacked four young nationalists in Malvern Street, killing eighteen-year-old Peter Ward.

The nationalist population looked around for their traditional protection from the IRA but that organisation had almost died out. All that was left was a talking shop where the Army Council discussed Marxist and left-wing theories and how they could be used to unite the working class of all shades and thereby solve the problem. This was idle thinking because the *modus operandi* of 'a Protestant parliament for a Protestant people' was still to exclude nationalists from any jobs that were the State's to give. This applied from the highest civil servant position to the person sweeping the street. Loyalist company owners who were members of various organisations, such as Orange Order or Black Watch, were encouraged not to employ nationalists. Loyalist workers were not interested in sharing these jobs with their nationalist neighbours – they viewed them as their privilege. Prime Minister O'Neill may well have introduced reform under pressure from London, but his then minister for home affairs, William Craig, and Ian Paisley spoke for the vast majority of unionists who were always against reform and were not prepared to concede. The reformer would have to go instead. Confronted with this unionist monolith that refused to budge, members of the new nationalist middle-class cautiously went about organising campaigns to highlight injustices in housing, jobs and electoral malpractices. Eventually most of these local groups became part of the Northern Ireland Civil Rights

Association (NICRA), or the Civil Rights Movement.

There were some within the various affiliated groups who relished the extreme confrontational street politics of the day and saw them as an opportunity to expose the brutality of a corrupt political system to the world media. During 1969 their protest marches were continually attacked by loyalists with the acquiescence and, in some places, the assistance of the Royal Ulster Constabulary and their reserve, the 'B Specials'. In Derry the previous November a Civil Rights march had run into trouble and television showed nationalists having their heads bashed by police batons and being dragged along the streets. After that there were regular small riots in Derry through out the following year. Taking this into account it was rather cavalier of the authorities to allow the Apprentice Boys march to take place on the twelfth of August: at this stage vigilante street committees were in place to prevent a repeat of the previous November. The inevitable riot took place and the police, followed by loyalist mobs, tried to enter the Bogside part of the city. They were prevented from doing so, 'Free Derry' was established and British soldiers arrived on the streets. It would be a year before the IRA would be a major player in Derry.

Calm returned to Derry but the trouble spread to Belfast and other urban areas. The attacks on nationalist areas of Belfast were well co-ordinated and thousands of people were burned out of their homes and whole streets torched. Young people in my home area assisted the distraught families across the border and this experience changed the course of their lives. It changed mine too. I had been used to seeing refugees in other countries, but the sight of families fleeing south in my own country had a profound and lasting effect on me. All people were asking for was equal treatment for everybody and this was the answer they had got. Should I get involved? What could I do? I decided to wait and see what way things would develop over the coming months.

* * *

We returned to Singapore in September to finish the few remaining months on my contract. While we were there I was offered a three-year contract with Gulf Aviation, a small, private airline operating out of Bahrain in the Persian Gulf. There were some regrets leaving the Malaysian area. Caroline was leaving a job she enjoyed very much; Kelly would have to settle into a new school and the Middle East would be quite different from the crowded Far East.

I had not considered the effect our departure would have on Sai Keo. On the day we left she started to cry, and we could not get her to stop. All she could say was that we were taking the children away from her. I had burnt all our bridges and there was no turning back so we boarded the aircraft with the sound of her lamentation ringing in our ears. About five years later we called to see her. Although Glenn was over eight years old, she again had him in a hammock suspended from the ceiling and played with him. She told me that during the intervening years she often imagined that she heard Glenn's voice. I think seeing the children again helped her to let go.

PART IV
LIVING A DOUBLE LIFE

CHAPTER 10

The Middle East

Caravans of camels shall fill you
Dromedaries from Midian and Ephah
All from Sheba shall come
Bearing gold and frankincense
and proclaiming the praises of the Lord.

Is 60: 1-6 (20)

Going to the Middle East did not hold the same excitement for me as my first journey to my beloved Africa. Still, I was drawn by that strange attraction that hot dry areas of the world have for some northern Europeans. Also, when you are exposed to other cultures, it leaves you bored with your own kind, and when you reach this stage other people tend to regard you as a little bit eccentric. 'He is a bit funny; who would want to go to that place where there is nothing but sand and Arabs' I had heard said!

It had been a difficult three months, two spent studying the BAC 1-11 aircraft systems with British Aircraft Corporation at Hatfield, and a further month of practical work and experience with British United Airways at Gatwick airport. I had successfully completed my examinations for my multi X ticket (license) at the Civil Aviation Authority offices at Redhills. This license gives authority to certify inspection, repairs and maintenance carried out on the specified aircraft's instruments, flight control and guidance systems. Work such as this is something that the average passenger never sees or thinks about. The passenger generally judges the quality, safety and calibre of an airline by the appearance of the flight attendants, their service, the decor and ambience of the aircraft. The passengers go by what catches the eye.

An hour prior to the departure of the aircraft the feeling I get is tantamount to being involved in the preparation and countdown required preparing a rocket for launch. Except that in the case of space flight only six lives are involved, whereas with an aircraft one or two hundred lives or more are involved. There is a good deal of controlled drama in it, which I always found exciting.

Fuel trucks have to be positioned to pump the calculated fuel load on board. Mechanics check engines, adjust oil and hydraulic fuel levels, check wheels and undercarriages, aircraft fuselage and flight controls, toilets and water systems. Others check passenger call and entertainment systems, cabin and seats, cleaning inside and outside, all co-ordinated with cargo and baggage loading and catering uplift so that it moves forward step by step as the time of departure approaches. At the same time the captain and his flight crew step through the pre-flight checks ensuring the serviceability of all aircraft systems. Any faults encountered will be brought to the attention of the engineer for rectification. Inertial navigation systems are initialised, instruments set, flight paths selected from flight data computers or entered into flight instrument systems, all moving to the final moments of take-off. When all outside operations are complete, all doors secured, activity converges on the cockpit; the chief cabin attendant reports passenger status to the captain, load and balance sheets are delivered to the cockpit and the engineer signs the aircraft technical logbook certifying the aircraft fit for flight. The captain signs the logbook also and accepts the aircraft for take-off. The final door is closed and start-up procedure commenced with the engineer communicating with the crew through headphones. When the area around the aircraft is totally cleared, the request 'clear to start 1 or 2' is received from the cockpit, the engines are started in sequence; 'remove checks' is requested and the removal of handset from the aircraft completes the sequence and the aircraft moves away from the stand for take-off.

* * *

Sweet to ride forth at evening from the wells
When shadows pass gigantic on the sand,
And softly through the silence beat the bells
Along the Golden Road to Samarkand.

James Elroy Flecker

Arabian Gulf – Arabia – what images these words conjure up for me: Bedouins slowly trekking by camel caravan from oasis to oasis across endless bleak landscapes. Constantly struggling to survive hunger and thirst, blazing sun and blowing sand, they are a proud, hard, independent people with few possessions, living close to Allah and nature. It also conjures up images of beautiful, veiled women who dance to entertain sultans, and exotic perfumes fill the air, endless treasures and flying carpets, magic genies and glittering palaces. Stories out of childhood books – far removed, I discovered, from the harsh Arab world of tents, camel milk, brackish water and dates. As these thoughts passed through my mind I knew that I was going to be alone at first in this new location and I would have to find somewhere to live before my family could join me.

I must have dozed off. I woke with a start as I always do when I fall asleep while travelling on aircraft. My senses confused, I hear people sitting beside me talking as if they are far off in the distance. Looking out the window I could see clouds of fire, the burn-off of gas from the oil wells; they scorched the desert, producing a scene from a primordial world as we flew down the Saudi Arabian Gulf coast. A steep banking turn as we passed over Bahrain gave a night-time panoramic view of Maharak Island with its illuminated village, airport runway and large military air base. Turning in our final approach, like a great bird of prey moving its feathers, the aircraft enlarged its wings by extending its flaps. Buffeting started as the undercarriage emerged into the slipstream, disturbing the airflow, the wing flaps extended fully, allowing the lifting air to escape as we sank slowly on to the runway. On contact, the reverse thrust spooled up the engines again, directing the air from the engines forward to slow down the aircraft with a mighty roar.

It was three o'clock in the morning as I stepped out into the humid night air; yesterday's heat radiated from the concrete under my feet. The arrivals building was a small jumble of prefabs and a low, one-storey building which contrasted with the large military air base at the other end of the runway. The arrival formalities were conducted in silence. The officials seemed to be in a hurry to get rid of the couple of people that arrived and return to their disturbed rest.

Picking up my bag I made my way to the small area that served both as arrival and departure hall. It was deserted, apart from a few bodies in '*thobes*' (ankle-length skirts) stretched out sleeping on the bench seats with their coloured '*gutras*' (square head scarves) over their heads and faces. I stepped outside and looked around at the sand in an area illuminated by one street light; there was no sign of life except for one person stumbling along on an erratic course towards the entrance where I stood. As he drew near I realised that he was quite drunk, barely able to remain on his feet. He was dressed in a khaki shirt, which hung partially out of his khaki shorts, sand-coloured, knee-length socks and hush puppies that dragged through the sand as he stumbled along. 'Did you arrive on the BOAC flight?' he asked in his slurred Scottish accent. 'No,' I replied, 'that arrived hours ago.' He pushed past me, half-falling as he entered the building.

In a short time he reappeared. I explained my problem. I had missed my pick-up, now I was lost. 'We are all lost out here,' he replied, but not to worry, he would take care of everything. We found his car, which he had abandoned in the middle of nowhere, the driver's door left hanging open. It was impossible to say if we were driving on the desert or the road as we meandered toward distant lights. He explained that his girlfriend, a stewardess, was due to arrive for a few days' stopover, but as usual he had some drinks with his friends. The car hit timber with a loud, rumbling sound and started to sway from side to side. We were crossing the wooden causeway from Maharak Island to Manama.

We arrived safely at the BOAC rest house. Rooms were built in a square to form an enclosed Arab-style courtyard; they had been constructed in the 1940s to serve as a hotel for BOAC flying boat crews who stopped to rest here on their slow journeys to the Far East and Australia. The security man told us that people who had six-month rental agreements now occupied all the rooms, and visitors now used the Gulf hotel, which had opened three months previously. When I went to the hotel to check in I was surprised to find that a room had been booked for me. I parted company with my friend, feeling enriched. I had returned to a land where a helping hand was willingly extended to a stranger. My friend left, enriched by my bottle of Blackbush whiskey.

Rising next morning I looked out of my room window. It was one of those halcyon days with no wind to stir the Gulf waters. They lay still and calm. I decided to go outside before eating. Opening the door I was hit by a blast of hot air, which took my breath away, forcing me to step backwards. Taking a deep breath, I stepped out into a world of diamond-bright light that dazzled the eyes, brilliance never experienced in Northern Europe. The hotel, ten storeys high, the tallest building in Manama, was built in the shape of a letter 'V,' on a peninsula of reclaimed land with its backdrop of turquoise Gulf water. I met the manager of the hotel; he was from the Whitehall district of Dublin. He organised a phone call to Gulf Aviation to let them know I had arrived.

After lunch Tom Ryan arrived to take me to the airport. He was a tall, blond Welshman who had worked with me in Malaysia-Singapore Airlines and had moved here a year previously with his wife and two children. His wife was Mary Hughes, a native of Claregalway. They met when she was working as a nurse in England in the early 1960s; he was then employed by British European Airways. We had established a friendship that would last a lifetime through many hard times. Summer can be a bad time in the Arabian Gulf, even if you are like me and can stand it. When the temperature reaches 57°C tempers get ragged and nerves become strained, and the slightest thing can have you fly into a rage even with your best friend. Sadly, Tom's life ended in 1977 when he died of a heart attack in Bahrain at forty years of age, leaving Mary to bring up three children. Tom, the Welshman, is buried in Claregalway; Mary returned to Galway city and successfully steered their three children through a university education, and she now rests beside him. Sitting here in prison now, it is strange to remember how they used to worry about my wellbeing.

We retraced my journey from the airport the previous night. The natives, being wiser than 'mad dogs and Englishmen', were all on their afternoon siesta and the roads were deserted. The road from the hotel passed by the Sheikh's town palace on the right. At Sulmania roundabout we turned down along the sea to the wooden causeway. On the seashore, before reaching the airport roundabout, people were living in barasti huts – the sea air passing through the bamboo construction providing free air conditioning. On the roundabout facing the causeway stands a mosque with elaborate mosaic-decorated twin minarets. The causeway connected Maharak Island to Bahrain Island; it was part roadway and part wooden construction to allow boats to pass through. Years later this whole area would be reclaimed and hotels and new roads built on it, but this was a time before the sweeping changes that followed the OPEC quadrupling of oil prices in late 1973.

The civilian part of the airport was comparable in size to a small private airfield in Europe. One small hangar provided cover from the scorching sun for people working on aircraft, the largest of which was a DC3. This was to be my base for the next five years, years that would bring great changes to the Arabian Gulf, and to my own life.

* * *

By the time I was leaving for the Middle East the civil rights protests at home had forced the British government to try and get the

Stormont administration to introduce various reforms. The most significant of these was to disband the 'B Specials' and disarm the RUC. Loyalists would see this as the first step in undermining the foundations of the unionist state. Reactionaries within the unionist family could arouse resentment over this and it was only a matter of time before there was a resurgence of loyalist random killing.

Events in the six counties over the next twenty months would cause me to change my views on using violence as a weapon for change. Stormont was still alive and standing in the way of implementing reforms. Perhaps unionists were hoping, as turned out to be the case, that their friends in the Conservative party would win the June elections. The Conservatives were more sympathetic to their cause and could be expected to give the security forces a more aggressive role in suppressing dissent. The harsh behaviour of the soldiers during the Falls Road curfew in May, where they used 1600 canisters of CS gas, was a sign of things to come.

The arrival of Brigadier Frank Kitson in the six counties in September that year as adviser to the army on counter-insurgency policy was another indication of Conservative thinking. I had become familiar with his approach during my time in Kenya where he had been involved in the Mau Mau war; he had also been in Cyprus and had taken part in the twelve-year war in Malaya. I had also read his book *Low Intensity Operations* and I knew that if he stuck to the methods outlined there, we were in for a very dirty war indeed. Traditional military responses were simply not his forte: information, psychology, superstition, religion and black propaganda was the name of the game. I think it was Churchill who said that the truth is so important during war that it should be protected by lies. Eighty percent of operations would be covert to avoid alienation of the moderates within the insurgent population.

Uniformed soldiers on the streets would be reduced as far as possible and diverted to collecting information on the population generally and suspects in particular. Special forces, such as the SAS, would be used for surveillance, intelligence gathering, snatch-and-termination in high-risk areas. Special reaction groups would be set up to respond with maximum force when deep undercover forces located groups of insurgents or individuals on their sighting list or on the photo montage that they carried. Pseudo-terrorist groups would be formed from lawless elements in the population loyal to the government to do their overt killing in an effort to shield the authorities from international scrutiny. Every effort would be made to 'turn' captured insurgents so that they would supply information on operations and personnel, sabotage equipment and carry out acts to discredit their former comrades. The only question remaining for me was how far into the gutter we would have to follow them.

Stormont was still responsible for security and refused to implement changes suggested by the British. It was business as usual: a 'Protestant government for a Protestant people'. After the disbanding of the 'B Specials' most former members moved on to the newly formed Ulster Defence Regiment. Nothing had changed except it was now controlled by the British army. Stormont had also prevented the disarming of the RUC and was pushing for internment without trial. They eventually got their way – against the advice of the military, we are told.

When internment arrived, at 4.00am on 10 August 1971, most of the IRA volunteers were unknown because under normal circumstances their families would be opposed to militant republicanism. These volunteers first became involved in the early days through loyalist mobs that poured through the barriers in cities and towns in the wake of the army's clearance operations. Internment was a disaster for the authorities. They failed to get the people they were after, and the brutal way in which it was introduced further alienated the nationalist population. Repeated house searches had already increased the level of resentment against the army, now it was stoked to a fever pitch by a stream of allegations of torture and ill treatment of internees. One man who was interned then told me that after supporting his weight as he leaned against wire with his legs spread for twenty-four hours he started to hallucinate and imagined that the wire was passing up between his fingers. Every time he tried to move he was kicked from behind or hit with the butt of a rifle.

I was at home that year on vacation during the months of August and September, and stories were circulating that a number of internees were being systematically tortured in Magilligan prison camp in Derry. It was hard to believe it, but it transpired that fourteen people were selected as guinea pigs for sensory deprivation experiments – later their case was taken to the European court and upheld. They were hooded and deprived of food, water and sleep and enclosed in a cabinet where they were exposed to constant electronically generated 'white noise'. It was a scientific attempt to find the best way to weaken and disorient the prisoner, psychologically and physically, so that more reliable information could be extracted faster than with the traditional method of physical beating. It has been shown that beating can get the interrogator to a certain point, but that information extracted beyond that point can be unreliable as the subject agrees to anything to avoid further physical torture. These revelations enraged the nationalist community so that many put aside their opposition to physical force and assisted any way they could. Even the mainstream nationalist party organised a 'rent and rates boycott' and many people stopped paying car tax, rent and television licence fees. It was a supercharged time and I saw law-abiding citizens do extraordinary things. I was aware that revolution could be intoxicating, like a love affair with a goddess, with unblemished ideals. History shows that, like all things, revolution has its own time-frame and in the final phase, when the politics must be involved, you find that she was no goddess. After internment the war spread to the countryside and, right or wrong, the young boys and girls were going to fight. Most of them, like me, had no history of republicanism in their families, were unknown to the authorities, and had very important skills.

I was aware of what they were up against in South Armagh. It would be classical rural guerrilla warfare against a NATO army. There would be no civilian or police involvement; the army would be in control and they could call on all their NATO allies to assist them. It was fortunate that this type of warfare has a low civilian dimension. People always ask about this aspect of war and the truth is there was no desire to injure or kill civilians. Leaving aside the moral aspect of this, it is essential to protect the civilian population at all costs lest you lose your support base for the war effort. But it is an unfortunate aspect of war that you are only as good as your collected intelligence; often this is defective or incomplete and civilians get killed and injured, but we made great efforts to prevent this happening.

In the beginning the attitude of the British army and their extremely bad treatment of the local people was a constant reminder of their power and control. As a consequence most of the population either supported the war or remained neutral. So, I felt, here was an army that had all the latest training, weaponry and technical know-how: was there any way that I could help to face down such an army? Could I confuse their technicians, second-guess their strategies and their tactics? I returned to the desert of the Middle East to work out how the cutting-edge technology of that time could be integrated into modern guerrilla warfare to offset all these enemy advantages.

The Civil Rights movement was still active and seeking to have reforms implemented by holding peaceful marches. On 30 January 1972 they had organised an anti-internment march in Derry in defiance of a Stormont ban. The First Parachute battalion killed thirteen marchers and wounded a further thirteen in what seemed to be a calculated strike to prevent further protest. This reminded me of the General Dyer action at Jallianwala Bagh (Amritsar) in India in 1919 when hundreds of marchers were slaughtered. The British had learned nothing after hundreds of years of colonial wars. Was it Joseph Conrad who said that terrorism is a weapon that feasts on its own suppression? The old thinking still prevailed: kill a few protestors and the 'Taigs' would keep their heads down and return to their proper place in society. That was the last straw and it pushed many people over the top. There would be no turning back after that.

* * *

The island of Bahrain and its capital Manama, where I was stationed, was a modern-day commercial and trading centre in the Arabian Gulf. In the past it had formed part of one of the world's first trade routes. But when Britain announced in 1968 that it would end all its protection treaties in the Arabian Gulf in 1971, the Gulf State leaders viewed the rolling back of the British presence east of Suez with alarm. To me it was inconceivable that Britain could leave this jugular oil-vein unprotected as two thirds of the oil exported by the Gulf States passed through it. The Gulf States rulers feared for the stability of this oil-rich area but they failed in their efforts to persuade the British Labour party to allow troops to remain even when they offered to meet the costs. These fears were well founded because there have been five major wars in the region since: between Pakistan and India in the 1970s, between Iran and Iraq in the 1990s; between Afghanistan and the USA in 2002, and the two wars between Iraq and the USA in 1991 and 2003.

Prior to their pull-out it seemed that Britain had lost its former influence in the area and was being replaced by the Americans. When they vacated Jufair naval base in Bahrain in 1971, an American battle ship moved in overnight. When the British finally left, Bahrain and Qatar opted for independence separately, while the crucial sheikhdoms of Abu Dhabi, Dubai, Sharjah, Ras al-Khaimah, Umm al-Qaiwain, Ajman and Fujairah joined together to form the United Arab Emirates. The government of these states agreed to take control of Gulf Aviation and make it the national airline. I was to work for this new airline.

At the end of the 1960s the gulf towns of Manama, Dubai, Abu Dhabi, and others that became well known during the gulf wars, were no more than fishing villages. Their trade depended on the activities connected with oil and the British military presence. Dhows were still the workhorses of the gulf waters and goods, including cars, were all carried on them to their final destination around the gulf. In Dubai I watched gold bars being loaded into dhows that were souped up to make the high-speed smuggling run to India. Hotel accommodation was non existent, and often I was glad to share a room with four other Gulf Air male and female crew members.

After three months I was able to move into a house about three hundred metres from the entrance to the British naval base at Jufair.

My family was then able to join me in Bahrain. At that time Bahrain and its capital Manama were very quiet, particularly after the noisy far east and one saw few signs of the turbulent history of the area. Manama was still a town where raw sewage flowed, with its distinct aroma, through open sewers along some streets. This helped to create for me the unpleasant task of dragging the family in for cholera injections every six months.

Under the protection of the British, life for the quarter million inhabitants was dull, but employment and business were provided by the large contingent of naval personnel stationed at Jufair, the RAF personnel at Muharak, and army people inland. Most military and associated civilians were accompanied by their families, who rented accommodation and lived among the local people. Oil production revenues after the 1930s permitted the development of an educated and reasonably skilled local labour force, who worked at ship repair, aluminium smelting and light industry. Aramco (Arab American Oil Company) operated an oil town in Awali, providing accommodation and services for its employees.

Little things make life pleasant – and unpleasant – in any climate and situaton. Like most hot countries, Bahrain had its share of cockroaches. These large, dark brown insects are about one inch long, and can take to the wing when necessary, but prefer scurrying into hiding places. They spend the daylight hours in sewers, bathrooms and shower drains; at night they appear in great numbers. There was a communications engineer who worked for a British company that operated airport control towers and serviced ship communication systems east of Suez. He had returned home one night after a few drinks and later in bed he was disturbed by something at his mouth; gathering his senses he realised that he had swallowed a large cockroach. His immediate reaction was to drink more beer to dull his senses, and, he hoped, drown the cockroach.

An Arab town's focal point is generally a junction where the police station, post office and other government buildings are located. We had a Dublin gentleman working with us, and being ex-Royal Air Force he liked to take a constitutional stroll in the evening. On occasion, this pleasant walk would be marred by groups of teenage boys daring one another to see how close they could swerve their bicycles to a pedestrian as they pedalled past at high speed. In time the gent became irritated by this practice and decided to put a stop to it. Getting his timing right as the rattling bicycles approached from behind, he stuck out his walking cane, which went into the spokes of a front wheel, bringing the bicycle to an abrupt halt and sending the boy through the air to land in a cloud of dust. The other boys altered their course and careened down the street and around the corner at high speed. Unfortunately for them, a group of policemen was standing outside the police station and the boys crashed into them. An amusing spectacle greeted our man when he reached the corner, the policemen in their khaki shorts, knee-length stockings and hobnail boots were stomping up and down on the boys and their bicycles in the dust.

Before the British left, Sheikh Isa Ibn Salman al-Khalifa exercised almost absolute power in Bahrain. When they left, growing political pressure and serious unrest saw him appoint an assembly to draft a constitution which was adopted in 1972. A thirty-member elected assembly was the new law-making body. They had a voice in the granting of licences to exploit natural resources and they granted trade-union rights and women's rights, unusual in the Arab world at that time. However, political parties were still prohibited.

Sheikh Isa, a very pleasant, happy, smiling man, was loved by his people and by the expatriates, including the British forces stationed in Bahrain. The people felt that they had access to their ruler, and that their wants and needs were heard, and their rights protected. Muslim law, based on the 'Sharia', was accepted by the Muslims as a just system – it was a religious-based system and as such would not be acceptable to democratic countries, but while there, we were all bound by it. Any citizen could come to the emir's daily '*majles*', stand before or sit down beside him, call him by his first name, petition him for help or assistance in righting a wrong. He maintained palaces in Manama and out on the Awali road. On the West Coast he had a house and gardens on the beach. The grounds of this seashore retreat were restricted to European residents, and the Arab host had afternoon tea served to all visitors – and he usually used the opportunity to have an encounter with an irresistible female, available at a price.

The Arabs of the Gulf States still lived in a male-orientated and male-dominated society, and most women were trained from childhood to be wives and mothers and to devote their lives to the home. Most people followed the strict, puritanical religion practised in Saudi Arabia. The Arab family is more than father, mother and children; normally it is centred on all the brothers, their wives and children, grandparents and unmarried aunts and uncles. The Arabs put great store in self-respect; they regard menial labour as demeaning which may account for the large number of foreign workers in the Gulf States.

The compulsion to maintain face in public takes away from an Arab man who otherwise has a deep sense of hospitality toward his fellow man. Should you express a liking for an object while visiting his home, you will not be permitted to leave without taking it with you. He will shake hands with everybody he meets, regardless of financial circumstances or rank. In the late 1960s when women were first allowed to drive cars in Bahrain, men considered it an affront to their self-respect. One Englishwoman, forgetting where she was, drove down the street in Manama as if she were in London. On being passed out by the woman, an Arab gentleman took offence and speeded up, cutting tightly in front of her car, making it necessary for her to brake violently. This manoeuvre was repeated many times by both parties until the man became infuriated. Bringing his car across in front of the woman's, he jumped out and proceeded to argue with her in a loud voice. Finally, in total frustration, he grabbed the top of the woman's dress and ripped it off her. Initially it was the Arab who was offended – he had wanted to establish the supremacy of the male over the female. He satisfied his anger by ripping her top apart and then his eyes awakened to the prospect of booty. There was a chilling realisation in him that the heat of anger simply opened the treasure chest, but the contents could not be enjoyed except in a calculating, cold approach, and in that the Arab is profoundly gifted. He is the master of intrigue, strategy, simulation and deception, one who can summon all powers, domestic and cosmic, to the service of his libido. On this occasion, the woman drove off, rejecting his charming approach.

The woman considered that she had been assaulted and proceeded to take the man to court. Those who understood that Islam is the official religion in the Gulf States, and the 'Sharia' the basis for law, and that the government's function was to enforce that law, tried to discourage her from this course of action. However, in typical British righteousness, she was determined to have her day in court. The judgement, when translated from the Arabic, stated that she was at fault for being in public dressed as an unbeliever, and had inflamed his anger and offended his sensibilities, causing him to lose control of his actions. The case was dismissed.

Kuwait was a 'dry' state; the consumption of alcohol was forbidden. A friend of mine who worked there frequently travelled to Basra to have a drink. He travelled along the road that would become famous as the 'Road of Death' during the war with Iraq in 1991. Returning one afternoon, he was conscious for a number of miles of a car parked ahead in the empty desert, facing towards the road. As he drew level, the car shot off the sand and smashed into his. A young Kuwaiti gentleman struggled out of the large American car, obviously under the influence of a good time spent in Basra the night before. He was most apologetic and offered handfuls of cash to compensate for the damage he caused. The money was refused. My friend felt that there was an element of deliberation – how could his car come down a road in the barren desert, with ten miles visibility, and not be seen? His fine-tuned English concept of right and wrong must be upheld, in court if necessary.

He made the wrong choice. Within five minutes the religious court brilliantly overturned thousands of years of Western logic. My friend was a guest in the country; if he weren't there the accident would have not occurred, therefore he was guilty and would be required to pay a two hundred-dinar fine.

At work, the lowest employee will sit down with his employer to talk or drink tea. I found no difficulty adapting to these customs at work, and should an employee come to the office at break time coffee would always be offered. In most cases the man preferred to sit on the floor, tell stories and crack jokes while he drank his coffee. Moving about in the workplace, people would offer food as they sat in a circle eating from their communal dish. I always respected this offer and took a few minutes out to chat while I ate a couple of fingers-ful of spiced rice or dates.

These interludes allowed me to develop a better understanding of a people with a vastly different culture. It is normal for westerners to make a simple, precise assertion in English and expect it to be taken at face value. Arabs, however, are not convinced of the value of a simple assertion; it must be analysed, talked over at length, reasserted, and exaggerated before being considered satisfactory. Arabs are more skilled at using verbal threats and venting hostility than westerners, but the words are usually a substitute for action. The exceptionally high value that Arabs place on this colourful conversation often affects their attitude towards work. They can get so deeply involved that they forget about what they are doing, and drift off, involved in a loud exchange. When necessary, I found that they would use praying as an excuse for being absent from the workplace.

The older Arabs who worked for Gulf Air were devout in observing the practices of their religion and invoked God's name frequently in their conversation. This group possessed a high level of independence, honesty and friendliness, and they poked fun at everybody. Looking back after passing by them, you could see one of them mimicking your mannerisms and the way you walked, to the delight of his companions. They came from a time when a man who could tell stories, recite poetry, and use language to stimulate and entertain enjoyed great esteem within his community. They talked about pearl diving in the beds north of Bahrain, the length of time spent under water, the great depths reached and, sadly, when some of their fathers and uncles perished there. When young, they watched a man ordered to jump off the mosque because the court could not decide his guilt or innocence, and related memories of such a man crippled after surviving this ordeal. God – God the merciful – he already knew everybody's destiny before they were born; they all nodded their heads in agreement.

Bahrain had a long tradition of education and a liberal approach to outsiders and business. The revenue from its oil after 1930 allowed it to expand its educational facilities and develop a modern government administration. In the late 1960s a technical college was opened in Isa town; this was a newly constructed town in the desert outside Manama on the Awali road. Graduates of this college were recruited to work for Gulf Air. Some were sent overseas for further training and a training school was set up in the former RAF base at Maharak. This introduced its own problems: some of the local workers who transferred over with the old private company, Gulf Aviation, to the new State-owned Gulf Air were employed at a time when such education was not available, and it was difficult for them to cope with the extensive training required to keep up with rapid changes in the new company. People who had worked with the airline for ten or fifteen years were unhappy to find themselves passed over for the new arrivals. Many young women graduates were employed, and a young Arab lady was assigned to my office in 1974 to receive training from the existing Indian male clerk, which was unusual in the Arab world at that time.

Gulf Aviation was a private airline set up in the late 1940s to fly passengers and freight in the Arabian Gulf area. Over the years it had remained a small operation, and in 1970 it operated a Beechcraft, and a couple of DC3s. When the Gulf states took over the airline they named it Gulf Air, and purchased an F27 aircraft and one BAC 1-11 jet aircraft in 1970. The latter was a British Aircraft Corporation manufactured aircraft, which was supplied with water injection engines. This was necessary due to the high humidity and temperatures encountered in the Gulf region. Normally an engine's power rating is calculated at 15°C standard temperature; for every degree above this nominal temperature the engine's ability to maintain its power rating drops off. In order to recover this loss, water is injected into the engine where it cools the compressed air and passes through the combustion process. The alternative to this is a reduction in the aircraft's take-off load, basically less than its full load of passengers.

When the British withdrew their forces from the Gulf States in 1971, Gulf Air moved from the small hangar near the terminal building into the vacated Royal Air Force complex next door. This proved a readymade facility to bring all sections of the airline together and allow for continued expansion; however, the departure of so many people in so short a time span did not instil confidence in the future success of the airline.

The initial stages when we first introduced jet aircraft on our routes were disheartening. I remember our first flight to Shiraz in Iran: we took off from Bahrain with *one* paying passenger! Still, life was lived at a slow pace and it had its lighter side, like the night my wife and I gave a BAC representative a lift home from a party in our open-topped MG Midget car. When we reached his hotel he was no longer with us! Retracing our route we met him walking along the road – he had decided to sit up on the back of the car with his feet on the seat; at a corner on the road he had quietly rolled off, and with the wind blowing in our faces we heard nothing.

The tragic location of the Gulf and the word of Allah would ensure that it would remain a focal point for conflict even at the end of the twenty-first century. All this oil, Sunni and Shia religious rivalry, royal kingdoms, communist guerrillas and territorial claims keep a deadly cauldron on the boil where two-thirds of the oil exported by the Gulf States must pass. War broke out between Pakistan and India in 1973. Airlines now switched their scheduled stop from Karachi airport to Bahrain. A beautiful new terminal facility was built to cater for the increase in the number of aircraft and passengers. During the war Bahrain established itself as a first-class duty-free airport, and it became the preferred stop for aircraft *en route* to and from the East and Australia.

In 1960 oil producing countries set up the Organisation of Petroleum Exporting Countries (OPEC) to try to stabilise their share of the oil market by fixing prices. They also demanded that the oil companies operating in member countries treat the governments as equal partners. The industrialised countries, at first, did not look seriously at OPEC's demand for a greater share of the wealth from their oil revenues and for greater participation in their development. However, the Arab-Israeli war in 1973 brought a complete upheaval to the Middle East oil countries.

The war rolled over the Suez Canal and ships wrecked there closed it to traffic, leaving the West short of oil. Libya had succeeded in forcing the Occidental Petroleum Company to pay a substantial increase for its oil at a time when Kuwait, Algeria, Bahrain, Iraq and Saudi Arabia were operating an oil embargo against countries that assisted Israel in the war. In 1973 OPEC countries controlled about 80 percent of the world's oil exports. Iran took over control of all oil production in its territory, Iraq and Algeria soon followed and Libya nationalised some foreign oil companies. A greater shock was yet to come. In late 1973 OPEC quadrupled oil prices. Industrialised nations were forced to pay whatever price the oil-exporting countries agreed on as disruption of supplies could prove disastrous to the economies of some countries. The United States' oil production had declined; she was no longer the world's leading producer.

The large increase in oil prices caused a great shift in world monetary reserves. The oil producing countries took in more money than they could spend, but they followed a responsible course and avoided swamping the international monetary system. The OPEC countries used much of the increased revenue for the import of manufactured goods and technical services from the West, but the rise in the cost of energy meant that the price of food, transportation and industrial goods also increased. This caused fluctuation in the value of currencies and inflation during the 1970s.

For Gulf Air the sudden increase in surplus oil money manifested itself in a dramatic increase in the number of foreign business people travelling to and around the Gulf states. Western companies realised that the Arab states had purchasing potential – they had a lot of catching up to do, and contracts for hotels, hospitals, schools, oil products, radio and television stations were signed; there was also a market for luxury goods. The renewed interest in the Gulf area, and the increase in the number of people travelling there, tempted Gulf Air to purchase a couple of Lockheed Tristar aircraft. While we waited for their delivery, we leased two VC-10 aircraft from BOAC to operate flights from London to Dubai and Bahrain.

To support the increase in the number of aircraft, local and expatriate technical personnel were employed. During my time working for Gulf Air, from 1970 to 1975, the staff increased from about one hundred to approximately one thousand. The number and type of aircraft also increased where we had four Islander, three Beachcraft, four Skyvans, three BAC 1-11s, two VC 10s and two Tristars.

Rapid change can, in itself, cause unrest; when coupled with high inflation it creates a volatile environment. A strike for increased wages started at the docks in Manama, and soon spread to the airport on Maharak Island. Expatriate contract engineers were

expected to report for work an
sans from the Indian subcont
during the strike. Armed police
the airport; only authorised pe
workers who remained inside h
unpleasant task to perform oth
is in progress: to do so when
repugnant. One afternoon as
Maharak Island on my way to w
workers standing by the side of
As I drew level, some of them
to take some food in to their s
moral dilemma – break the sec
and drive away? I motioned to
after a quick flurry of activity
at the airport entrance. Fortuna
to open the car boot that day, a
keys to the first person on strik
my spare wheel for air pressu
my office and the incident wa

Some days later mass meet
ball pitch in Manama; here, to
was born in Kenya and becan
Mau Mau war. He was a maj
and successfully used pseudo
fight against their former com
nal security in Bahrain. The
persed; a few days later hea
swept the airport clean of stri
trucks. During the remainder

* * *

We lived in Jufair outside what was the British naval base before the Americans took over. The house was a one-storey, flat-roofed Arab design with three bedrooms, kitchen, dining room, lounge and two bathrooms. No matter how much work was carried out the plaster always seemed to part from the walls to form undulations. In the larger rooms the flat roof always drooped downwards and fell in on regular occasions. Nevertheless, it was a cool, airy place to live; the bedrooms were connected through the bathrooms, and the children could play 'tag' and 'hide and seek' without being cornered in one room. I often got involved in these games, and it was possible to do a right or left circuit – the children never knew what direction you would come from, or even if you stopped your pursuit. On one occasion when I was pursuing them, our daughter, Kelly, looked behind her and crashed into a doorjamb, making a visit to the Sulmaniya hospital necessary. Our son ended up there also, after he decided to jump on to a branch of a thorn tree; the branch used by the preceding boy lashed back to split his eyelid like a lance. The hospital followed that wonderful Arab custom of providing sleeping facilities for a parent whose child has been admitted, thus removing some of the terror a child must feel when left in a strange place.

The outside of the house looked like a sand-coloured blockhouse. Two large thorn trees, a pomegranate tree and a broadleaf creeper offered some shade from the scorching sun. Exposed concrete absorbed the heat during the day and became a brick oven. If you walked close by in the relative cool of the night, you could feel the heat radiating from the walls.

I enjoyed gardening and I planted flowers and tomatoes in January in the small strip of sand enclosed by a wall surrounding the house. It was a good feeling to get things to grow in the desert: the ripe seeds of the sunflowers attracted birds, including parrots and bulbuls. By June the growing season was over; the scorching heat dried up and returned the garden to fine dust.

* * *

While this ordinary, everyday life was taking place, I was living another life in parallel with it. In order to produce some equipment for the war effort at home I purchased components from around the world and built devices. Out on an isolated part of the desert I tested them out for operating distance, reliability, effectiveness and resistance to electronic countermeasures until I had what I was looking for. With seven weeks' leave per year I was able to return to Ireland at intervals to check the devices in the battlefield and, if satisfactory, put them into service. When I returned to the Persian Gulf, radio reports allowed me to follow their effectiveness. In time, as skills were developed, they became more successful and helped to force the British army off the ground and into the air.

* * *

One of our neighbours was an Englishman in his sixties, and was what we called one of the 'when we were' brigade – a colonial type – forever lamenting the decline of the British empire. As a young man he had served in the Royal Air Force, and told stories of a time when he was stationed on the northwest frontier in what is now the Pakistan-Afghanistan border. In ancient times this area was a crossroads for conquerors and a natural barrier between Tsarist Russia and the Indian subcontinent. In the nineteenth century the British tried to conquer Afghanistan to use it as a buffer state. This was nothing new to the Afghani tribesmen whose forebears rode against endless waves of invaders who had funnelled down into their land through the high mountain passes. Alexander the Great, Arabs, Mongols led by Genghis Khan and Tamerlane, the British and later the Russians, and now the Americans have all tried to tame this land without success. The British finally gave up in 1919 after many Anglo-Afghan wars, and retreated to hold their line of defence along the northwest frontier.

George talked of journeying up the Wakham corridor, which arcs eastward across the Hindu Cush mountains to China. In the 1270s Marco Polo, the Venetian explorer, followed the Oxus river to this valley, on his way to China. George was stationed north of Charsadda to the Malakand Pass, and he visited the Vale of Swat, a beautiful princely state ruled by the Wali. As I write this in prison, amazingly there is one prisoner here from the Vale of Swat. He said that after the British left, Pakistan took it over and it went downhill after that because Pakistan did not have the money for the upkeep of roads and schools. Why he was in prison was never discussed, but he said that his father had been in the British army and was assassinated after they left.

The British engaged in endless punitive expeditions against the Pathan tribesmen in the hills and passes of the northwest frontier. When the tribesmen became bored and spoiling for a fight they raided the British outposts in the lowlands. A British expedition was mounted to sweep the mountain passes clean, burn a few villages to teach the tribesmen a lesson, then retreat, leaving the high ground to the returning tribesmen who in their own way acted as a buffer against would-be invaders. While in support of one of these expeditions, all hell broke loose in their camp one night. George was too tired to get up and went back to sleep. Next morning when he got up the ground all around the tents was covered with steel balls, fired from cannons by tribesmen during the night.

George suffered a nervous breakdown while he was working in Accra, the capital of Ghana. On Easter Sunday morning, shortly after his return from convalescence in England he was sitting on the balcony of the British club having a drink, when one of his friends released a pink dyed rabbit, which bounced across the lawn below. He looked at the pink rabbit, and then his pink champagne, considered his health, and waited for the pink elephant.

* * *

After the entertaining, bustling, teeming life of the Far East the silent, empty, sand-coloured sameness of the Middle East was a cultural shock. Bahrain had its *suq*, beggars crying '*baksheesh*', shops, mosque, government, schools, playgrounds and all-male cafés. However, clubs and places of public entertainment were lacking; it is not an Arab custom to participate in public entertainment or to join clubs. Social life is generally carried on within the home. Camel racing at Awali town on Fridays was an exception, but even here it was a male-dominated affair, with only a small number of non-Arab women present. I found the camel a rather unpleasant animal, forever moaning, complaining and snapping; it sprays its excrement down the back of its hind legs, exhales a raw animal odour, and one of its nasty parasites, the camel tick, flies into your hair if you get too close.

Within the last generation the camel has been brought to the edge of extinction, though the rise in popularity of camel racing may help to preserve it in the future. On these 'ships of the desert' the Arabs travelled for millennia on another sea, the waves of the shifting Arabian sand. Domesticated around the eleventh century BC, the single-humped camel's slow canter set the pace of Arab life and the number possessed was a measure of a man's wealth. It carried warriors into battle, provided all transport, and other essentials – milk, hide and fuel. Now the camel stands obsolete, the Bedouin are giving up their old ways.

The Arabs seem to dislike animals that serve no purpose in their life, a product perhaps of a harsh desert existence. When the British forces left the Middle East, cats which had become particularly wild were left behind, especially around military bases where they had been tolerated and occasionally fed by the soldiers. Those remaining around Maharak air base came under attack when we moved in. On one occasion I was shocked to see one cat cornered, picked up by the tail, swung in circles, then flung, head first, at a wall, which killed it instantly. On another occasion I was inspecting test equipment in a room when I came upon a small kitten hiding underneath. Remembering what I had previously seen, I decided to take it home with me. Seeing my intention, an Arab man warned me to leave it, but I possess my own measure of stubbornness. As I reached to pick it up, the kitten sank its teeth into my finger, piercing it to the bone. It refused to let go, no matter what I did, and there I stood like a fool, in great pain, the kitten in my left hand and its jaws firmly locked on to my right index finger, until someone hurried up with a screwdriver to pry its jaws open.

The people of Bahrain were endowed with more than their fair share of friendliness, hospitality and generosity; however, when it came to government departments and officialdom, things could get clouded in red tape and paperwork. In order to facilitate flexible travel, our children's names were entered into both parents' passports. Returning from leave one time, Caroline proceeded through Immigration, claiming the two children on her passport and immigration form. When I submitted my papers the official wanted to know where the two children were. I explained that they had already passed through on their mother's passport. 'If there is an entry visa on both passports, there must be four children!' he declared. 'Stand over there until this matter is cleared up.' Soon my eight-year-old daughter, blond hair and blue eyes, appeared around the edge of the door. I discreetly waved her away lest she add another dimension to the complication.

After an hour the children were getting bored waiting in the baggage area and our son Glenn amused himself by placing his hand on the baggage belt and walking around, humming to himself. He allowed his hand to go under a roller. He was fortunate that a gentleman standing nearby had the presence of mind to grab him and pull his hand out. The action of removing his hand left all the skin of the palm on the abrasive belt, but this was much better than losing an arm. The arrival of Caroline with the boy covered in blood and the weariness induced by the long flight caused tempers to go off the clock at the Immigration desk – however, I still had to wait until a senior official arrived to stamp my passport.

Education for the children up to eleven years was quite good in Bahrain. The government ran a school using Arabic as the teaching medium, and Italian nuns ran a school attached to the only Roman Catholic Church in the Gulf. Our two children attended St Christopher's school, a British council school staffed by qualified teachers. They prepared students for entrance into second-level schools in Britain, where most pupils returned to attend boarding schools. Together with the normal subjects, they got the children involved in team games, singing and taking part in stage productions. The dedication and hard work of this small group of teachers set the course for our children to pass smoothly through higher education and for both of them to obtain their PhD in later years.

The Bahrain drama club staged regular productions, which

provided a pleasant diversion in a society devoid of public entertainment. The proximity of so many British military bases allowed the staging of ambitious productions, including wonderful musical shows where the music was provided by the military.

The fish-filled turquoise waters of the Gulf provided another pleasant family activity. Families clubbed together and hired a large dhow to go fishing or relax in the sun on the deck. An experienced crew always seemed to know where the fish were, and the children usually ended up fishing by the time the contents of the picnic baskets were consumed; most adults preferred to laze about in the evening sun. Returning in the evening the blood-red orb of the sinking sun set the water of the Gulf on fire in its short-lived farewell flush.

On one such occasion the wind picked up after the sun went down, and as we pitched along in the darkness the cry 'man overboard' rang out. I immediately thought of the children who had been running up and down the deck. With my heart in my mouth I reached for a buoy, having decided to jump into the water to be close to where the accident occurred. At that moment, our daughter Kelly came flying down the deck and came to a swinging stop with her arms around my leg acting as a brake. Thus restrained, I soon saw Glenn's blond head as he passed by, pursued by his friend. Cold sweat broke out on my forehead as I gazed at the dark choppy water, realising that sharks patrolled there. The cold sweat was joined by the skin crawling on the back of my neck as I listened to the high-pitched wailing cry of the crew: 'Aaahmi-id, Aaahmi-id' they called as they searched the pitiless dark water. Silent, white-faced passengers, heard only a lament played by the wind in the rigging, where graceful wind-filled lateen sails billowed.

* * *

Gulf Air embarked on a policy of expansion in the Gulf region while I was there in the 1970s. A decision was taken to open up routes to Oman, using modern jet aircraft. I was asked to assist, and an Oman national named Fahud was transferred from Bahrain to work at Bait al Falaj, the capital's airport. This airport was a military base set in an extinct volcanic crater.

Oman, a Muslim monarchy, lies at the eastern tip of the Arabian Peninsula. The interior is a sea of burning sands, the east lava mountains, the west – Dhofar province – a scene of bitter fighting in recent times. It is bordered on the north by the United Arab Emirates, and an ill-defined border with Saudi Arabia through the vast and sandy 'Rub al Khatl' (empty quarter). Fighting took place here in the 1950s between the two states. In the east lies the Gulf of Oman and the famous Strait of Hormuz. The Arabian Sea skirts the south coast, and to the west lies Yemen, formerly know as Aden. Opening up this ancient country to twentieth-century travel was a difficult task. Sultan Said Ben Tainur, thirteenth ruler in the dynasty stretching back to 1749, lived a secluded, eccentric life in his palace at Salalah, a town on the Arabian Sea coast. He imposed a policy of strict isolationism, rejecting the materialist values and cultural features of the twentieth century. It was said that he wished his country to remain as it was during his childhood.

This policy was to prove disastrous. During a century of great change, no country could stand still or remain an island unto itself. The former British colony of Aden had received independence and the new name Yemen with a Chinese-supported Marxist government, which propounded revolution to the Omani people who longed for change.

The province of Dhofar was ideal terrain for insurgents. For years the Popular Front for the Liberation of Occupied Arabian Gulf (PFLOAG) had waged war against the Sultanate, trying to seize control and install a Marxist government. From 1968 British soldiers on secondment 'advised' Omani forces attempting to quell the uprising. 'FINGA' companies, made up of former rebels who changed sides, and commanded by SAS men, proved very successful at containing the revolt, but not ending it.

When I visited Oman for the first time, we flew over the northern desert, an undulating sea of scorching sand as big as Texas. Its permanent population is zero; in summer the northerly 'Shamaal' blows stinging sand-storms. At noon in this arid, barren wilderness, the temperature reaches 125°F. Flying over it, not even a shadow broke the glare of this blinding landscape. Finally the desert gave way to the northern mountains; below us was Nizwa, ancient capital of Oman. Further south the lava hills reflected the blinding sun, their peaks shaped like needles by the ever-present grinding sand and swirling wind. Descending across this moonscape we approached Muscat; on crossing a lava ridge the runway appeared below in a shimmering cauldron surrounded almost totally by a volcanic rim. A rapid descent was necessary to put down as near as possible to the end. Hitting the runway solidly, applying full brakes, flaps, reverse thrust and lift dumpers, we roared to a thirty-knot crawl as the towering rocks approached at the other end.

Fahud stood on the hot concrete as I stepped out into the 127°F temperature; it felt like an oven. It *was* an oven – sweat began to ooze from my body, my feet burned through the soles of my shoes, I felt as if the volcano below was still heating the ground under me. I looked around at the volcanic rim surrounding us, here with its wild and awesome walls focusing the sun's rays into the centre like a mirror. It is difficult to imagine the extreme cold of winter when you are sitting in the heat of a warm summer's day, and vice versa. Here in this cold prison in the Appalachian Mountains I struggle to get my body to sense again that level of heat and I find that even in memory it can hurt the senses.

The Oman security forces stationed helicopters and Viscount and Caribou aircraft to support the war, code-named 'Operation Storm', in the Dhofar province. The aircraft, built in a benign climate with meticulous exactitude, catches the eye in flight as a gigantic, frolicsome bird – a regurgitated member of a species long extinct. Here in Oman, on the piping hot tarmac amidst a screen of heated particles of powdery sand, there is the constant illusion that these huge planes are in the process of fading in and out of their surroundings. Here also lived military personnel, including British expatriates in a compound some distance away from the hangar and arrivals area.

During my stays in Oman I would use the Petroleum Development Oman Limited (PDO) facility at Matrah, a coastal town separated from Muscat by lava hills. Hostels housed oil-well personnel in transit to and from oil wells in the interior. PDO had a contract with us and operated two of our Skyvan aircraft to ferry food, personnel and drill spares in and out of the desert. The aircraft operated out of a small clearing not far from Matrah called Sib, soon to become Oman's international airport.

On one occasion one of these machines refused to start when it was out at an oil-drilling rig and we had to travel over the desert with spares to recover it. Driving across the trackless desert at noon in the burning live air, it is difficult to judge distances. The oscillating air brings down the sky on the hills and creates a silvery expanse of water in the valleys. I looked at the driver and wondered if he really knew where he was and if we had enough water and food if we got lost. I remembered that Wilfred Thesiger crossed here on camel in the early part of the twentieth century and I felt ashamed. At night out here you became aware of how still the desert was, and that you were surrounded by hundreds of miles of undulating sand with no fences, ditches or roads. This produced a sense of space which was difficult for the mind's eye to comprehend, but now it is very useful to my imagination in prison. And when lying on your back at night in the desert the vault of the nocturnal sky moves slowly over your head and the stars grow big and radiant beyond anything you saw before, then slowly retreat to points in the sky as the sun's dull red ball appears in the east.

As we drove to Matrah the landrover became a crucible; unlike me, Fahud was dressed in a turban and grey gown suitable for the climate. He was five feet, five inches tall, and lightly built. As the landrover travelled along the road out of the Middle Ages, he bounced about like a doll in the cabin: his feet losing contact with the control pedals produced a jerking, bouncing motion which, together with the heat and dust, made the journey intolerable. Stopping at Sib we inspected the Skyvan aircraft, and talked to one of the pilots over a cup of coffee. As a test pilot he had flown the 'flying bedstead', the forerunner to the vertical take-off harrier. Flying alone across this inhospitable land offered a challenge and tested his undoubted skills.

The sunset cast a henna glow over the desert, and it lost its harshness. Subtle shades and colours appeared. As I walked across the sand-packed runway into the desert, the still evening air carried the sweet scent of flowers. The southwest monsoon had dropped nourishing showers here during the previous weeks. Flowers shot up, giving the desert a delicate hue of colour; tomorrow they would disappear in the heat of the eternal sun. Still, with water, life was possible, even here.

The following evening Fahud insisted that I visit his family in Muscat. We entered the town through one of its medieval gates, which was still closed at nightfall and opened at sunrise. A short distance inside the gate a burial was in progress. The body was wrapped in a shroud and burial took place on the same day as the death. Packs of wild dogs often raided graves – for this reason, and because dogs don't sweat, the Muslim world regards them as unclean and despises them.

The sun was sinking toward the summit of Al Jabal al Akhdar (the green mountain) as we reached the *suq* where Fahud lived with his family. The mud-brick houses and shops were virtually unchanged since the seventeenth century. Fahud lived above his father's house in a '*barasti*' extension built with palm fronds and cane. On entering the house I was introduced to his father, with whom I started the usual Arab greetings:

'Peace be with you.'

'And with you, peace.'

'God grant you life.'

'Our family, our home is yours.'

Sitting on the flat roof of the seemingly fragile construction, we ate a meal of mutton and spiced rice from a communal dish; using our right hands only, we rolled rice into compact balls and popped them into our mouths. We drank coffee spiced with cardamom and ginger root, poured from a long-beaked pot into tiny china cups. Normally a guest accepted the customary three servings, then shook the cup in a rapid movement of the wrist to signify that they had finished.

Fahud had bowed to his father's request and married his uncle's daughter, a custom designed to keep the family clans strong. They had two children. On hot, humid nights the family slept on the flat roof to escape the unbearable heat indoors. But sleeping under the stars had its down side, since malaria was endemic in the region.

With our hands washed after the meal, an incense burner was passed around to be held under head cloths until the fragrant smoke soaked into beards and hair. This signalled the end of the gathering and people started leaving. This custom is the origin of the old Arab saying '*Bak hkhir wa-ruuh*', (take the incense and go).

Wandering through the *suq* in the evening was a social event in Muscat, and the variety in the people strolling there represented the country's turbulent history. Pale-coloured eyes stared out from brown leather faces that tapered to pointed chins, reflecting the mixture of ancient Persia, early Portuguese explorers and Indians, all mixed with the ancient tribes that lived here. Men were dressed in '*dishdashes*' (long white robes) and turbans had '*jambiyyas*' (traditional daggers) thrust under heavy cartridge belts clasped around their waists; they moved slowly and carefully; with heads held high, they looked down their noses at me, the '*uhudi*' (unbeliever), like proud, alert hawks. Dates, dried fish, cloves, cumin, cinnamon, saffron, sandalwood and frankincense scented the night air, making it an unforgettable journey into the past.

Next day I flew to Salalah, and we dropped rapidly out of the Dhofar sky, straining to reach the runway as quickly as possible to reduce the chances of being hit by insurgent fire. A man beside me, whom I suspected was a British soldier, said that the insurgents had fixed mortar plates in the surrounding hills. It was a simple matter to fit the launch tube and let off a few rounds and then disappear. Salalah lies on the coast five hundred miles southwest of Muscat town, across barren mountains and vast dune lands. The plain inland from the town forms a crescent hemmed off from the interior by the Qara Mountains. The southwest monsoon blows life-giving rains into this oasis from June to September. It allows green pastures, palm groves and fields of grain to flourish in contrast with the barren interior.

* * *

With the increase in the number of people employed by Gulf Air, the job became more impersonal, more narrowly defined out of necessity. I found that the pioneering spirit of the original small group was dispersed and diluted by business meetings, travel and a mountain of paperwork. There was no place for determined individualism. Some of the old corps started drifting away to other parts of the developing world, where their special drive and talents were more suitable.

For me, this drifting lifestyle would soon end. Our children reached an age where a decision on their education had to be made: send them away to boarding school or return home and provide a stable base for their Europeanisation? They had spent all their lives overseas in a protected environment, with no concept of what it was like to live in Europe. Simply being white meant they were part of an upper class, an elite, in the Third World, and as such were privileged and also forced to conduct themselves in a civilised and honourable manner. This give a sort of democratic flavour to the foreign colony where white children from different classes all mixed together and no doors were closed to any of them. When they visited Europe the children found it difficult to understand that there were different social groups among white people, some of which they did not mix with or talk to. Arriving at European airports, they would ask: 'Dad, why is that white man carrying bags?', a sight never seen in their experience. When out in public they would hear people use common swear words that were never used overseas: 'Dad, what is the meaning of the word fuck?'

In talking with some teenagers attending boarding schools I found that quite a few resented being sent away from their parents when they were so young. They set about trying to hurt their parents by misbehaving at school and ended up being moved from one school to another. The change to the boarding school programme was very disruptive for the children. The father was also locked into a financial regime that required him to remain overseas to meet the high costs; the mother ended up spending most of her time in Europe close to the children. The father was now on his own most of the time, with the added burden of a second home to support. In time, the family drifted apart or broke up under the pressure. One of my friends in such a position experienced bad periods: the loneliness and the dreadful summer heat affected his nerves so badly that he allowed small problems to grow out of all proportion and drag him into rows with his fellow workers. Later he would retire to his house to indulge in a bout of drinking that lasted a couple of days.

Time was the enemy. We decided to return home to live in Swords, a satellite town of Dublin, where we had had a house since the 1960s. As the time to depart drew near I was surprised to hear that the Arab employees had organised a special farewell party for me. When I arrived I found that I was the only non-Arab person there, and during the evening I was asked again and again why I wanted to leave their country, was I not happy with them? I explained that I had spent some of the happiest days of my life with them, but family requirements made it necessary to move on. During the presentation of a gift the speaker said they were gathered that night to show that they had not forgotten the man who had taken food to them when they were starving.

The following evening we arrived at Bahrain airport to leave for the last time. I parked the car haphazardly in the sand and handed the keys to Raza Butt as he ran up in front of a group of local workers who had come to see me off – and I said goodbye to them and the near east.

CHAPTER 11

The Bahamas and Trinidad

In 1975 Ireland was not a good place to live but the children had to go to second-level school and we had a house in Swords, so it was suitable. The events that I had experienced in the Middle East were now having an economic effect in the west and more so in Ireland. The uncertainty of oil supplies and the huge hike in price caused interest rates to reach 18 percent. Unemployment was very high and there was little hope of employment in the airline industry. I worked as a service engineer with Corning, an American-owned company that sold and serviced analytical equipment to industry, hospitals and colleges around the country. My job required me to travel all over the country, installing, servicing and repairing these machines.

The hospital element made the job very demanding. When equipment malfunctioned the staff demanded immediate attention and on one occasion I had to work on a machine that measured the gasses in the blood during a heart operation in the Mater hospital. One New Year's Eve I arrived home at 10.00pm from Letterkenny to find a note asking me to call to Temple Street children's hospital. There I spent the early hours of New Year's Day repairing a flame-photometer that measures the levels of various chemicals in a baby's urine.

At home now, I was more involved in the war in the north than I was when overseas. The research that I had carried out in the desert previously was now in place and had helped to restrict the movement of British forces on the ground. Their operations were now very dependent on their air superiority. Because it made sound military sense, weapon research and development in the following years would lean heavily in this direction. If we wanted to advance to the next phase of the struggle we had to neutralise their air superiority. With the increased ability of our side to carry the war forward, we expected the recently elected British Conservative party to pour great resources into the conflict, which they did. Our contacts in the universities in England told us that they had started to provide millions of pounds for research to counter our technology.

As luck goes, I got an opportunity in my next job to return overseas and again had the opportunity to search out new technology to lessen the expected shock. The location was close to the US, which was perfect for that work. The search for answers to keep us ahead of the enemy would last for the duration of the struggle. Though I was very heavily involved, all things associated with the war were ultra-secret and neither my family nor friends were aware of my involvement. I did not make fools out of people, but certain subjects were simply not commented on if they came up in conversation. This did not cut me off from relationships, I felt, but they were approached with caution, and I found that most of the time this attracted people rather than repelling them. One does not deliberately choose such a secretive, double life, nor does one have the knowledge or foresight to anticipate it, but security considerations slowly move you into it and after eight years I was used to it.

When the economic climate changed I decided to return to the aircraft industry and joined Aer Lingus in 1978 to do much the same work as I had done overseas. At that time Aer Lingus had started to capitalise on their engineering and maintenance expertise by supplying personnel to other airlines to carry out this work on a contract basis. In 1979, after working for a year in Dublin, I was requested to go to the Bahamas as part of a team on a technical contract with Bahamas Air. My family would not be with me now because the children had to remain in school and could only visit when school was closed.

The intervening years since my return to Ireland had been very difficult for me. In my area of operation in the six counties, 1979 was a horrific year, and on a number of occasions I had stared down the last great spectre of life – death. I felt war-weary, and now that I was on my way abroad my thoughts remained focused on those I was leaving behind who must have felt the same way. Yet it was their lot to face a NATO army in the day-to-day struggle on the ground. Thinking about them in prison now, I remember them as unusually brave, incomparable comrades. I tried to think of what lay ahead and come to terms with the fact that I had returned to my wandering ways again, what the Spanish call a *camino san salida*, a 'road with no exit' . It was a very dangerous road and was the start of another phase of my double life. Success can trap you: if you get results you are given other, more difficult assignments, and I would remain on that road for the next ten years. It would be a different experience travelling to a new location without my family for the first time. But over the previous five years I had been away from home a lot because of the service engineering job and the war in the six counties. I hoped that this experience would help me to settle into a new routine without my family.

The Spanish thought was appropriate since it was the Spanish, under the leadership of a Genoese sailor, who discovered this cluster of seven hundred islands in a hundred thousand square miles of sea and called them Baja Mar or 'shallow sea'. As its name implies, the Bahamas is a barely submerged plateau of gravel, sand and limestone on a turquoise parchment. With the exception of the mile-deep 'tongue of the ocean' between Andros and New Providence islands and the northeast New Providence channel, most of the plateau is only a few metres below the surface of the water. To the west of the reef is the great Bahama bank, and the Gulf Stream rushes north between the Florida Gold Coast and Bimmi Islands, once thought to be the location of the lost city of Atlantis.

My destination was Nassau, the capital, on the island of New Providence. It is a small island, only eighty square miles, yet half of the nation's population lives there. To the people living on the 'out islands', Nassau is a crowded, noisy place that sucks away the young from the close-knit friendly hamlets on pristine islands. Some locals refer to Nassau as Gomorra. The island communities have been held together for generations by religion, farming and fishing, and a shared African heritage. For the young, the fast dollar and the high life of Nassau is more attractive than scraping a living from depleted soil and a sea that can become a monster and eat you up.

We approached Nassau airport from the north across reef-churned water, then Love Beach and Orange Hill, before setting down on the runway. When the aeroplane doors opened, the balmy salt air, with its tropical fragrance, drifted in and I could hear a band playing songs of the islands for tourists in the arrival hall. The whole arrival process was so entertaining that I was not aware of the formalities involved, which was quite a contrast to my experiences in other parts of the world. I exited to the car park with a sense of restfulness that was reinforced by the journey downtown.

This was the Caribbean. If you forgot about the tourists for a while the same tableau that the conquistadors found still spread out before you like the unfolding of an ancient map. Palm trees on the edges of bleached white beaches fringed warm turquoise waters, and red and lemon hibiscus, purple and pink bougainvillea and red acacia trees were everywhere. This is what I had longed to see and I sensed that it could be difficult to keep one's mind on the job when you entered such a seductive environment.

The road outside the airport was lined with royal palms; it was the first time on my travels that I saw these magnificent trees with their smooth trunks, beautiful in colour and symmetry, with their umbrella tops. Travelling along John F Kennedy Drive to Blake Road, Lake Killarney is on the right and bears little resemblance to the real thing. At the end of Blake Road where it meets West Bay Street stands Conference Corner where Macmillan, Kennedy and the Canadian Diefenbaker planted trees during a conference in 1962.

West Bay Street is really a road that runs along the north shore of the island east into Nassau town and west to the south ocean side of the island. In the late 1970s there were few buildings along this stretch of the coast to the west. The exception was a bar and restaurant called Traveller's Rest. It was very popular on Saturday and Sunday afternoons. A fellow prisoner who stands nearby at work as I write this is a native of the Bahamas and he says it was also famous for soft drugs. He remembers waking up one Sunday morning at home, not remembering how he got across the island or where his car was. He learned later that he walked all the way, forgetting his car after smoking pot and drinking. It is the middle of winter here in the Appalachian mountains – the buildings, ground, trees and grass are encased in black ice as if it was carefully sprayed on during the night. It is minus 30^0C and there is a wind chill to add another twenty. All the clothes that I possess are on me and I am still cold. In the line for breakfast this morning nerves were frayed and already two prisoners are on the way to the hole. The Bahamas is not a bad place to travel to in my mind today.

Life in the Bahamas was and still is largely influenced by the island's proximity to the North American continent and the sea routes created by the Trade Winds. During the first two centuries after discovery the islands were plagued by pirates. Prosperity depended on a sequence of events in the United States. During the American liberation war with the British, loyalists fled here with their slaves, and, because of blockade gun-running during the American civil war, that was a period of great prosperity. Depression followed until prohibition in the 1920s when rum-running brought back the good times to Nassau. Depression returned until the Second World War came, and things were very bad in the 1930s. After the Second World War an effort was made to prevent the return of the bad times during peace. Tourism and off-shore banking were established, and, later, pharmaceuticals and other industries were put in place. In the late 1970s cruise ships packed Nassau harbour and tourists flocked to casinos and shops; over one and a half million tourists visited this small nation which had a population of only two hundred thousand people, a long way from the five hundred who visited in the nineteenth century. Tourism now provides most of the country's gross national product.

This was the Bahamas I arrived in, and Nassau, crowded or otherwise, would be my home for the next six months. Eighty-five percent of the people were descendants of African slaves, and this African and European mix allowed the population to make some of the most vibrant music on earth. This produced a wealth of entertainment on the islands, and the people possessed a natural rhythm.

The tendency to move with music manifests itself most strikingly during the Junkanoo festival which takes place on New Providence island on the nights of 26 December and 1 January. It is called after John Canoe, a popular slave leader, and is loosely derived from African culture and customs, but its exact origins are unknown. It is thought to have grown up around slave celebrations on the only days they had off during the year. Local businesses sponsor groups who spend most of the year producing exotic costumes. When dressed up in these costumes participants dance wildly on Bay Street until dawn. The whole population gets involved, beating cow bells and shak-shaks and blowing whistles, and the dance becomes loud and boisterous, snaking around in circles.

I worked permanently on nights at Nassau airport, a great vantage point from which to observe the pale-skinned northerners arrive and the partially-broiled ones leave. Work started at 8.00pm and ended when all of the maintenance and technical problems were cleared, usually 6.00am. The local workers were very laid back, and I usually got stuck in and assisted in the manual work. Sometimes they would take advantage of this and just stand back and let you get on with it. One such occasion comes to mind now. We had to replace an engine on an aircraft and to reduce the time I had breakfast and a shower, then returned to prepare the motor for installation. As I worked in the heat I noticed one of the day workers entwined around the stand that was holding the motor, and he was fast asleep. I tapped the metal he was hanging on to and asked him what his problem was. 'Oh man, I dying! Met this Canadian-Chinese chick last night, went out to her yacht and spent the night licking champagne off her cunnie, oh maan.' Perhaps he had a rougher night than I'd had! I could only laugh.

That was the lifestyle, women did most of the work and men

entertained the tourists. After a short period it was possible to recognise local men with a new arrival, having waved goodbye to his now sun-tanned guest after her two-week stay. They rarely strayed far from their charge, even sitting close by while she tanned on the beach. It reminded me of a dog watching a bone. If your eyes lingered too long on the lady you expected him to turn and snarl at you, which he often did. The tourist got value for money – these men were very attentive, good dancers and entertaining. A woman's age did not matter. I often wondered whether these women, who came here for an island boy, would bid them the time of day if they met in New York, Toronto or Berlin. Be that as it may, this was often the man's only meal ticket; he was guaranteed a dinner and perhaps an air-conditioned bedroom for a period. Life was not great for most Bahamians who lived away from the tourist haunts in a section of Nassau known locally as 'over the hill'. The terrain on which Nassau was located rises very sharply to form a ridge west of Bay Street. In the late 1970s this ridge separated the commercial district from the rather dilapidated dwellings of the unemployed and low-income people on the west side of the hill. Tourists may never go there but may sample some of the friendliness of the Bahamians around the markets, particularly at Potter's Cay under the bridge to Paradise Island. Here they find the local banter and jokes flowing in an endless exchange between the vendors and customers alike, as they sell tropical fruit, vegetables and fish from the outer islands.

Working constantly at night and living alone led to an unusual lifestyle for me. Some of my days off were spent in the United States visiting outlets and companies that produced technical products to see if they had anything that could be adapted for use in the war at home. Other days were spent studying components that I got there to see if they could be adapted. When I was working I rarely got out of bed before one o'clock in the afternoon, and this left only six hours free. Outside of doing the normal household chores I generally had brunch and went fishing or snorkelling for a few hours in the afternoon. Later I went for a five-mile run across a ridge from Cable Beach Manor to Blake Road and back. In the seventies there was a track there but no houses – sand flies biting you was the only discomfort. Though on one occasion as I was returning to my apartment a dog came out and decided to check me out. Seeing him coming, I stopped and stood still – he came up and placed his jaws very gently around my ankle and looked at me with one eye as if to ask, what are you going to do now? I stood there until he let go, but each time I went to move away he reapplied his grip. Eventually, the lady of the house had to come out to release me. It felt as if he had come out to catch a man for her!

My favourite areas for snorkelling was Cabbage Beach on Paradise Island and Coral Harbour on the south side of the island. Coral Harbour was a casualty of Prime Minister Lynden Pindling's policy on restricting the right of foreigners to own land or property in the Bahamas and to exercise some control over immigration and foreign labour, which was guaranteed under the British to large, foreign-owned companies. Construction sites such as Coral Harbour, with miles of canals and roads, came to a standstill while still only partly built and soon tropical vegetation took over. It was a rather deserted area during weekdays and snorkelling alone can be dangerous anywhere. On one occasion I did not pay enough attention to the tide and wind changing and when I looked up the shore was very far away. With the sea running against me, I was forced to swim at an angle to shore and land about a mile and a half away from where I entered the sea. Because it was a relatively cool

February day I felt chilled and decided to find a sheltered spot, where I lay like a lizard on a huge rock to warm myself. I fell asleep for some time and when I awoke there was a three- or four-foot snake sitting on the rock not far from my face, looking at me. Holding back panic, I decided the best escape was to roll away off the rock on to the ground. Fortunately the snake decided to roll away in the opposite direction and disappear into the undergrowth.

South Ocean was a beautiful beach west of Coral Harbour. There was only one hotel, South Ocean Beach and Country Club, on this coast and the beach was almost deserted during the week. The water here was very shallow and I spent hours snorkelling in this area. I saw a lone fisherman with his small boat using oars and a small sail disappear over the horizon and return in the evening loaded up with fish. On this shore I also saw aircraft lying, nose down, in the shallow water. Perhaps they had been on a drug run and ditched there, the owners fading away into the bush. A prudent person doesn't ask about such matters. As natives say, 'This the Bahamas, who knows about these things, maan.'

Cabbage Beach is on the north shore of Paradise Island. This beautiful island was originally called Hog Island. To reach it you have to take a water shuttle or cross a toll bridge: walking 25 cents, car one dollar. I heard that the charge was to deter locals from crossing to the gambling casinos.

The water on Cabbage Beach is deeper than it generally is on the north shore of New Providence. This leads to better fishing and snorkelling where the fish are larger and a greater variety. I often found myself surrounded by grunts, butterfly fish, jacks, goat fish, surgeon fish, parrot fish, cardinal fish, gobies, grouper, pogies, yellow tag, puffer fish, blow fish, trigger fish and barracuda. When my family were on vacation with me my son speared a parrot fish and somehow while I was recovering it from the spear my finger ended up in its powerful jaws which are used to crush coral. I remained with the spear in one hand and my finger in its mouth until the handle of a spoon was used to prise it open. My son and I also played games on the sea floor with a sponge and sticks. He always won because I had to surface for air more frequently. Occasionally a large ray would cast a shadow on us as it glided overhead or a large barracuda would prowl around us at a discreet distance. When snorkelling there alone one day, I saw a man swimming under water towards me with a knife in his hand and the instinct for imminent danger kicked in. Thinking about my involvement in the war back home, I feared the worst and positioned the spear gun to protect myself. This action made him hesitate and point to the surface; when we surfaced he asked for my spear to recover his watch which he had dropped among the coral.

On my way home I stopped regularly at the cloister on Paradise Island and watched the sun setting on Nassau Harbour. The cloister was the remains of a fourteenth-century Augustinian monastery imported by a rich person and placed above the harbour with steps going down from the pillars to the water's edge. The ancient stone structure retreated across the island and this section was called Versailles Gardens. I also stopped occasionally at Brown's Point on Cable Beach. The fast-disappearing sun turned the strip of sea between there and Long Cay blood red, pink and later rusty as it slipped below the horizon. Calmness descended as dusk rapidly followed the last flicker of sunlight.

This was an unconscious signal for the tourists to leave the commercial districts and return to the cruise ships and hotels to prepare for the long night's entertainment. It was also a signal for me to prepare for work. However, if it was my night off, I might go the way of the tourists. To make it easier to work constantly on nights I remained up late into the mornings on my rest days. When the sun went down the temperature dropped, the trade winds made the nights balmy and the scent from tropical flowers added excitement to the endless nightlife on New Providence. There were very few hotels on Cable Beach then. Balmoral Hotel had a night-club and also a nice quiet area where a man played a piano. Further down the road Nassau Beach had a club called the Rum Keg where there was dancing to live music until early morning. The Ambassador had the Playboy Casino, with the glamorous bunny girls, where the dices rolled and the dollars flowed and gamblers sipped free drinks to cushion the loss. King and Knights Club, Saunders Beach, had a good show, which borrowed from the Caribbean islands generally, mixed with American country music. Later you could retire to the disco at the rear that remained open until morning. At the western edge of Nassau there were a few hotels and opposite these sat the Drumbeat Club, where they staged a fine native show and locals often joined the groups on stage. In the Bridge Inn on Mackey Street at Paradise Island bridge, there was a magical piano player who seemed to know every piece of music people could think of. Sometimes an old lady down on her luck dropped in there and would entertain you with stories for a drink. Then again a lovely lady might wish to dance and in the early morning this piano bar could transport you to the Casablanca of your dreams with Sam playing on.

The Pink Pussy Cat was frequented by Bahamians and was very lively, for they knew how to sway to music. At exactly 1.00am the owner, a Greek lady, made her spectacular entrance in flowing robes. This seemed to signal a change of mood and to the delight of patrons the place went wild. Grey Cliff was an upmarket restaurant-guest house – the Beatles and ex-King Edward had stayed here in different eras.

The Green Shutters Inn on Parliament Street was one of those places for people who enjoyed an Old English atmosphere. The only time I attempted to go there was a Monday night, but it was closed. I met a lady there who had the same idea; she was the wife of a fellow worker. I became friendly with her because of a mutual interest in music and literature. She was the first person who managed to get close enough to me in twelve years to form a friendship. I had erected a protective barrier around myself to keep people at a distance where they would not know me well enough to ask questions. You know how easily a female's smile can open the doors of your mind and touch all its secrets and I did not want anybody to know my secrets. In this case we could be in each other's company without questions or romantic involvement. After seven years the split between the two sides of my life had become well established. The natural reserve, ingrained by my early years growing up on a relatively isolated farm where the next-door neighbour was a mile away, allowed me initially to stand back and observe people and situations. This was not so obvious that it isolated me, rather it aroused interest and I was not short of company. The only reaction I ever got to it was curiosity and a comment from some of the more forward females: 'You are a very alert and suspicious person.'

That evening we continued on to the Holiday Inn on Paradise Island. Here they had music and dancing in the foyer between seven and nine-thirty in the evening. After that it was possible to choose a meal from any of the twelve restaurants on Paradise. If you felt like a stroll after your meal, you could go for a walk in Paradise Beach or Pirate's Cove. Perhaps you could enjoy the sound of the star-lit sea as the balmy trade winds rolled in from the east, swaying the palm tree and causing the fairy lights to dance in time with the steel band playing in the distance; truly a romantic place. Afterwards you could take in the late spectacular show in the Le Cabaret Theatre or try your luck at the tables in the casino where the 'working ladies' or 'ladies of the night' drifted around slowly in seductive attire. After a period you got to know most of them. I was approached continuously until they realised that I was not a tourist. They respected your wishes and afterwards greeted you when you passed by.

There was one occasion when I was sitting at the bar there and a new arrival glided up. I must have been staring because her approach was, 'What do you find so interesting?' She was the most beautiful coloured girl that I had ever seen in my life and I told her so. Straightaway I asked her if she was a 'working lady' and she said, 'Yes, just in from Cincinnati for a few months' tour.' I observed her minder paying attention some distance away and asked her if she worked alone or had she a man friend. She told me a lie and said she was alone. After a short time, when there was no business coming from me, I saw him catching her eye and she then said she had to go. Such were the encounters one had on Paradise Island.

Out through a corridor to the foyer of Leow's Hotel, was my favourite nightclub, a place of which I never tired. It was appropriately called the Trade Winds. For the cost of two drinks consumed on the premises, I could enter before the first show at ten o'clock at which there was fantastic music for dancing, followed by the late show at 12.30am. You could never prevent your hips moving with the rhythm of the island music. My favourite artist was Jay Mitchell; very few people could match his Afro-Caribbean voice when he sang 'Another Place and Time' or 'Three Times A Lady'.

Here in prison my Bahamian fellow prisoner also remembers Jay. When the sky at last starts to turn golden and the sun burns away the curtain of darkness it is time to make for home. Perhaps a short stop at Nassau Beach Hotel on Cable Beach for ice cream or coffee before retiring.

It might seem that I spent all my time enjoying myself. That was far from the truth. I spent a lot of time in Florida searching for parts to integrate into new equipment for the war effort at home. This consumed hundreds of hours and in some ways this project occupied my thinking process during my waking hours, even when I was out for a night. Often during those periods of abstract thought a solution to a problem suddenly flicked into my brain. It is possible that in prison your survival makes it necessary to remember the good parts and blot out the bad, but this was the other side of my double life at this time. Communications and other electronic devices were under continuous assault from counter-measures by the enemy. Eventually they were rendered inoperative or dangerous to use and it was necessary to increase their resistance to electromotive attack or to move to new equipment. Some of the systems that I produced on the desert in the Middle East were in use since 1972 – although I gave them a life expectancy of six to twelve months they had lasted for eight years. This seems incredible when one considers that Britain had access to the latest NATO technology.

Perhaps the British believed their own propaganda. Their enemy in Ireland was portrayed as a bunch of bandits lacking support and possessing a low level of intelligence, therefore they were receiving supplies and assistance from outside the country and that could be closed off. We made every effort to encourage them to follow this line of thinking, for the art of deception is a very important element in war and it diverted their attention away from seeking out our 'cow-shed' production system. It seemed that this portrayal of the enemy as sub-human was also part of a soldier's training for Ireland. In the 1970s some soldiers stationed in the Persian Gulf, not realising what my position was, said to me that they were going to Ulster 'to shoot me a bogtrotter'. Some time later the attitude had changed. Some members who had survived a tour in South Armagh were using it as a mark of courage to taunt those of their group who had not been there.

On other occasions I flew in a light aircraft with a fellow worker to visit the out islands – out of Nassau. For generations farming, fishing and trading across the archipelago had supported small, close-knit settlements. They were mostly of African origin and had a strong attachment to church and community. The islands have remained pristine, but immigration towards tourist jobs on the larger islands has depleted the villages. Out of all the islands I visited, the most poignant was Samana Cay, now called San Salvador and once called Guanhani by the native indians. It languishes in isolation with its four hundred and fifty inhabitants in the eastern Bahamas. It is believed to be where Columbus first landed in the New World – or, as he thought, Asia – on the morning of 12 October 1492. It was a momentous moment in human history. It brought profound changes; the earth turned out to be much larger than people thought, new plants were discovered and weaker civilisations were practically swept off the face of the earth in a short few years. The handsome, sturdy people who inhabited these islands, including San Salvador, would be exterminated within forty years.

The trade winds and the constant heaving of the wave that once brought the ships *Nina*, *Pinta* and *Santa Maria* to these shores so long ago were ticking off the days and hours and too soon it was time for me to go. Time to return home to war, time to introduce new systems higher up the electromagnetic spectrum, time to help prevent the special forces, paratroopers and marines, gaining the initiative. When the aircraft banked away after take-off I looked down and wondered if I would ever see this place again – and I did.

I was fortunate to return to work for another year in the Bahamas in 1981 after a spell in Trinidad. I spent a year back in Ireland working with Aer Lingus and devoting my energies to war work before I went to Peru to work for Faucett Airlines in 1983. Peru, this land that the Spanish Pizarro brothers stole from the Inca in the early fifteen hundreds, was poverty-stricken when I was there. The descendants of the Incas still live there in abject poverty in *barriadas* (slums) on the outskirts of cities or in the high mountains. There are only two classes, very rich and very poor, but the Indians, though poor and uneducated, are infinitely enduring and they have not integrated into present-day Peru. Living at altitudes up to fifteen thousand feet, their lungs are larger than normal and they have about four pints more blood than people living in the lowlands. Lima, the capital, sits on a desert looking out to sea with the Andes at its back and the traditional Indian capital sits two miles higher in the mountains to the south at Cuzco. The white man and the Indian are as far apart today as they were when Cuzco was built, with different language, dress, attitude, food, manners and lack of material goods on the part of the Indian, and even the physical world in which they live is different. Lima, where I worked, sits in desert plain between the sea and the mountains. There remained signs of colonial times in the luxurious homes of the Peruvian rich but the country as a whole was in flux. There was a guerrilla war in progress at that time and some of their comrades in Lima jail took two visiting nuns, including one from Belfast, as hostages. The authorities agreed to let the prisoners go and provided minibuses for transport, but the prisoners took the hostages with them. When they exited the prison, police opened fire and killed everybody. It is a beautiful country but the police were corrupt. The dreadful poverty made my time there rather unpleasant. I don't really want to dwell on it here. Let me think instead of the Caribbean.

As I write these words in this cold federal prison in the Appalachian Mountains I can feel the pain in my face from the cold. I walked backwards to work this morning as it was minus 25°C with a high wind-chill factor. The work pays twelve cents an hour and I can't refuse. When I look at the Bahamian prisoner across from me his voice and body language triggers memories that I put down here – they are like a glowing ember and my soul stays warm.

Trinidad

The winter of 1980/81 found me in Trinidad, land of the sweet Calypso. I was dispatched by Aer Lingus to this most southern Caribbean island nation to work for 'Bee-Wee', as British West Indian Airlines was familiarly known. I was stationed at Piarco Airport southeast of Port of Spain, the capital. Before returning to the Bahamas I spent a winter working in this beautiful country, which kept me within striking distance of the United States.

I choose to write about beautiful places during the long winter months in prison in this high country. Prison is a harsh environment at any time in the United States, but the winter in the mountains makes it cruel. The deep snow reduces your freedom to get outside and if you are confined in a small walled area it affects your long sight. It takes from you the freedom to experience the normal ebb and flow of events that happen, even in the prison. There are no pleasant surprises or entertainment to make you remember any day more than another. As I sit here writing I realise how much I miss the vitality, sense of enjoyment and freedom enjoyed by the people of Trinidad. With total abandon they immerse themselves in exploring the pleasures of music, dancing and partying more than any other people I have lived among. To escape the freezing cold and monotony in this prison I will try to relive in my mind the vivid enjoyment of life I found there.

When I arrived in Trinidad in the early eighties there were few tourists there. The island had got rich on oil in the seventies and tourism was left to Tobago, the other island to the north, which makes up the nation of Trinidad and Tobago. The drop in oil prices made life harder. In spite of this the people still remained happy, with an incomparable appetite for fun, music, rum and carnival. Some of the parties are the world's greatest. They never seem to end; when one celebration finishes, preparation starts for the next. This meant that most nights I was lulled to sleep by the distant sounds of steel bands practising new tunes. But did I care? No. And I would happily lie awake now tossing and turning because of such things.

The hotel where I stayed overlooked Queen's Park Savannah. This famous two hundred-acre park is located in the northern part of the city at the foothills of the Northern Range. Both poor and affluent neighbourhoods surround it. In rich areas large villas climb up the hillside, in others shantytown-type buildings crowd above the capital.

The park is something of a focal point for the people of Trinidad. It is home to a football pitch, a race-course and a famous cricket pitch where the West Indies team shows off their great skill. During the day the temperature here reaches 90°F (36^{0}C), at night it drops to about seventy-five. In the relative cool of the evening, vendors set up stalls around the perimeter to sell all kinds of tropical fruit. Traffic follows a one-way system around the park. Coming from the airport I would join the road about fifty yards from my hotel entrance, but I had to drive two miles around the park to get in. For exercise, I ran around the racecourse after dark. The fireflies were so numerous here that their pinpoint light flashes disrupted my vision and made it difficult to keep my balance. Looking up at the stallholders' bright lights on the perimeter and down to the ground again had the same effect.

The park itself is not much to look at but it comes to life when the people crowd in to cheer on their cricket team or celebrate Trinidad's most important event, Carnival or Mardi Gras. The carnival is a way of life here and an opportunity to give free expression to the people's natural gaiety. The steel band tunes and calypsos carry the crowds away and they get swept up in the excitement and participate in their own exuberant sideshows that last for days. In the main event, huge steel bands with over one hundred 'pan-beaters' blast out music that rocks the town as men and women compete for the Calypso crown and King and Queen of the contest. God help anyone looking for peace and quiet. This is not the place to get it. But the noise is such a happy one it lifts the spirits. The leading figures in the masquerade costume section struggle to show off their elaborate creations to best advantage, some of which are twenty feet high. The street parties continue until dawn and they bring together people of diverse backgrounds on this multi-ethnic island.

The Spanish did not establish a settlement on Trinidad until about one hundred years after Columbus first arrived. This settlement signalled the end for the native people. Work was anathema to those early people – slavery, revolt and disease wiped them out. Because of difficulty in getting Spanish workers, French nationals were invited to settle here. In the late eighteenth century thousands arrived with their black slaves to become rich on the cultivation of sugar and cocoa. Unfortunately this wealth attracted British attention and they sent their navy to take over a decade or so later. They remained in control until the island became independent in 1962.

Things have changed little over the years in northeast Trinidad. This may be due to the difficulty in completing the Skyline highway east through the rugged mountains and the existing long and difficult route there at present. To get there one has to drive across the centre of the island to the east coast and travel north on a potholed road to the town of Toco. The journey can be difficult, but the forested hills have great tropical beauty, full of giant butterflies and hundreds of beautiful birds. Rounding a corner, you are looking down on a valley covered in flowering trees with the African tulip tree, or Flame of the Forest, taking pride of place.

The isolation of this area has preserved the French language of former days; often the initial greeting is in French when you meet an elderly person. Mostly they are of African descent and live in quiet little villages at the foot of great forest-clad mountains that rise up into the clouds. Religion plays a large part in people's lives here. Many of the older types of religious belief and practices still survive, even some that were banned by the British centuries ago.

When you work with airlines overseas you often stand out because of your colour and accent. Many people are interested in learning why you are there and where you come from. I was invited to many people's homes and this was an opportunity to get to know a little about them. In Trinidad most of the hosts were descendants of people who had come from India as indentured workers, others were descendants of African slaves. They all were westernised and well removed from their roots, and very friendly, entertaining people.

Piarco airport where I worked is south-west of Port of Spain on the Caroni plain. International services connect the island to Europe and, most important for me, North America. This allowed me some flexibility and the security of entering America on a flight from a different area of the world – other than Ireland – thus reducing the possibility of drawing attention to myself. Travelling to the United States where the necessary technology existed allowed me to continue my research and development work for the war effort at home.

Working with the people in so many different countries allowed me to see them at their best and worst. In Trinidad I found that the different cultures often stood apart from each other and there was some tension. But when there was work to be done they stepped in and interacted well until the job was done; then afterwards they tended to retreat again into their own community. Somehow, in the end, they seemed to feel that they were one nation and lived peacefully together.

[illegible] were [illegible] and [illegible] with their [illegible] and [illegible] mechanical people.

[illegible] support [illegible] the [illegible] plant. [illegible] independent, [illegible] the same flexibility and the [illegible] from a different area of the world – [illegible] including the [illegible] the United States, [illegible] and [illegible] at a [illegible].

Working with the people of so many different countries [illegible] them, I [illegible] found that the different cultures [illegible] and there [illegible] that when there was work to be done they [illegible] and [illegible] the job was done. [illegible] to find that [illegible] possible.

PART 5
ON THE RUN

Chapter 12

Hiding Out in Nigeria

Beware of the bite of Benin,
one comes out though forty goes in.

The third phase of my double life had lasted from 1979 to 1989. It was not always possible to get the opportunity to work close to the United States where the high technology was located but I was able to spend quite some time close by in the Caribbean. All that finally came to an end one day in July 1989. I was back in Dublin again, working at the airport. I got up at six-thirty that morning and on my way to work I was shocked to find myself named in the first item on the seven o'clock news. Four engineers had been arrested in the United States the previous evening and charged with conspiracy to manufacture a guided missile system. Somehow the American security services were aware of my involvement in the project and would be seeking my extradition to stand trial with the others. Although there were five engineers including myself indicted, as time passed and the case dragged through court in Boston, the group became known as the 'Boston Three.' There was no point in reporting for work so I just kept driving north; I was 'on the run' now. This came as no surprise to me. I was amazed that it took almost twenty years to happen. I was automatically out of a job, but fortunately my two children had finished their university education and the economic consequences were not too great.

My family were shocked, but it was not unexpected. When I was in Nigeria in 1997 the police had searched my home and property in Dublin. This alerted my wife and children to the fact that I was involved in the struggle in the six counties, though not the full extent of that involvement. That was as far as it went until the American 'sting' happened. My brothers and sisters in Ulster, who had been surrounded by the war for years, also became aware of my involvement then. Some of them communicated with me while I was in prison, others did not.

I laid low for a year and during that time I was still able to help in the struggle, but in the longterm I thought it would be better to leave Ireland for a while. I expected the Americans to come after me, big time. This was confirmed several years later, in December 1992, when I was arrested in South Africa and the following was part of an article on me in the *Boston Globe* newspaper: '"We never stopped looking for Maguire [sic]", says US Attorney John Pappalardo. "He was the lead defendant in the case. He was the leader."'

I had moved around quite a bit after my stint in the Caribbean. After working for a period with Faussett Airline in Lima, Peru, in 1983, I spent a couple of years at home before going to work in Nigeria in 1985; I returned there again in 1987/88, working in Benin city for a small airline called Okada. The airline had grown large in the intervening years. Now I was able to get employment there again as engineering manager, and I hoped that the Americans would find it difficult to locate me in that remote place. At the end of 1990 I left Ireland and went 'on the run' in Africa.

* * *

Nigeria – that troubled nation, half Muslim, one-third Christian, and the remainder practising various native religions, nestled in the westward bulge of the African continent – was my destination. In time I would come to love the people. I never felt intimidated or in danger, although I may have been one of only about fifty Europeans living in a hundred-mile radius. There were days when I got hassled, jostled, even threatened. Baked in the heat of the northern desert or steamed in the humidity of the south, I felt the veneer of western civilisation occasionally slip from me as people pulled me this way and that to gain advantage. The Nigerian climate is basically six months of tropical rain and six months of the harmatan, a wind from the north that is filled with Saharan dust that irritates your eyes and throat. Without being exposed to this harsh climate it is difficult to understand why feelings are always near the surface ready to explode into aggression or kindness. Arguments and fights break out over minor issues, but most confrontations end as suddenly as they begin and are forgotten just as quickly. The Nigerians are a happy-go-lucky people.

Boarding an aircraft bound for Nigeria can be amusing or an ordeal, depending on your temperament and attitude. People who are used to preferential treatment at home in Nigeria under local customs tend to demand the same at check-in counters in other countries. They push to the top of the line, causing it to disintegrate and become a free-for-all. This leads to loud verbal confrontations between groups of passengers and check-in staff, and it takes hours to get everybody processed. Another practice that caused problems in the 1980s and made flights uncomfortable was the enormous amount of hand luggage that ended up in the cabin. The Nigerian government's policy up to the late eighties insisted that the nira (local money) was worth two US dollars and currency controls made it difficult to import essential commodities. Passengers, therefore, did not declare all their hand luggage at check-in and arrived at the departure gate loaded down, with only minutes left before take-off time. It was impossible to repeat the fracas at the check-in and to take off in the time slot allocated. If you missed the take-off slot it would be hours before you'd get another.

My first journey to Nigeria in 1985 was a UTA flight from Paris; this was the French equivalent to BOAC, set up to serve the French colonies. On this occasion, I was in line at the boarding gate in Paris and a lady passenger noticed that I had no hand luggage and asked me to carry one of the many bags she was laden down with. As I took hold of the selected bag, the weight took me by surprise and it pulled me down, hitting the floor with a metallic clunk. The attendant checking the boarding passes heard the sound and looked at me knowingly and said, 'That's not your bag?' As an airline employee caught in the act, I had to admit it wasn't mine. It turned out to be part of a Peugeot car engine.

The long approach to Lagos airport at Ikeja on that first occasion gave me a quick synopsis of what lay ahead. Ten miles out it was possible to see the high-rise skyline of Lagos Island in the background. Underneath the path of the aircraft thick evergreen vegetation covered the ground and it persisted along the approach, broken occasionally where a small allotment was hacked out of the bush, exposing the red soil. Closer in, the shacks with their rusted, corrugated iron roofs grew in number until the ground was almost totally covered, leaving narrow, disorganised, potholed dirt tracks between. It was an unsettling introduction to Nigeria, which would be more disturbing when viewed from the ground where one could see the flies on the shack walls and on the dirt-encrusted faces of children playing in the dust.

The final approach was across small, cultivated plots, which ran right up to the taxi and runways. There was no security fence here which allowed for some easy pickings for nimble-footed thieves. As the aircraft moved in line along the taxiway for take-off they would run out of the vegetation, open the cargo door, grab the nearest suitcases and dash back into the bush. On one occasion they struck it rich when they grabbed a box containing a quarter of a million nira. The usual suspects were gathered up, but I imagine that it was an inside job where airport staff was involved.

Lagos airport was called Murtala Muhammed, after a Brigadier in the Nigerian army who led a coup against a civilian government in 1975. Today most Nigerians choose to forget that and regard him as a saint or a prophet who could have lead the people back from the abyss of violence, corruption and inefficiency. Like some other leaders, he did not live long enough to prove or disprove that theory as he was killed in a counter-coup in 1976 with less than a year in office.

The airport is a modern construction, not necessarily a good thing when NEPPA or the electrical supply is unavailable. When the cooling system was off it could be a sweatbox and after a long flight nerves could get frayed. Other irritants could be encountered at the immigration desk where an enterprising official looked at your passport and set it aside to soften you up later for 'dash'. This is not necessarily a harsh practice; perhaps all that was required was the pen or cigarettes in your breast pocket or your foreign change. Usually the friendly greeting was, 'What have you brought me?' It was an old custom in the villages that when a person returned from the outside world they were expected to bring gifts.

I have only parted with hard cash on one occasion. One New Year's morning, I arrived in Lagos at 3.00am. On my way to the Hilton hotel two armed policemen stopped the taxi. Their greeting was directed at me, 'Happy New Year, *Oyibo*, [white person] we work New Year's night and the cold is scratching, have you a present for us?' I ignored the question and greeted them, intending to wait them out but at the same time keeping in mind an incident reported in a local newspaper when I was here in 1988. It seems that a truck was stopped in the same manner as this in Rivers state, and the newspaper reported that 'the gun leaked and the man died'. They walked around asking questions and eventually hit the jackpot by asking what was in the car trunk. Because of the medical situation in Nigeria I carried a blood plasma kit with me in case I got ill. Since it contained syringes and other items I suspected that I might end up explaining myself in a police station where more people would like a New Year's present. It was a game we played and I had lost; it was time to fold them: two five-dollar bills and a Happy New Year.

Having passed through all the formalities at the international side on that first occasion I had to 'dash' a local worker with items worth the equivalent of fifty cent to drop me over to the domestic terminal. Most of the internal flights departed from there to outlying towns and cities. When I arrived there it was chaotic. I had never experienced anything like it during my travels. Tickets were sold without seat allocation, and when the aircraft was full, the remaining passengers waited for the next flight. When boarding, there was a free-for-all, and people tried to gain advantage by jumping up the line that snaked across the tarmac. Loud arguments and fistfights broke out. When passengers entered the aircraft and found no seat available, they refused to leave and stood in the aisle.

Others crowded on the steps outside and held firmly to the handrails while more pulled themselves up the steps between the legs of those already there. It got so bad that the captain shut down the machine and left the cockpit. The heat forced the people out on to the tarmac and the loading eventually got underway again.

I had worked at Lagos airport for long periods on my first trip to Nigeria in 1985. Due to the small area in which the internal flights loaded and unloaded passengers the aircraft had to make tight turns to get onto parking stands, increasing engine power to do so. Passengers queuing for other flights had to continually move the line to avoid getting injured. Even this snaking about did not prevent them from being exposed to the jet engine exhaust, which blew their headgear and other loose articles up in the air and away.

Working there had its lighter moments, it was not all doom and gloom and often it was amusing. On one occasion an aircraft arrived from Jos city. As the engines ran down it was normal to carry out a walk-around inspection and open the cargo hold doors for unloading. As I opened the rear door a flash of white passed over my head, causing me to drop to the ground on one knee with surprise. A large white goat had chewed through its tether – and it took off. In its bid for freedom it crashed into a line of Muslims boarding a flight to Kano – they ended up in a tangle of fancy embroidered robes, hats and hand luggage. The goat changed direction and headed for the bush under a barrage of Allah's revenge from the holy men. The place was now in uproar as everybody got involved in apprehending the goat. Helen, a lovely Yoruba woman dressed in an elegant blouse tucked into layers of richly coloured wrappers fastened around the waist, strolled across the tarmac in her plastic flip flops with a red plastic bucket in one hand and a mop in the other. A shout from the pursuing crowd caused her to dash into the path of the oncoming goat with her mop and bucket swinging in the air. In its confusion the goat ran straight into her, sending her tumbling in a flurry of green and scarlet. The bucket flew up into the air and landed on the goat's head as it covered the final few yards before disappearing into the elephant grass. Helen rolled around the tarmac, laughing uncontrollably.

It was precisely the chaos and lack of organisation of the place that made me choose to go 'on the run' in Nigeria in 1990. I felt it would be more difficult for the American authorities to corner me here and I could allow myself to wind down a little.

The question most often asked about being on the run is how do you cope with the stress of watching your step at every turn? I believe that you must have a natural temperament to handle stress and live with danger, otherwise you would avoid anything that would put you in such a position in the first place. If you possess this ability it will develop over time, and I had over twenty years' exposure for it to do so. The natural survival instinct becomes finely tuned and after a while you don't think about it – scanning faces, reading body language and listening to sounds runs on an embedded programme in normal day-to-day living without disturbing you. The self-conscious feeling, familiar to most people, that everybody is watching you is soon replaced by the cold fact that nobody is watching you except the person that may be 'tailing' you and they soon become apparent.

As engineering manager I had plenty to occupy me, but there was always time to brainstorm about the technical problems back home in the hope of finding theoretical answers. In Nigeria, as in other countries, the average person doesn't want to know or think about what is happening in other parts of the world. In Nigeria people were not aware of who I was and, even if they knew about me, they would not suspect that I was the same person who was named in America. It was up to the American security services to track me there and unfortunately, in April 1991, an article in *The Reader's Digest* called 'The Breaking of the American Connection' pointed the way to Nigeria and, of course, put me on my guard. Most security services check you out or have some other source 'look you over' before taking action, and this process can show their hand if your security is good. It would be unlikely a European would come to see if you were the person they were looking for – better to send a local. Those closest to you were the best source of information. Anticipating this, I bought off those who worked with me or for me, so that they would warn me if any person asked questions about me.

* * *

In 1990 I was bound for Benin city, then the capital of Bendal State in the Republic of Nigeria, to work for a local airline called Okada (I had worked here before for a short period). The job required me to see that the maintenance and repair work was carried out as laid down in government regulations and ensure that proper records were kept. When I arrived back in Benin that December, I was taken fully by surprise. As I walked down the steps one of the workers let out a cry and all the technical staff rushed up the stairs and picked me up bodily with their hands and placed me over their heads. Carrying me aloft they paraded off, singing about how they had suffered since I had left. The lead man told the story while the others clapped in time; the chorus was wild shrieks and loud ululating. I thoroughly enjoyed it. I find that I like the extreme differences between peoples and I hope it doesn't disappear altogether in the modern world. I have worked in many places across the world from the early sixties and I was never troubled by loneliness or homesickness: it was always an adventure and the more unusual the local customs the more I enjoyed them. People who spend their whole life in the country of their birth have difficulty understanding how I can be like that and not miss what they call home. But I never stayed at home long enough to miss it. My existence was 'out there', and I always settle in quickly to my new surroundings.

Benin city is located in a tropical rain forest, hot and humid; it is less than a hundred miles west of the mighty Niger river. The airport was very small with few buildings, but it had a concrete runway. It had only one navigation aid, a radio beacon, to fly in on. Often when the electricity failed the backup generator did not work and a bearing on the local radio station was all you had to locate the airfield.

In pre-colonial times the city was the political centre of a vast empire. The present *Oba*, or king, is the thirty-ninth of his dynasty. The city was called Ile Ibinu, 'the land of vexation', but most outsiders called it Benin. In the late nineteenth century a British trade mission, led by a consul called Phillips, was present during a ceremony of 'making father' at which human sacrifices were to be carried out. It seems that Phillips intervened and a chief and others decided to act without the Oba's knowledge and put Phillips and his party to death. The Oba was well informed of the British feeling about human sacrifices and he expected them to invade his kingdom. He acted in the only way he knew how, which was to carry out more human sacrifices in order to appease the Gods and spirits of his ancestors and beseech their protection. As the British forces approached even closer to Benin the sacrifices increased in number and when they entered a near-deserted city they found corpses at every shrine and an indescribable stench. This gave Benin a new name: 'the city of blood and skulls'.

When I arrived there twenty-five years had passed since the British had left. Not a great amount of time and most people over thirty remembered them. I asked people to compare conditions under both systems. Most said that there was good and bad: when the British were there the roads, sanitation and disease control was better, but now jobs and schools were available to a greater number of people.

The chief that I worked for was the *Uzama* (senior chief) of Benin, the highest-ranking order of chieftaincy under the *Oba*. Although, as custom dictated, the *Oba* did not venture outside his palace, he was well informed. In the mid-eighties the *Uzama* had purchased a horse-drawn Buckingham palace-style carriage to ride in on ceremonial occasions, complete with a British ex-cavalry man dressed in royal livery. The *Oba* had a quiet word with him and this display of opulence ceased.

The ex-cavalry man did not appreciate the strength of local customs and decided he wanted rid of a local worker in the stables. He asked the chief to sack the man, which he did. However, old customs still filter down from the village chief to modern times. In a village the chief was the law, and he usually banished offenders into the bush, a dreadful place to be for a person who believed in juju and evil spirits. Later, the demented person would crawl back on all fours to the chief begging forgiveness, saying, ‘I beg you – I beg you,’ and all would be forgiven. Thus, the attendant in the stables was reinstated a short time later. When the ex-cavalry man saw him return he went to the chief to complain, but got little joy and his language became abusive. The chief’s reaction was that of an African father to his disobedient son, an open hand-slap to the face. This infuriated the *Oyibo* who instinctively reacted with force and ended up buried beneath the chief’s eight security men. Not a comfortable position – the descendants of the Edo warriors who established the large Benin kingdom were not something to trifle with.

The chief threatened me with a slap on occasions; it is part of a Nigerian businessman's way of getting what he wants. This is particularly true if you stick to regulations that he sees as an inconvenience. I always held my position without letting things get out of hand. I enjoyed the utmost respect from the chief because I refused to give way where matters of safety were involved. After a heated argument he would storm off. Later I would be welcomed into his residence and treated like a member of the family. On occasions when I arrived early in the morning to conduct business, he would be with religious people of various denominations. I would be waved to take a seat, but if I had anybody with me they would be required to wait outside while he conducted his affairs. When the religious people were shown out he would come over to me and say, 'Now, Irishman, say some prayers', and I would do so.

Not all Europeans could handle the ceremonies that took place in the throne room. These were conducted to install subjects into various ranks in the local political system and to reaffirm old loyalties and obedience. Two pilots arrived to work at Benin airport one evening in 1990. Naturally, for security reasons, I stayed in the office until I saw all the passengers had disembarked. The two men came in my direction because I was the only white face there, although I often forgot what colour I was. I put them in the car and went down to the chief's residence to introduce them and see what arrangements were made for their accommodation. When we arrived there, a ceremony was in full swing and the chief used his eyes to indicate that we should take a seat.

Normally I would look straight ahead and show little interest in the proceedings but on this occasion I watched the chief with peripheral vision. He was quite a character, with a strong sense of humour, and I could see him watching the newcomers getting uncomfortable. In one ceremony the novice entered the room, raised his hands in various gestures while crying out his pledge of loyalty and obedience in the Edo language.

This loud wail in a strange language, in a large decorated chamber with an echo and low-level lighting, could be unnerving to a person fresh in from Europe. The two men did not know what the outcome was going to be and I was not in a position to explain while the ritual was in progress. The general atmosphere of the rainforest and the absence of others of your own kind was not a good first-time introduction to Africa. The novice then prostrated himself, face down on the floor, with arms outspread. This action was repeated as he moved closer to the throne, at which point he knelt and was touched on each shoulder with a double-edged, fan-shaped ceremonial sword. Now he got up, turned his back to the chief, sat on his knees and had the sword placed on his head. I assumed that this unprotected position was a sign of trust and obedience in the chief. It was all very dramatic.

After the proceedings the grinning chief came down to us and discussed business. Later I dropped the pilots off at their accommodation and made arrangements to see them later after work. We went to a bar run by a local woman, some would say a cathouse, and after consuming some alcohol the men expressed their uneasiness with events since they had arrived in Nigeria. I cited my own experiences and asked them to give it some time because first impressions could be misleading. I left them home, indicating that I would pick them up next morning – and the presence of a lady of the night assisting one of them into his room held out some hope that all was well.

Next morning when I called they had checked out and I was concerned when I could not locate them. I contacted Lagos office by high-frequency radio; this was the only way I could stay in contact with other stations, and I asked them to check the usual watering holes and use the bush telegraph. The following morning a radio message said that they left on a flight the evening before.

I had a very good relationship with local workers. Trust was everything; keeping your word once given would generate loyalty; remaining calm and civilised when mayhem broke out was also important. I had one local worker who had been educated in England, went to the best schools and got all the qualifications. He did not pull his weight and came in late. This was a very bad example to more junior employees but there was little I could do, considering local customs. I felt that I should try and do something about it within the parameters I had. One morning he was late and I was very busy. He was dressed in tennis gear with his towel and racket over his shoulder, ready to drift off after presenting himself. I picked up the attendance clipboard and pen and walked out to him saying he was marked absent and he was free to go. This was a useless exercise, but I wanted to embarrass him in front of his people. He turned on me saying, 'You can't do that to me', I said I could, to which he replied, 'If you do I will juju you.' Instinctively I reached out with my white pen and touched him on the chest saying, 'I will white-man juju you.' He jumped back with surprise and his fellow workers rolled around on the ground in convulsions of laughter. I had no further problems with him.

Witchcraft, juju and a mist of superstition touched most of the local minds. You found it everywhere; mostly it stemmed from a lack of knowledge and was similar to beliefs of earlier times in Europe. My own upbringing in the country before the coming of electricity gave me an understanding of all of this. Terror seized people when the God of Night unleashed his demons. Everything was governed by these beliefs. I did not realise at first that these fears and taboos still lingered on, and were just as prevalent in towns as in the bush.

A friend of mine was married to a local girl from a well-to-do family in Benin; she insisted that he sprinkle magic dust around the house each night to keep evil spirits away. Workers coming to the airport one day suddenly piled out of the minibus because one of them got hysterical and said someone had jujued him and stolen his 'willie'. After a lot of loud argument they finally simply boarded the bus as if nothing had happened and arrived late for work! Concerned about the absence, I enquired quite firmly why nobody had decided to check his private parts to see if, indeed, they were missing. I was told that it would be unwise to interfere with juju. It always intrigued me too that the corn growing along the roads or tracks was never touched, although there were many starving people around. When I asked about this I was told that the owner had poisoned some of the cobs and only he knew which ones. In my time there, animal and chicken sacrifices were common. Often a sacrifice would be left outside a Christian minister's house or blood splashed on the door. Rumours circulated about the occasional human sacrifice. I saw letters in the local newspaper complaining that the reason crops went bad was because the land was not nourished by blood. It was true that people who called themselves Christian drifted out of the Christian church when they did not get what they wanted, returning to the ancient religion and then back again.

In one case further south in the delta, a local man was big into a Christian faith and provided the land for a church. Later he fell out with the minister and decided to start his own church next door. In my time he had some of the local mentally impaired people tied to stakes in the ground there and he went around occasionally sprinkling blood from a sacrifice on them. I was told that when the Oba died in 1978 he was buried completely surrounded by human heads so that no earth touched his body. I asked the son of one of the court's close advisors about this and he agreed that it was the case. He also added that the heads of albinos were prized for this purpose; perhaps he was trying to scare the *Oyibo*! I was told another story about a Norwegian who set up a wood mill in the district some years previously. It seems he decided to get rid of one of his employees who did not take it lightly and said that he would juju him. The mill owner took all the precautions he could to prevent any ill befalling him, including poisoning. He still died. It turned out that there are poisons in the rain forest that you can put on the surface of glasses or cans that seep into the body through the skin. When he started to feel unwell the possibility of juju took a grip on his imagination and finished him off.

There were other threats too. A lady that I knew to speak to owned a hotel in Benin in which her boyfriend had a financial interest. One evening she arrived home early to find him in bed with her sister; she said nothing then, but one night soon afterwards he woke up and there was a shotgun barrel under his chin. He was handed a pen and a form to sign away his interest in the hotel. When I asked about this episode I was told that it wasn't unusual for a woman to poison successive husbands until she became very rich.

Port Harcourt is the capital of Rivers State in the low delta rainforest. It was one of the towns and cities that we operated flights in and out of. I had to visit it on a regular basis to ensure everything was kosher. During the rainy season, April to September approximately, massive storms rolled in from the bite of Benin and produced the most incredible fireworks display of lightning that I ever saw. Flying can be hazardous at that time of year. Strings of thunderstorms meant flying hundreds of extra miles to get around them. I recall one such evening when we decided to fly through a hole in a storm necklace. When we exited on the other side we flew straight into the centre of another storm that had moved in behind the first one. It turned the cockpit into a chamber of horrors and my eyes were vibrating so rapidly that I could not focus on the instruments until we were cast out the other side again.

I went to visit a priest from Ireland in a parish near Port Harcourt. Only those who have lived off the beaten track can imagine the excitement that contact with a fellow countryman can have on a person such as this man who had been shut off from the outside world for so long. His parish was such that he had to pack his mosquito net and set off in his canoe for periods of two weeks or more, visiting communities along the many creeks where the Niger river filters into the sea through the delta. The river flows between the solid banks of greenery; the tall trees, with climbing vines trailing over their massive trunks, grow to the river's edge. What a thrill it was for me to glide along, even if the water was a brown colour and you could not see beyond the jungle wall.

It was here on this trip that I first saw women carrying large limbs of trees on their heads. I passed the remark to the priest about how strong they must be and he took me along to a village to see the result of their labour. Their frames had collapsed under the strain and most were crippled. They knew that their time was fleeting. By thirty they were old, by forty they were considered ancient and their looks reflected that change

My steward (a house man servant) was from Rivers State. Servants played a very important role in one's life. They came to you in various ways. You could select one by random, inherit one from previous incumbents, or one servant brought another, or they simply turned up at your door with their reference 'chits', a book from previous employers. I had the same one both times I worked there. He appeared within twenty-four hours of my return in 1990; how he knew I was back I do not know. Most would prefer to work for *Oyibo*s because they received many perks that they did not get elsewhere. They always arranged the shopping at the market so that they could purchase some food for themselves. I ignored this because there were two prices anyhow, one for the Europeans and a cheaper one for the locals. The end result was the same money spent and more people fed – and the steward knew where the best supply was. In truth, you formed a close relationship with your employee and took care of his family. When his wife or children were sick, which was regularly, you paid for medication. In return you got loyalty, and a reliable tap into what was going on locally, a useful commodity when you were one of very few Europeans for hundreds of miles around. He was first to know if another white person or government official arrived in the general area. This was useful security for me and it allowed me to relax my guard a little. I remained undisturbed in Benin for a year and a half before the article appeared in the *Reader's Digest*, after which I prepared for the inevitable and was on high alert.

The local currency, the nira, had been de-regulated in the late 1980s under pressure from the international monetary fund and the cost of everything had rocketed out of reach of the workers. Over the following years I made every effort to get a better deal for them. While I was there I always changed one hundred dollars a month to use as 'dash' or to give to people who truly were starving.

This became a habit some years before. The first time I lived in

Benin, a lady who was just skin and bones came to me in my office; because I was white, she saw me as a rich person, and asked for money for food, which I gave her. Every week after that she arrived to collect the same amount from me – the equivalent of one pound sterling. It seems that she could purchase the basics for about 15 pence per day. When I arrived back in 1990 she appeared again as if by magic – the bush telegraph was alive and well. This time she had a little girl with her. I asked where the father was and she said he just ran away, so I continued to help her and the child.

Another day I was called out of the office because somebody at the security gate wanted to see me. As I walked out I saw one of our workers running across the runway and disappearing into the elephant grass. At the gate I was directed to a lady who was expecting a baby, and had one child on her back and another by the hand. It was obvious that they were starving. I enquired about her request to see me and was told that her husband, the very man I had seen running away, had not been at home for some weeks and they had no food. I gave her some money and said I would see what I could do with her husband, not promising anything because I fully understood the local customs. Later I talked to the husband and he just said he was finished with that family as he had a new wife. I asked about the support of the children and he said that that was her problem.

Two young girls came to see me, aged between ten and fourteen years. It wasn't difficult to find me as there wasn't many *Oyibo*s around. I asked them what I could do for them and they replied 'You could take us home with you.' I refused to have anything to do with them. I lived alone and did not wish to get involved with children or upset the local people. Before I sent them away I gave them the equivalent of two pounds sterling and told them not to come back again, and they did not. Some months later I was called to a meeting with the administration officer and the subject was a letter received from an angry parent about a daughter who was staying away from school and living with one of the workers. I was asked to use my influence to get her back home and I related my experience about the two young girls. After much discussion I got up to leave and the older gentleman at the table said, 'Those little girls are nice but remember to send them home afterwards.' A sense of hopelessness descended over me.

The people looked upon you as a 'fixer', but you couldn't do very much for them. Because you were white, they expected you to be able to move things along. Perhaps this expectation was a carry-over from the British Colonial District Officer who would listen to their problems, try to fix them or plead their case with the colonial office. My employer trusted me with responsibilities which tended to bring the best out of you, but any feeling of superiority was tempered by the knowledge that your effectiveness depended on the co-operation and consent of others, and power was itself something of an illusion. Wealth brings power and influence, and in some parts of the world the colour of your skin can create the same illusion, so I felt a bit of a humbug. My inability to do anything of lasting consequence often filled me with humility.

Even in the 1990s life was hard in Nigeria. Yam and cassava were the staple food; meat of any kind was a luxury for most people. Around stagnant pools, in intense heat and high humidity, mosquitoes abounded. Children got high fever and died within twenty-four hours. Yellow fever, black-water fever and parasites were everywhere. Guinea worm laid its eggs in water, and if you drank it without boiling and straining it the eggs hatched inside you. The worm wandered around inside you until it got stuck in some extremity such as your leg, which then swelled up. The tumbo fly laid eggs on clothes that were drying after washing; the lava entered the body through the skin, producing a sore similar to a boil. The filaria fly lava wandered about the body until it lodged somewhere, producing a large bump, and the black-river fly produced blindness. In the middle of all this, many orders of nuns worked hard to bring some relief.

The group that I had most contact with was the Medical Missionaries of Mary from Drogheda in Ireland. Their Nigerian headquarters, then run by a local nun, was located on the south east outskirts of Benin. When I had some time off I often visited them to repair equipment and assist in whatever way I could. The Medical Missionaries were relative latecomers to Nigeria. Their first outpost was in Anna on the south coast and from these humble beginnings they spread across central Africa, numbering about 150 members when I was there. At one stage they administered to about twenty thousand lepers.

I used to visit a leper colony in Assiomo, north-east of Benin. It was really a village because when the lepers were cured they were not readily accepted back into their families and had to stay on there. This attitude is understandable to some degree, because close proximity promoted a communicable disease such as leprosy.

Another outpost run by the Medical Missionaries was a maternity hospital at Uromi. On my way there I called to see a monastery set up by monks from Glenstal Abbey in Limerick. They were in a remote and lonely area, but seemed quite happy, although I felt that their manner of dress did not protect their ankles and feet from mosquitoes. I also called at Asaba, a town on the banks of the great Niger river. I was told that there was an outpost for Irish priests there. When I arrived there I found no European priests except those who lay in the small graveyard. Those priests arrived here in the 1920s, shortly after ordination, and had been laid to rest between the ages of twenty-two and twenty-five, in some cases less than a year after arrival. Their missionary zeal was not enough to sustain them against tropical diseases. The roads were very poor and I got a puncture out there one afternoon. Rather than continue without a spare wheel I decided to go down a dirt track to see if I could get it fixed. In a little village with half a dozen shacks I found a local handyman who was delighted to assist me. While I was there I was astonished to see the game the children were playing. They had captured butterflies and tied a thread to them; setting them free, they ran after them, holding onto the thread. It reminded me of a distant time at home when discarded items were turned into toys and children ran after a bicycle rim using a stick to keep it rolling.

The hospital at Uromi was well run by the nuns but funds were very low. The water supply was unreliable and when I was visiting there they managed to drill for water, though it required a thousand-foot bore hole. It also required a high-powered pump to get the water up, as Uromi was situated on a high plateau. Money had been donated in Ireland for the project. The electricity supply was erratic and the back-up generator did not have the necessary power to drive the pump motor. The storage tank had to be topped up by manually turning the on–off control switch when the mains supply was available. Some time later I heard that the switch had been left on and the expensive pump burnt out.

Most of the laboratory equipment did not work. Since I had worked for a period as a medical service engineer and had some knowledge of such machines, I used what spare time I had to repair what I could find the parts for. Unfortunately, as soon as they were working, they were stolen. The wiring from the control to the X-ray machine ran through a duct in the floor, but here rats chewed the plastic insulation of the cables. At least the thieves were unable to take that when it was repaired.

Such was life on the run in deepest Nigeria. It wasn't a bad life – in fact it held many interesting and colourful things that I found fascinating. But after a year and a half in this remote place, the bush telegraph, my security system, warned me that the Americans had tracked me down and were ready to close in. It was time to move on. I headed for the border with Benin State, which was part of the old French empire. I could not locate my passport, not that it was going to be of any use to me. Clandestinely crossing over the border, I reached the city of Cotonou and flew to Paris. In Paris I renewed my travel papers at the Irish embassy and later made my way to Ireland to go on the run there for the next six months.

Chapter 13

The Last Refuge: Mozambique

The six months at home after Benin were difficult because I had to keep on the move while I assisted the war effort. Keeping ahead of the security services in Ireland was not easy and I decided to go overseas again as soon as possible. In January 1992 I boarded an aircraft bound for Mozambique. Fortunately this aircraft had stopped at Dublin on a delivery flight from Seattle to Maputo, and I was able to travel without the usual requirements that apply to regular passenger flights. Now I was leaving the war zone at home but going to another war zone to work on contract for Mozambique Airlines. I would fall asleep most nights to the sound of gunfire.

January is mid-summer in the southern hemisphere and when I walked out of the aircraft at Maputo after twelve hours' flying, the heat was like a slap in the face. We had to stand around on the hot tarmac while members of the government inspected the Boeing aircraft, the first sent to a country that America was not very happy with due to its connections with the eastern block. The airport was very well laid out; obviously it was meant to cater for large numbers of passengers, but it looked deserted. Two old Boeing 737s stood there, the only reminder of the local Portuguese airline that thrived here up until 1975. A once-a-week flight to Lisbon and a few light aircraft from South Africa were all that called here in

1992. But things were changing: Mozambique Airline was getting two modern 737s and a Boeing 767 to fly internal as well as international routes to Europe. The collapse of the Soviet Union and the shift of power in South Africa meant that there was little need for the West to continue to support the unspeakable savagery of Renamo. They were a pseudo guerrilla organisation set up by Rhodesia, South Africa and Portugal in 1971 to frustrate the then original freedom fighters who were now in power.

At the other side of the airport Russian twin-engined prop jets sat at the military base. They lay silent because there was no cash from Moscow and no fuel. Prior to the collapse of the Soviet Union those gifts were the only things that held this country together. Strangely, many Russians decided to remain in Mozambique rather than return home. They continued working at the jobs they had been sent to do, mostly doctors, dentists and engineers. Others less qualified also remained, regardless of the difficulties. I even heard of one Russian man living in a bamboo or cane shelter in a shanty village on the northern outskirts of Maputo.

Here I was, in a country run by a socialist government, again hiding from the Americans. I did not know how long my situation could continue because the local regime's supporter – Russia – had collapsed and it seemed that the government was getting ready to do business with the West. In the short term, I hoped that the chaos in this wartorn country would help preserve my anonymity. Being on the run can get tiresome eventually – never trusting anybody and always expecting someone to recognise and betray you, which eventually happened here in my last refuge. But it never troubled me enough to make me consider giving up. The very thought of that goes against the grain.

I was staying at the Polana hotel, which unfortunately was being renovated after decades of neglect. I lived in a room with no air conditioning in intense heat for quite some time. The hotel is located on Julius Nyerere Avenue, the Beverly Hills of Maputo. The avenue runs along the rim of a high bluff, which overlooks Riviera-type beaches. I was surprised at the sophistication of the architecture: white towers and apartment blocks with walls faced with colourful mosaic patterns, sidewalks paved in patterned tiles, sharp spires and chimneys that looked like mushrooms – all very Mediterranean. But in 1992 the cracks of the previous seventeen years of socialist rule and war were showing through. When you looked closely the tiles were missing in places, leaving gaping holes; some buildings had cracks in their high walls with shrubs growing out of them.

President Joaquim Chissano lived two doors down from the Polana and his wife owned a restaurant across the avenue where you paid six dollars for a drink. Not many locals could afford to eat or drink there. It was estimated that seventy-five percent of the population of Mozambique lived below the poverty line and about one million were infected with HIV. Times were changing in 1992. African socialism had failed, it was now get-rich time, even though famine ravished the population and Alfonso Dhlakama's Renamo forces controlled the country outside the major urban areas

The Polana hotel was a beautiful building, designed by Walter Reid and completed in 1922; it was one of Maputo's best-known landmarks. It was being rehabilitated after seventeen years of neglect and run in a joint venture between the state and a South African hotel company, Karos. I stayed there through most of the renovation, which cost sixteen million dollars. When it was officially reopened in July 1992 the then president of South Africa, FW de Klerk, arrived for the celebrations. Since I was a resident I had a degree of freedom of access to events taking place there, and I attended the ceremony. President Chissano did not let him off lightly, accusing South Africa of working with Renamo. Many other issues were brought up at a press conference including the prosecution of military intelligence officers involved in various acts such as the mission to London in an attempt to assassinate South African defector Captain Dick Coetzee. But relations were improving and there was talk about the Mozambique state returning confiscated property and businesses to original owners.

Late at night after work I usually took time out to sit on the hotel patio wall overlooking the warm Indian Ocean with its palm-fringed shores and consider my security and how long I could remain in this country. I was one of a small number of western Europeans living there and we stood out from the other nationalities. One evening I was required to attend a function, associated with my Mozambique Airline job, with the American ambassador present! Their security people must have looked closely at those attending; I suspected that they were aware of my presence in Maputo and a 'snatch' operation was always possible. It was a dangerous position to be in where such an operation could go wrong and I could be killed. But then, I could have been killed at any time over the previous twenty years and it had not worried me. Danger has its own attraction and raises living to a higher level of consciousness, where you are alert and aware of what is going on in the world around you. It also makes you aware that you cannot run every time you suspect something is wrong before you take time to check it out.

While I was sitting in the patio one night, in the cool breeze coming in off the Indian Ocean, two South African men slowly drifted across an otherwise deserted patio where I sat. This was unusual, as for the best part of a year nobody had ever come out there, so I was very alert to their movements. They greeted me from a discreet distance and seemed interested in engaging me in conversation. They asked questions about the opportunities for setting up in business in Maputo and produced business cards. I found it strange that they should ask me since they could get much more useful information from their embassy or the hotel manager. I suspected that they were intelligence officers giving me the 'once over' for the Americans and I felt that time was running out for me.

Over the years I developed the ability to temporarily park threats that were down the road a bit and concentrate totally on what was happening at a given moment in time. Now this new sense of insecurity made me appreciate the luxury of the quiet balmy night in Maputo, and looking around I tried to imagine what it must have been like here before 1975 when the state was taken over by the socialist regime. I was told that there were one hundred and eighty thousand Europeans living in Maputo, then known as Lorenzo Marques. In 1975 they had to choose between becoming citizens and having everything taken over by the state, or to leave. Most took the latter option. For those who remained, life was not pleasant. Often they had to share their home with other families and run their former businesses for the state. When most of the Portuguese left Mozambique, the Africans moved into the cities and were assigned to the vacant accommodation. They were unable to pay the rent that would cover the cost of upkeep and everything went into decline. Maputo had the musty odour of things left unattended in a humid climate; perhaps it was the smell from the trunks of the beautiful jacaranda trees along the avenues that the locals used as latrines. Whatever the reason, Maputo was no longer the pearl of Africa. Even the Portuguese cemetery in the city centre had been vandalised, with the doors of over-ground vaults prised off their hinges and the coffins stacked on shelves and smashed, exposing the remains. There was a security man here, but everything of value was long gone. Still, he made a living from the human bones scattered around: the odd curious person like myself called to have a look around the graveyard and the old custom of 'dash' applied, even here. He accompanied you on your walk, hoping that you would give him some cash.

It was difficult to understand why the people involved in this African socialist experiment did not give up and take another road when it obviously did not suit the people any more than western capitalism did. Perhaps it was due to exposure to the particularly backward colonial system of the Portuguese. Mozambique was not dominated by the colonising power's wealth; such capital was not available because Portugal itself had many features of a Third World economy, exporting labour and raw material and importing manufactured goods. As in other parts of Africa, the pre-colonial societies were disrupted and reshaped to serve the interests of the dominating power and as a result of Portugal's weak economy, Mozambique's dependency and underdevelopment took a very unusual form. Portugal exercised political control, but Mozambique became an integral part of a British regional sub-system dominated by South Africa. As the Portuguese colonial grip weakened on its African colonies, Mozambique found itself increasingly under the control of its neighbour and this proved a troublesome relationship when independence arrived.

In 1969 the two northern provinces of Cabo Delgado and Niassa were under rebel Frelimo control. By 1971 they had poured down the middle of the country and the Portuguese were worried. And if they were worried you can imagine how the South African apartheid regime and Ian Smith in Rhodesia felt. Victory for Frelimo would cut Rhodesia's access to Indian Ocean ports and encourage the rebel Zanla forces fighting in Rhodesia. In order to prevent this outcome, intelligence officers from the three countries established a joint operations unit. A decision was taken to form special pseudo guerrilla units to undertake covert action in Mozambique and spread confusion and mistrust among the Frelimo fighters and their supporters. Operations would be based on tactics developed by the British as their empire diminished around the world. This simply delayed the inevitable and caused needless suffering.

With the collapse of Rhodesia, South Africa had lost a loyal supporter in the north and there was a socialist country to the east. They decided to prevent Mozambique from prospering. This could act as an example for those with revolution on their minds in the land of the Boer. With the help of intelligence agents who had fled to South Africa from Rhodesia they took control of MNR, which had been set up by Rhodesia. They gave them a new name 'Renamo', re-equipped and trained them and returned them to Mozambique under the leadership of Alfonso Dhlakama. Their inability to attract recruits was solved by conscripting people, mostly children, who were forced to commit acts of savagery so that they could not readily return to civilian life. They put forward no alternative political programme except the destruction of the government.

South Africa's proxy army had the finance to continue doing what they were trained for, reducing Mozambique to rubble, but they lacked popular support to become a political force and terror became the objective. Roads and railway bridges were destroyed, government employees killed, health, water and rural development stations destroyed. South Africa assisted by attacking oil installations and harbours. The country spiralled downwards into widespread famine, millions of people were displaced, towns and villages depopulated by abductions and massacres. Over a million people died in this war fought at the behest of South Africa.

This was the situaton in which I worked at that time. The night of 4 July 1992 was very bad. Renamo guerrillas tried to enter Maputo through the suburb of George Dimitrov and a fire broke out, spreading to the Zona Verde district. At least five people died. On the 25 July they attacked Benfica suburb; that was a major operation and one night they would get through. It is not in my nature to feel vulnerable and I went to sleep to the sound of war most nights. Now that the cold war was over, the West was making an effort to bring this conflict to an end. To achieve that it would be necessary to give Dhlakama a say in any future government and it would take some time to rehabilitate his men who were used to a barbaric way of life.

In 1992 the capitals of the provinces were government-controlled islands in a sea of conflict and it wasn't safe to venture outside them. It was impossible to go sightseeing in Mozambique, and after eleven months I was weary of famine and the suffering all around me and longed for something different. I had worked sixteen hours, seven days a week for the previous month. My birthday is 14 December; I hoped that I could get away from it all and spend a few days in South Africa. Renamo forces controlled the country along the border with South Africa, thus travelling by road was not an option. All traffic had to run the gauntlet of the Renamo guerrillas: trucks and cars were looted and burned, their occupants often killed. I decided to fly out in a light aircraft.

Unfortunately, decisions are not made with hindsight. Someone like me is not readily deterred from doing something just because there is an element of danger involved. All the possibilities and dangers in making this trip were carefully analysed on the basis of the information available to me and the decision was made on a better than fifty-fifty chance that I could enter and leave South Africa without drawing attention to my presence there.

In order to keep my residence papers in order in Mozambique I decided to go through Immigration before leaving so that if I had to return by some other route I would have an exit stamp. This simple procedure can be made difficult as the officials try to augment their salary by dragging the process out until you decide to 'dash' them with some money. On principal, I never bow to this pressure and on this occasion I walked away, deciding not to travel after all. I was in my airport uniform and the official knew me well. He called me back and waved me through. If I had been a little more stubborn I would have walked away, avoided the well-organised trap waiting for me at Nelspruit air strip. I had avoided such snares for years. Unfortunately, the Americans were aware of my plans and had the South African police waiting there to arrest me.

EPILOGUE

It is almost ten years since I wrote this book in prison. As I reflect now on my life's journey and where it finally brought me, I find the cost was very high. Everything I had is gone except the dreams. I would never leave them behind for they are the stars by which one plots one's course through life. They also keep you moving on and prevent you living in the past.

I tell myself that I took part in the event of a generation and I am glad that I survived, yet the faces of lost comrades keep dragging me into the past. Most of my comrades were ten years younger than I was. Some possessed the wild hope of youth and were not the kind of people to grow old. Like a storm they swept across the land and were gone. The memories of these people can pop into your head at strange times and switch your focus, even in company. People will observe the vacant look in your eyes; they know your mind is elsewhere and they call you back to the present. I think of the tens of thousands of prisoners of this uprising and wonder if their fiery hearts were fanned by dreams similar to mine? I hope it was so. It is difficult for the general public to understand how normal people make the transition to activist or soldier, and back to normal again. When I left prison I was fortunate that I was able to work in a high-tech job that helped me reintegrate into normal society. But in combat survival is the primary motivator and unit solidarity is the best way to achieve this. It forges the strongest bonds I know. I have no regrets about the action I took and the price I paid. It was a different time from the present and conditions were dreadful under the Stormont administration. It had to go.

Looking back now, my life was like riding on the wind with death travelling at speed not far behind. I never knew when it might catch up and often wondered how it would feel. That was all right with me. It is the same for all life forms, except they don't think about it. As a young man in Africa I learned that I could not protect myself from the assaults of fate and nature, and I learned to accept such things with a great degree of calmness.

During the war years I saw myself as a soldier. Soldiers do not start wars, they have to fight them when politicians act aggressively against other nations, ignore injustices or fail to resolve them peacefully. The British and Irish governments were aware of the injustices in the six counties for over forty years and made no effort to introduce reforms until the lid blew off, and even then Stormont refused to reform. War is the art of terror and savagery; there is no nice way to conduct it. It is about killing and there is no good way to die. It is an unforgivable fact of war that civilians get killed. Civilians get killed whether it is a B52 bomber cutting a swathe five hundred metres wide and two kilometres long through Baghdad, or a small misplaced home-made bomb in Belfast. I wish that my saying sorry would make the pain go away, but I know from experience that that is not the case.

Most activists do not wish to inflict terrible pain on people who are not involved in the war, but modern war has no boundaries. You may start out with high moral principles in a people's war, but soon the enemy will drag you from your ivory tower into the gutter with his black ops and black propaganda. He controls the media and will even ignore bomb warnings on bombs against economic targets and allow civilian casualties to take place to try and turn the people against you or force you to give up the struggle. He refers to his own civilian victims as 'collateral damage' and most people forget about the tens of thousands and focus on the one or two that he highlighted in the media. The lack of sympathy for a little girl losing half of her face to a police plastic round on an otherwise deserted street because she belongs to a nationalist family has to be lived with also. Do you give up? There is always a price to pay for freedom. Most Irish people like to forget about the civilians killed in Dublin during Easter week 1916 or the tens of thousands of women and children recently killed in Iraq.

Many things changed and yet many stayed the same in Ireland over the nine years that I was away 'on the run' and in prison. The 'Celtic Tiger' was born and a cease fire came into existence in the six counties. A referendum relinquished the Republic's claim on those counties and a majority of the people accepted the proposed peace terms. I now accept them too.

Looking back at the uprising, it seems that there was a window of opportunity presented in the 1970s to take the first step to freedom by the mobilisation of the nationalist population in the six counties against the treatment they were receiving. The timing was critical. I had seen the initial break at the right time lift the heavy hand of colonialism in other countries. Should the time-frame run out, then fatigue sets in and the stress rather than the hope of that intensely emotional time seems to be passed on to those coming behind, and the struggle falters. The changes brought about by the war raised the physical and emotional wellbeing of young nationalists in the six counties, and the grievances that existed in their parents' time do not move them. You do not get something for nothing, and so it was in the six counties; in a sense, the war generation was 'a generation lost', along with the dead the imprisonment of one in ten nationalists was the price paid for the 'privileges' now enjoyed by young nationalists.

For fifty years the Stormont government indulged in cultural imperialism against almost half of its people. When it fell, loyalism fragmented and the resulting vacuum left their various group leaders with no clear direction. They reacted to events rather than guided them.

The economic insecurity due to the decline in traditional jobs that were exclusively loyalist and the narrowing economic gap between nationalists and loyalists fanned ancient fears in loyalist low-income areas. There was the predictable loyalist swing to the right in elections. It was the purest expression of the politics of tribal survival. Fear drove them to the right: fear of change, fear of the future, fear of republicans, but most of all fear of the loss of political control and tribal disintegration.

Their elected leader, Ian Paisley, now lectures people on democracy. If he was a democrat and had not opposed the introduction of human and civil rights for nationalist people, he might well have prevented thirty years of war. He is no democrat. His utterances show that he is still a holder of outdated beliefs and a prisoner of his isolationist electorate. He is unable to bring himself to genuinely share power now or in the future. No concession, except a return to the past, will satisfy him and when one obstacle is removed he will introduce another. I see no real progress in the near future.

In the south the government propaganda machine works overtime. This is prompted by the struggle to hold on to power against a vibrant Sinn Féin party. Yet Sinn Féin have delivered on all their promises in so far as it is within their power to do so. They are deemed to be responsible for the actions of IRA volunteers who have departed over the years and gone their own way. This equates, in my view, to holding the minister for defence and the government of the day responsible for soldiers who commit offences years after they have left the military. We get lectured about democracy from members of the main party in the present government – about the qualifications necessary to enter government – but they suffer from selective amnesia. The founding fathers of Fianna Fáil refused to accept the will of the people in a similar situation in 1922 and dragged the country through a civil war. They did not dispose of their arms and some members carried weapons *into* the Dáil. Did this action prove that they were not capable of governing democratically over the years? When the people of Ireland spoke in the referendum on the settlement in the six counties we, the activists, responded to their wishes, and went further and disposed of our weapons of war. But the British and Irish governments have left the loyalist murder gangs fully armed; strangely, there is no outcry as they continue to murder. It will be interesting to see what decisions the electorate will make in the future about such issues.

Republicans have faced the fact that the war is over because the people were asked and they have said so. The nationalists rose up against an unjust system, and this was the first step in the struggle; the destruction of Stormont was the second. The third step has to be political because we must unite all our people and move on. Having said that, the question arises: was it worth the price to get this far? I believe it was. One must think about how bad things were prior to 1969 before answering that question. It is hard for a person far removed from those conditions to imagine what it was like. But ask yourself why did almost half the population rise up against the government unless things were intolerable? At least one in ten was willing to sacrifice themselves for change. I believe that we would not be where we are now without the war and I hope that our politicians will see sense and govern justly so that our people will never have to endure twenty-five years of horror again.

> Know that we fools, now with the foolish dead,
> Died not for flag, nor King, nor Emperor,
> But for a dream, born in a herdsman's shed,
> And for the secret Scripture of the poor.
>
> Tom Kettle

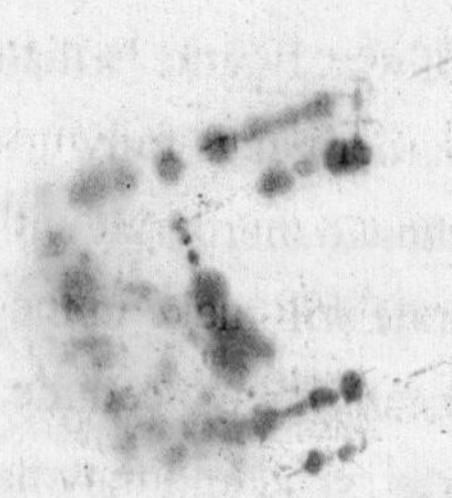